CW01619069

THE GOLF MISCELLANY

First published in 2007

This edition published in 2011
by Sevenoaks an imprint of the
Carlton Publishing Group
20 Mortimer Street
London W1T 3JW

Copyright © Carlton Books Limited 2007, 2011

All rights reserved. No part of this publication may be reproduced, stored in a retrieval system, or transmitted in any form or by any means, electronic, mechanical, photocopying, recording or otherwise, without the prior permission of the copyright owner and the publishers.

A CIP catalogue record for this book is available from the British Library

ISBN: 978-1-86200-918-9

Editor: Martin Corteel
Project Art Editor: Darren Jordan
Production: Janette Burgin

Printed and bound in Great Britain by CPI Group (UK) Ltd, Croydon, CR0 4YY

THE GOLF MISCELLANY

JOHN WHITE

SEVENOAKS

❋ DEDICATION ❋

I am dedicating this book to a friend, a truly good friend, whom I lost forever on 5 January 2007, David "Wilson" Steele. I met Wilson 17 years ago and we became friends instantly. When Wilson died the world lost one of life's true gentlemen, a loving, caring, sensitive, intelligent man who had time for everyone especially my two sons, Marc and Paul. Wilson was like a grandfather to my boys whom he loved very much and who loved him in return. Wilson created warmth wherever he went, his very presence lighting up a room and I still remember with fondness the many wonderful times we enjoyed together going to see Manchester United, a team he supported passionately, play.

Wilson, I miss you; Marc and Paul miss you; Janice misses you; the members of the George Best Carryduff Manchester United Supporters Club miss you; your former work colleague miss you; your friends and family all miss you but above all else the world will miss you because it is a less enjoyable place to be without you here among us.

However, I know you will look down on us now and again from heaven and I can only hope that we live as rewarding a life as you once enjoyed.

Your friend for ever,
John

❋ FOREWORD ❋

I was delighted when John, a fellow Northern Ireland man, wrote to me and asked me to write the foreword to his *Golf Miscellany.* Golf has provided me with so many fond memories from the time I turned professional in 1990, on both a personal level and on a team level with my fellow Ryder Cup team members. I will also never forget the reception you, the fans, gave me when I walked on to the first tee on Day 1 of the 2006 Ryder Cup at the K Club. That most precious and moving of moments will live with me for ever.

I was impressed with Carlton's kind offer to make a donation to Cancer Research UK, a charity close to my heart following the death of my wife, Heather, from this debilitating disease. And if you wish to make a donation to Cancer Research, and I urge you to consider doing so, you can contribute by visiting their website:

http://www.cancerresearchuk.org.

There have been many wonderful golfers throughout the history of our sport. Legends such as Gary Player, Jack Nicklaus, Arnold Palmer, Tom Watson, Seve Ballesteros and not forgetting my close friend, Tiger Woods, have all graced the greens with their own charisma and exciting style of play. Television has transformed our sport, and today more than ever we golfers are under the microscope. However, we accept our responsibilities and I only hope we can continue to bring pleasure to the many millions of fans who follow the tournaments in person and on TV.

You know golf is a truly wonderful sport, and a great leveller, because any player can beat a fellow player, as we have seen all too many times over the years, on their day. There have been many tournaments, and indeed Grand Slams, where the favourite has failed to win, instead being beaten by a rank outsider or a player just coming into some good form. Naturally a little Lady Luck can often play a part too.

So I really do hope you enjoy John's *Golf Miscellany* as much as I enjoyed it. It is evident that John has worked on a labour of love here, because the entries in the book are not only extremely interesting but historical, factual, informative and almost encyclopaedic in nature. This really is a little goldmine of a book and one that I will dip into now and again between tournaments to satisfy my own thirst for knowledge of the sport.

God Bless, and Heather, I know you are watching over us.

Darren Clarke
Ryder Cup winner 1997, 1999, 2004 & 2006

❋ LIST OF ABBREVIATIONS ❋

CC	Country Club
GC	Golf Club
LPGA	Ladies Professional Golf Association
NGLA	National Golf Links of America
PGA	Professional Golfers' Association
R&A	Royal & Ancient [Golf Club]
R&CC	Resort and Country Club
USGA	United States Golf Association

❋ INTRODUCTION ❋

Some historians claim that the game of golf originated in China in the 11th century whilst the Netherlands claim to have founded a similar game, known as *kolf*, dating back to 1297. However, very few golf historians argue with Scotland's claim that they invented the game and fewer still dispute that the R&A and St Andrew's are respectively the modern custodians and home of the sport. Indeed, King James II of Scotland banned the sport in 1457 claiming that the citizens were playing too much "gowf" and not concentrating on their military skills, particularly archery: golf was described as an "unprofitable sport which should be utterly cryit doun and not usit".

Today golf is played all over the world and even beyond following the American astronaut Alan Shepard's famous golf shot on the moon when he landed there with the third Apollo moon mission in 1971. It is a sport that unites people regardless of race, colour or creed. It is a sport which almost anyone can play but above all else it is a sport which truly pits the individual against himself/herself in their search to become the best they can possibly be whether they are playing in a Major Championship or on a Sunday morning with friends.

I have never known a sport in which the losers are so dignified and this was never so evident than Tom Lehman's emotional closing speech at the 2006 Ryder Cup after Team USA had been given one of the worst beatings in the history of the famous competition by Team Europe. Lehman, the USA Team Captain, was the utmost professional and extremely dignified in defeat whilst his graciousness should serve as a template to all sportsmen and sportswomen when things just do not seem to be going to plan. And again four years later at the Celtic Manor Resort, Wales who will ever forget the magnificent performance of the European team and the emotion that poured out around the course when Northern Ireland's Graeme McDowell sank the putt which won the coveted trophy back for the Europeans, captained by a Ryder Cup hero of the past, Colin Montgomerie. Just as Tom Lehman had to do in 2006 at The K Club near Dublin so too did the USA captain in 2010, Corey Pavin, have to do in the Welsh valleys when he was magnanimous in defeat.

I truly hope you enjoy my *Golf Miscellany* and that some of the entries contained within it leave you feeling as if you have just hit your approach shot to the green straight into a nearby bunker – scratching your head in amazement!

John White
June 2011

❋ GREAT GOLF COURSES OF THE WORLD (1) ❋

Prestwick, Scotland
Opened: 1851
Designer: Anon.
Yardage: 6,544 Par: 71
Majors: Open Championship 1860–70, 1872, 1875, 1878, 1881, 1884, 1887, 1890, 1893, 1898, 1903, 1908, 1914, 1925

Prestwick is among the most historic golf clubs. Where better to tee off than at the Ayrshire venue where the first major championship was played almost 150 years ago? Prestwick Golf Club was founded in 1851 after a group of men met in a local hotel, the Red Lion, and decided to build a golf course. The inaugural Open Championship was held at Prestwick in 1860 and organized by the members who subscribed £25 to purchase a red morocco belt with silver clasps. Only eight players contested the first Open Championship, which was won by Willie Park of Musselburgh with a score of 174 over 36 holes.

❋ WIT AND WISDOM OF GOLF (1) ❋

"Keep close count of your nickels and dimes, stay away from whiskey, and never concede a putt."
Sam Snead

❋ CRANE SNATCHES PAR-THREE WIN ❋

On Wednesday, 5 April 2006, the day before the 2006 Masters began, Ben Crane won the par-three contest with a score of 23. Amazingly, three holes-in-one were made at the 9th hole, bringing to 61 the total of holes-in-one made in the par-three contest since its inception in 1960. The winner of the par-three contest has never gone on to win that year's Masters and Luke Donald continued that run in 2011.

❋ MASTER OF CLUB AND RACQUET ❋

Ellsworth Vines was a five-times winner on the PGA Tour and managed a semi-final place at the 1951 US PGA Championship when it was a match-play tournament. Vines only took up playing golf in his late twenties after he became bored with his first love, tennis. During his tennis career Vines won three Grand Slam singles titles: the US Open in 1931 and 1932 and Wimbledon in 1932.

❋ FIVE OR MORE MAJORS ❋

The following list details those players who have won five or more of golf's four Majors, up to and including the 2007 Masters. The list does not take account of Amateur Championship victories.

Jack Nicklaus – 18	Sam Snead – 7
Tiger Woods – 14	Harry Vardon – 7
Walter Hagen – 11	Nick Faldo – 6
Ben Hogan – 9	Lee Trevino – 6
Gary Player – 9	Seve Ballesteros – 5
Tom Watson – 8	James Braid – 5
Bobby Jones – 7	Byron Nelson – 5
Arnold Palmer – 7	J. H. Taylor – 5
Gene Sarazen – 7	Peter Thomson – 5

❋ THE GREATEST WINNING STREAK ❋

In 1945 Byron Nelson won an unprecedented 18 tournaments, a feat which today remains the Everest for golfers. In the same year he notched up another amazing record: 11 tournament wins in succession. Between 1944 and 1945 Nelson won 34 of the 75 tournaments he entered and was placed in the top 100 on every occasion. (He was exempt from war service as a result of suffering from haemophilia.) Nelson also held the record of "being in the money" in the most consecutive tournaments (113) – until Tiger Woods broke it in 2004.

❋ GOLF'S FIRST WORLD CHAMPIONSHIP ❋

In 1926 Walter Hagen and Bobby Jones played a 72-hole match in Florida which at the time was dubbed the "World Championship of Golf". Hagen won 12 & 11, and following his loss Jones said: "When a man misses his drive, and then misses his second shot, and then wins the hole with a birdie, it gets my goat." Jones was referring to Hagen's wild shots off the tee.

❋ BRIGHT STARS ❋

Two 15-year-olds, Ben Hogan and Byron Nelson, were involved in a play-off for the 1927 Caddie Championship tournament at Fort Worth's Glen Garden Country Club. Nelson defeated Hogan to win the title.

❋ WIT AND WISDOM OF GOLF (2) ❋

"I would like to deny all allegations by Bob Hope that, during my last game of golf, I hit an eagle, a birdie, an elk and a moose."
***Gerald Ford, US President** 1974–77*

❋ WHEN CHI-CHI MET MOTHER TERESA ❋

Chi-Chi Rodriguez once had a brief meeting with Mother Teresa of Calcutta. Speaking about the experience afterwards, the Puerto Rican golfer said that it was the greatest moment in his life. Indeed so inspired was Chi-Chi by Mother Teresa that he decided to help others less fortunate than himself and along with Bill Hayes and Bob Jones he founded the "Chi-Chi Rodriguez Youth Foundation", an after-school programme at the Glen Oaks Golf Course in Clearwater, Florida. The principal aim of the foundation is to rebuild the self-esteem of young people who are victims of abuse, or who have got themselves into trouble with the law.

❋ WATCH THE BIRDIES ❋

When Gary Player won his third green jacket in 1978, he secured The Masters with a superb final-round 64, including seven birdies on the final 10 holes.

❋ BRITISH OPEN SIXTIES ❋

The following players hold the record for the most career rounds in the 60s in the British Open Championship:

33 – Jack Nicklaus,
Nick Faldo
29 – Tom Watson
23 – Greg Norman
21 – Lee Trevino
20 – Seve Ballesteros
Nick Price

❋ THE PGA'S LAST MATCH-PLAY CHAMPION ❋

When Lionel Hebert defeated Dow Finsterwald 3 & 1 in the 1957 US PGA Championship at the Miami Valley Golf Club in Dayton, Ohio, he became the last match-play PGA Champion in what was the 39th edition of the tournament. Hebert went one up on Finsterwald with a birdie at the 32nd hole before closing the match and the Major with a par at the 35th. The following year, 1958, the US PGA Championship switched to a stroke-play format and has remained so since.

❋ SEVERIANO BALLESTEROS (1957–2011) ❋

Severiano "Seve" Ballesteros was born on 9 April 1957 in Pedrena, Cantabria, Spain. The young Seve took up golf at the age of three and often was found hitting a golf ball on the beaches near his home in northern Spain with a three-iron given to him by an older brother. Ballesteros was just 16 when he turned professional in March 1974, and only 19 when he burst on to the major stage in 1976. To the astonishment of the golfing world, Seve finished runner-up to Johnny Miller in the Open Championship at Royal Birkdale. He then won his first European Tour event, the Dutch Open, followed by the Lancome Trophy, and secured the 1976 European Tour Order of Merit title. Seve won four times to retain his European Tour Order of Merit titles in both 1977 and 1978, the first three of six titles, a record which was broken by Colin Montgomerie.

In 1978 Seve won his first PGA Tour event, taking victory in the Greater Greensboro Open. Then in 1979 the young Seve made the world sit up and pay attention to him when he won the first of his five Majors, claiming victory in the Open Championship at Royal Lytham & St Annes. His 1979 Open win made him the first golfer from continental Europe to win a Major since Arnaud Massy from France won the 1907 Open at Royal Liverpool Golf Club. Ballesteros's 1979 Open win came on the back of wild play during the tournament, including smashing his ball into BBC vehicles. However, Seve was a natural, and very few golfers have ever possessed his ability to turn a wayward drive into a magnificent shot from deep rough, woodland or bushes. Indeed Hale Irwin was left scratching his head at Royal Birkdale in 1979, pondering how anyone could win the Open with such poor driving.

He won four PGA Tour events in 1980, including The Masters. His Masters victory meant that he became the first European to win the green jacket and, at the time, the youngest ever Masters champion, aged 23. In 1983 Seve won his second Masters title, and in 1984 he captured his fourth Major, and his second British Open title. Four European wins and one PGA win came his way in 1985, followed by seven more wins on the European circuit over the next two years. In 1988 he claimed his third Open title, winning again at Royal Lytham & St Annes. During his career Seve won 44 European Tour events, nine PGA Tour events and 39 other events that included five World Matchplay titles and three Alfred Dunhill Cups. Seve won 20 points for Europe from 37 matches in the Ryder Cup.

Seve collapsed in a Madrid airport in October 2008, and a brain tumour was discovered. He died from the illness on 7 May 2011.

❋ BRITISH OPEN PAST WINNERS ❋

Year	*Player*	*Venue*
2010	Louis Oosthuizen	St Andrews Links
2009*	Stewart Cink	The Westin Turnberry Resort
2008	Padraig Harrington (2)	Royal Birkdale Golf Club
2007*	Padraig Harrington	Carnoustie Golf Links
2006	Tiger Woods (3)	Royal Liverpool Golf Club
2005	Tiger Woods (2)	St Andrews Links
2004*	Todd Hamilton	Royal Troon Golf Club
2003	Ben Curtis	Royal St George's Golf Club
2002*	Ernie Els	Muirfield
2001	David Duval	Royal Lytham & St Annes Golf Club
2000	Tiger Woods	St Andrews Links
1999*	Paul Lawrie	Carnoustie Golf Links
1998	Mark O'Meara	Royal Birkdale Golf Club
1997	Justin Leonard	Royal Troon Golf Club
1996	Tom Lehman	Royal Lytham & St Annes Golf Club
1995*	John Daly	St Andrews Links
1994	Nick Price	The Westin Turnberry Resort
1993	Greg Norman (2)	Royal St George's Golf Club
1992	Nick Faldo (3)	Muirfield
1991	Ian Baker-Finch	Royal Birkdale Golf Club
1990	Nick Faldo (2)	St Andrews Links
1989*	Mark Calcavecchia	Royal Troon Golf Club
1988	Seve Ballesteros (3)	Royal Lytham & St Annes Golf Club
1987	Nick Faldo	Muirfield
1986	Greg Norman	The Westin Turnberry Resort
1985	Sandy Lyle	Royal St George's Golf Club
1984	Seve Ballesteros (2)	St Andrews Links
1983	Tom Watson (5)	Royal Birkdale Golf Club
1982	Tom Watson (4)	Royal Troon Golf Club
1981	Bill Rogers	Royal St George's Golf Club
1980	Tom Watson (3)	Muirfield
1979	Seve Ballesteros	Royal Lytham & St Annes Golf Club
1978	Jack Nicklaus (3)	St Andrews Links
1977	Tom Watson (2)	The Westin Turnberry Resort
1976	Johnny Miller	Royal Birkdale Golf Club
1975	Tom Watson	Carnoustie Golf Links
1974	Gary Player (3)	Royal Lytham & St Annes Golf Club
1973	Tom Weiskopf	Royal Troon Golf Club
1972	Lee Trevino (2)	Muirfield
1971	Lee Trevino	Royal Birkdale Golf Club

1970 Jack Nicklaus (2) .... St Andrews Links
1969 Tony Jacklin .... Royal Lytham & St Annes Golf Club
1968 Gary Player (2) .... Carnoustie Golf Links
1967 Roberto DeVicenzo .... Royal Liverpool Golf Club
1966 Jack Nicklaus .... Muirfield
1965 Peter Thomson (5) .... Royal Birkdale Golf Club
1964 Tony Lema .... St Andrews Links
1963 Bob Charles .... Royal Lytham & St Annes Golf Club
1962 Arnold Palmer (2) .... Royal Troon Golf Club
1961 Arnold Palmer .... Royal Birkdale Golf Club
1960 Kel Nagle .... St Andrews Links
1959 Gary Player .... Muirfield
1958 Peter Thomson (4) .... Royal Lytham & St Annes Golf Club
1957 Bobby Locke (4) .... St Andrews Links
1956 Peter Thomson (3) .... Royal Liverpool Golf Club
1955 Peter Thomson (2) .... St Andrews Links
1954 Peter Thomson .... Royal Birkdale Golf Club
1953 Ben Hogan .... Carnoustie Golf Links
1952 Bobby Locke (3) .... Royal Lytham & St Annes Golf Club
1951 Max Faulkner .... Royal Portrush Golf Club
1950 Bobby Locke (2) .... Royal Troon Golf Club
1949 Bobby Locke .... Royal St George's Golf Club
1948 Henry Cotton (3) .... Muirfield
1947 Fred Daly .... Royal Liverpool Golf Club
1946 Sam Snead .... St Andrews Links
1940–45: *No Championships due to Second World War*
1939 Richard Burton .... St Andrews Links
1938 Reg Whitcombe .... Royal St George's Golf Club
1937 Henry Cotton (2) .... Carnoustie Golf Links
1936 Alf Padgham .... Royal Liverpool Golf Club
1935 Alf Perry .... Muirfield
1934 Henry Cotton .... Royal St George's Golf Club
1933 Denny Shute .... St Andrews Links
1932 Gene Sarazen .... Prince's Golf Club
1931 Tommy Armour .... Carnoustie Golf Links
1930 Bobby Jones (Am) (3) .... Royal Liverpool Golf Club
1929 Walter Hagen (4) .... Muirfield
1928 Walter Hagen (3) .... Royal St George's Golf Club
1927 Bobby Jones (Am) (2) .... St Andrews Links
1926 Bobby Jones (Am) .... Royal Lytham & St Annes Golf Club
1925 Jim Barnes .... Prestwick Golf Club
1924 Walter Hagen (2) .... Royal Liverpool Golf Club
1923 Arthur Havers .... Royal Troon Golf Club

1922	Walter Hagen	Royal St George's Golf Club
1921	Jock Hutchison	St Andrews Links
1920	George Duncan	Royal Cinque Ports Golf Club

1915–19: *No Championships due to First World War*

1914	Harry Vardon (6)	Prestwick Golf Club
1913	John Henry Taylor (5)	Royal Liverpool Golf Club
1912	Edward Ray	Muirfield
1911	Harry Vardon (5)	Royal St George's Golf Club
1910	James Braid (5)	St Andrews Links
1909	John Henry Taylor (4)	Royal Cinque Ports Golf Club
1908	James Braid (4)	Prestwick Golf Club
1907	Arnaud Massy	Royal Liverpool Golf Club
1906	James Braid (3)	Muirfield
1905	James Braid (2)	St Andrews Links
1904	Jack White	Royal St George's Golf Club
1903	Harry Vardon (4)	Prestwick Golf Club
1902	Alexander Herd	Royal Liverpool Golf Club
1901	James Braid	Muirfield
1900	John Henry Taylor (3)	St Andrews Links
1899	Harry Vardon (3)	Royal St George's Golf Club
1898	Harry Vardon (2)	Prestwick Golf Club
1897	Harold Hilton (Am) (2)	Royal Liverpool Golf Club
1896	Harry Vardon	Muirfield
1895	John Henry Taylor (2)	St Andrews Links
1894	John Henry Taylor	Royal St George's Golf Club
1893	William Auchterlonie	Prestwick Golf Club
1892	Harold Hilton (Am)	Muirfield
1891	Hugh Kirkaldy	St Andrews Links
1890	John Ball, Jnr (Am)	Prestwick Golf Club
1889	Willie Park, Jnr (2)	Musselburgh Links
1888	Jack Burns	St Andrews Links
1887	Willie Park, Jnr	Prestwick Golf Club
1886	David Brown	Musselburgh Links
1885	Bob Martin (2)	St Andrews Links
1884	Jack Simpson	Prestwick Golf Club
1883	Willie Fernie	Musselburgh Links
1882	Bob Ferguson (3)	St Andrews Links
1881	Bob Ferguson (2)	Prestwick Golf Club
1880	Bob Ferguson	Musselburgh Links
1879	Jamie Anderson (3)	St Andrews Links
1878	Jamie Anderson (2)	Prestwick Golf Club
1877	Jamie Anderson	Musselburgh Links
1876	Bob Martin	St Andrews Links

1875	Willie Park, Snr (4)	Prestwick Golf Club
1874	Mungo Park	Musselburgh Links
1873	Tom Kidd	St Andrews Links
1872	Tom Morris, Jnr (4)	Prestwick Golf Club
1871	*No championship*	
1870	Tom Morris, Jnr (3)	Prestwick Golf Club
1869	Tom Morris, Jnr (2)	Prestwick Golf Club
1868	Tom Morris, Jnr	Prestwick Golf Club
1867	Tom Morris, Snr (4)	Prestwick Golf Club
1866	Willie Park, Snr (3)	Prestwick Golf Club
1865	Andrew Strath	Prestwick Golf Club
1864	Tom Morris, Snr (3)	Prestwick Golf Club
1863	Willie Park, Snr (2)	Prestwick Golf Club
1862	Tom Morris, Snr (2)	Prestwick Golf Club
1861	Tom Morris, Snr	Prestwick Golf Club
1860	Willie Park, Snr	Prestwick Golf Club

*NOTES: * – Won in a play-off Am – Amateur Nat – All born in Britain but were granted American citizenship prior to winning the Open Championship*

❋ GREAT GOLF COURSES OF THE WORLD (2) ❋

MEDINAH COUNTRY CLUB, ILLINOIS

Opened: 1851

Designer: Tom Bendelow

Yardage: 7,508 Par: 72

Majors: US Open Championship 1949, 1975, 1990. US PGA Championship 1999, 2006

Medinah Country Club was founded in 1925 by the Medinah Shriners (from Chicago's Medinah Temple), and its sprawling 640 acres in Illinois contains three champion golf courses. Medinah CC is best known for Course No. 3, a 7,508-yard course that has hosted three US Open Championships (in 1949, 1975 and 1990) and two US PGA Championships (in 1999 and 2006). In 1930 Harry "Lighthorse" Cooper carded a 63 in the Medinah Open, the lowest score ever recorded on the course (and still a record, albeit equalled, in a Major Championship. Both of the US PGA Championships played at Medinah were won by Tiger Woods. In 2006 Woods destroyed the field and won the 88th US PGA Championship by five strokes. To commemorate Woods's achievement he was made a member of the club, the first player ever to be so recognized by the golf club. He recorded another five-stroke victory at the 2006 PGA Championship. Medinah CC will play host to the Ryder Cup in 2012.

❋ WIT AND WISDOM OF GOLF (3) ❋

"I play in the low 80s. If it's any hotter than that, I won't play."
Joe Louis

❋ 54-HOLE PLAY-OFF ❋

At the 1926 Metropolitan Open a 54-hole play-off was needed before Macdonald Smith finally beat Gene Sarazen. At the time 18-hole play-offs were the norm and if the players were still tied they played another 18. However, in this titanic battle Smith and Sarazen were still tied after 36 play-off holes and therefore had to play a further 18.

❋ SARAZEN HONOURED ❋

Gene Sarazen, the winner of 39 PGA Tournaments, was inducted into the World Golf Hall of Fame in 1974. He was the Associated Press male Athlete of the Year in 1932 and won the PGA Tour's inaugural Lifetime Achievement Award in 1996.

❋ GOLF'S FIRST $10,000 PURSE ❋

In 1926 the inaugural Los Angeles Open was held and became the first tournament in the history of golf to offer a purse of $10,000 to the winner. Harry Cooper scooped the bucks. The Los Angeles Open is the third oldest surviving PGA Tour event but is now known as the "Nissan Open". In February 2006 South Africa's Rory Sabbatini won the 2006 Nissan Open at the Riviera Country Club, Pacific Palisades, California, and took home the first prize of $918,000.

❋ TIGER'S US AMATEUR HAT-TRICK ❋

In 1996, aged 20, Tiger Woods became the first golfer in history to win three consecutive US Amateur titles. He won the NCAA individual golf championship the same year.

❋ EUROPEAN MONEY MEN ❋

In 1971 Neil Coles of England won the first ever PGA European Tour money list with winnings of £10,479. Thirty years later Retief Goosen of South Africa topped the European money list with winnings of €2,862,806.

❋ SWEET FOR SWEETSER ❋

In 1926 Jess Sweetser became the first American-born winner of the British Amateur Championship.

❋ HAGEN THE BASEBALL STAR ❋

Walter Hagen was also a very skilled baseball player and in 1914 he actually cancelled a try-out for the Philadelphia Phillies in order to play in a golf tournament. Later that very same week, Hagen won the US Open Championship and his sporting career was changed for ever, much to the delight of golf enthusiasts today.

Did You Know That?
Hagen won his first tournament in 1914 – the US Open Championship – and his last in 1936 – the Inverness Four-Ball (with Ky Laffoon).

❋ TOP OPEN LADY CHAMPIONS ❋

Australia's Karrie Webb was the only woman to have won three women's British Open Championships, with titles in 1995, 1997 and 2002. Her achievement was matched by American Sherri Steinhauer, who claimed the Championship in 1998, 1999 and 2006.

❋ BRIDGES OF AUGUSTA NATIONAL ❋

The three famous bridges at Augusta are dedicated to legends of golf:

Hogan Bridge: Dedicated to Ben Hogan on 2 April 1958. The Hogan Bridge crosses Rae's Creek, taking golfers to the 12th green. A plaque on the bridge commemorates Hogan's 1953 Masters victory, when he posted a then record score of 274.

Nelson Bridge: Dedicated to Byron Nelson on 2 April 1958. The Nelson Bridge crosses Rae's Creek, taking golfers to the 13th tee. This feature of the course commemorates Nelson's play on holes 12 and 13 at the 1937 Masters, when, on the final day, Lord Byron scored a two and a three on the two holes and made up six strokes on Ralph Guldahl to win The Masters.

Sarazen Bridge: The first bridge at Augusta named for a player, the Sarazen Bridge was dedicated to Gene Sarazen on 6 April 1955. It crosses a small body of water fronting the 15th green. It was on this hole in 1935 that Sarazen's "shot heard 'round the world" – a four-wood into the green that dropped into the cup for a double eagle – helped him win the 1935 Masters.

❋ WIT AND WISDOM OF GOLF (4) ❋

"The reason the Road Hole is the greatest par four in the world, is because it's a par five."
Ben Crenshaw

❋ MONTY THE GREAT ❋

In 1999 Colin Montgomerie topped the PGA European Tour money-winners' list for the seventh consecutive year, beating the previous record of six PGA European Tour money wins, which he had held jointly with Seve Ballesteros. In 2005, Montgomerie won his eighth PGA European Tour money-winners' award.

❋ EIGHT-YEAR WAIT ❋

Eight years after turning professional, Arron Oberholser finally claimed his first win on the PGA Tour by winning the AT&T Pebble Beach Pro-Am in February 2006.

❋ MIND THE COWS ❋

Stuart Appleby was born on 1 May 1971 in Cohuna, a northern country town in Victoria, Australia. As a young boy he practised hitting golf balls from paddock to paddock on the family's dairy farm. He turned professional in 1992 and won his first PGA Tour event, the Honda Classic, in 1997. He claimed his ninth win on the PGA Tour at the Greenbrier Classic in West Virginia in 2010 and won the 2010 PGA Tour Comeback Player of the Year award.

❋ SNEAD THE WORST FINISHER ❋

Sam Snead holds the unenviable record for hitting the worst finishing round by a champion in the British Open. In 1946 the American golfing legend carded a final-round 75 at St Andrews.

❋ SPEEDY PROGRESS ❋

In 2005 J.B. Holmes won the PGA Tour Qualifying Tournament and tied for 10th in his first PGA Tour start at the 2006 Sony Open in Hawaii. A month later, in his fifth event as a professional, he won the FBR Open in Arizona, his first on the PGA Tour. Holmes again won the FBR Open in 2008 and played on the winning Ryder Cup team.

❋ NICK FALDO, MBE (1957–) ❋

Nicholas "Nick" Alexander Faldo was born on 18 July 1957 in Welwyn Garden City, England. In 1975 Faldo won both the English Amateur Championship and the British Youths Championship at a time when he was training to be a carpet fitter. However, in 1976 he turned professional and joined the European Tour. The following year he won the first of his 27 European Tour events, the Skol Lager Individual. In 1977 he also played in the first of a record 11 Ryder Cups (and a record 25 points) and beat Tom Watson in his singles match. In 1978 he claimed another European Tour victory, and finished third in Europe's prize money list.

Further successes on the European Tour followed with victories in the 1980 and 1981 Sun Alliance PGA Championship and the 1982 Haig Whisky TPC. In 1983 he won the Paco Rabanne Open de France, the Martini International, the Car Care Plan International, the Lawrence Batley International, the Ebel Swiss Open-European Masters, and came first in the 1983 Order of Merit. In 1984 he again won the Car Care Plan International and also won his first ever PGA Tour event when he claimed victory in the Sea Pines Heritage. However, disastrous collapses during the 1983 Open Championship and the 1984 Masters made Faldo decide that his swing was not good enough to bag a Major. He turned to the golf guru, David Leadbetter, and spent a few years remodelling his swing. However, it was not until 1987 that the "Faldo swing" started to make a dramatic impact. He took victory in the Spanish Open that year before going on to win the first of his six Majors and the first of three Open Championships.

During the late 1980s and early 1990s, Faldo was one of the biggest names in the sport and topped the official world rankings for a total of 98 weeks. In 1988 he won two European Tour events and the following year he claimed victory in The Masters, his second Major. Three more wins followed in Europe in 1989 before he enjoyed his best year, 1990, when he bagged two Majors, retaining his green jacket at Augusta and winning his second Open Championship. A third Claret Jug followed in 1992, and a third green jacket was donned in 1996. Faldo was named the European Tour Player of the Year in 1989, 1990 and 1992 and the PGA Tour Player of the Year in 1990. During his career he won 43 tournaments (27 European Tour titles, 9 PGA titles and 7 others). In 1989 he was voted the BBC Sports Personality of the Year, he was awarded an MBE in 1998. His captaincy of the 2008 Europe Ryder Cup team was less successful as they lost 16½–11½.

⁂ WIT AND WISDOM OF GOLF (5) ⁂

"Golf is like solitaire. When you cheat, you only cheat yourself."
Tony Lema

⁂ MOST AMATEUR & PROFESSIONAL MAJORS ⁂

The following list details those golfers with the most men's professional Major titles – including Amateur Championships.

Jack Nicklaus – 18
Tiger Woods – 14
Bobby Jones – 13
Walter Hagen – 11
John Ball – 9
Ben Hogan – 9
Gary Player – 9
Arnold Palmer – 8
Tom Watson – 8

⁂ FOREIGN CHAMPIONS ⁂

In 1985 Peter Thomson of Australia became the first non-American to top the Champions Tour money-winners' list. Up to the end of 2010 only five other non-Americans have topped the list (two of them on two occasions):

2010: Bernhard Langer (Germany) – $2,648,939
2009: Bernhard Langer (Germany) – $2,139,451
2008: Bernhard Langer (Germany) – $2,035,073
1989: Bob Charles (New Zealand) – $725,887
1988: Bob Charles (New Zealand) – $533,929
1987: Chi-Chi Rodriguez (Puerto Rico) – $509,145
1986: Bruce Crampton (Australia) – $454,299
1985: Peter Thomson (Australia) – $386,724

⁂ THE VARDON GRIP ⁂

Harry Vardon, winner of the Open Championship a record six times (1896, 1898, 1899, 1903, 1911, 1914) and the US Open Championship in 1900, was famous for introducing the Vardon Grip, the grip that has become the most popular in the game. To form this grip you place the little finger of the hand lower on the club in between the index and middle finger on the lead hand. The lead-hand thumb should then fit comfortably in the lifeline of the trailing hand. The grip, although popularized by Vardon, was actually invented by Johnny Laidlay, a champion Scottish amateur golfer.

❋ THE TOREADOR DANCE ❋

During his early career Chi-Chi Rodriguez used to put his hat over the golf hole whenever he made a birdie or an eagle. However, when other golfers officially complained about his actions he decided to adopt his famous "toreador dance". Chi-Chi would pretend that a birdie or an eagle opportunity was a bull and that his putter was a sword he would use to kill the bull (sink the putt).

Did You Know That?
In 1992 Chi-Chi Rodriguez was the first Puerto Rican to be inducted into the PGA World Golf Hall of Fame.

❋ ITALIAN ROOKIE CLAIMS HUGE PRIZES ❋

On 9 April 2010, 10 days short of his 17th birthday, Italian Matteo Manassero, the 2009 British Amateur champion, made the cut at the Masters, making him the youngest player ever to achieve the feat. He finished tied for 36th and won the silver medal as the low (leading) amateur. Manassero turned professional in early May 2010 and was quick to make his name on the European PGA Tour. In fact on 25 October 2010, at the Castello Masters Costa Azahar in Spain, he finished 16 under par to win the tournament, thus becoming the youngest ever winner on the Tour. He was later named the 2010 European PGA Tour Rookie of the Year, and, to show he was no flash in the pan, Manassero then won the 2011 Maybank Malaysian Open.

❋ SLAMMIN' SAMMY ❋

In 1965 Sam Snead won his eighth Greater Greensboro Open, making him at 52 years, 10 months and 8 days the oldest ever player to win a PGA Tour event.

❋ MASTERS WIRE-TO-WIRE WINNER ❋

In 1941 Craig Wood won The Masters to become the tournament's first wire-to-wire champion with rounds of 66, 71, 71 and 72 and a three-shot victory over Byron Nelson. Only three other golfers have equalled Wood's Masters feat: Arnold Palmer (1960), Jack Nicklaus (1972) and Raymond Floyd (1976). Wood followed his 1941 Masters victory by winning the 45th US Open Championship at The Colonial Club in Fort Worth, Texas. This was the first time a player had won the first two Major championships of the same year.

❋ BRITAIN'S FIRST LADY FAMER ❋

In 1975 Joyce Wethered (England) became the first non-American female to be inducted into the PGA World Golf Hall of Fame. She is widely regarded as the greatest British female golfer of all time, winning the British Ladies' Amateur Golf Championship four times (1922, 1924, 1925 and 1929) and the English Ladies' Championship on five consecutive occasions between 1920 and 1924. In the Ladies Open of 1929 she met the great American champion Glenna Collett in a memorable contest. Joyce was five down after only nine holes, but clawed her way back to win 3 & 1.

❋ FIRST NON-AMERICAN FAMERS ❋

In 1974 Harry Vardon (England) became the first non-American male to be inducted into the PGA World Golf Hall of Fame.

❋ BRITISH OPEN OLDEST WINNERS ❋

Old Tom Morris, 1867 – 46 years, 99 days
Harry Vardon, 1914 – 44 years, 41 days
Roberto de Vicenzo, 1967 – 44 years, 93 days

❋ WATSON HONOURED BY THE R&A ❋

Tom Watson joined the Champions Tour after celebrating his 50th birthday in 1999. In the same year he was given an honorary membership of the Royal & Ancient Golf Club of St Andrews, which ironically was one of the few venues where Watson did not win any of his five Open titles.

❋ TOP MASTER ❋

Jack Nicklaus holds the record for achieving the most top 5 Masters finishes with 15, the most top 10 Masters finishes with 22, and the most top 25 Masters finishes with 29.

❋ SAM'S FRUITLESS CAMPAIGNS ❋

Sam Torrance lies in second place, one behind Dai Rees, for having participated in the greatest number of Open Golf Championships without ever tasting victory in the tournament. Sam played in the Open 28 times. Neil Coles played in 27 Opens without success.

❋ GREAT GOLF COURSES OF THE WORLD (3) ❋

Pebble Beach, California
Opened: 1919
Designers: Douglas Grant and Jack Neville
Yardage: 6,799 Par: 72
Majors: US Open Championship 1972, 1982, 1992, 2000, 2010

Pebble Beach Golf Links is one of several well-known courses situated in Pebble Beach, California. In 2001 it became the first public course to be selected as the No. 1 Golf Course in America by *Golf Digest* magazine. Pebble Beach Golf Links has hosted the US Open Championship four times and has a distinguished set of Open Champions, Jack Nicklaus, Tom Watson, Tom Kite, Tiger Woods and Graeme McDowell. It hosted its fifth US Open Championship in 2010. The course co-hosts the PGA Tour's AT&T Pebble Beach Pro-Am with the nearby Poppy Hills Golf Course and Spyglass Hill Golf Course. Many other high-profile championships have been staged on the course, including the 1977 PGA Championship, won by Lanny Wadkins, and several US Amateur Championships.

❋ HAGEN SNUBS ORGANIZERS ❋

Walter Hagen once refused to enter a clubhouse to claim his prize because he had earlier been denied entrance. During Hagen's era there was a wide gulf between amateur and professional golfers, and at many clubs professionals were not permitted to enter the clubhouse via the main entrance.

❋ US MASTERS BRIDESMAIDS ❋

Three players share the unwanted record of having finished runner-up in The Masters on the most occasions:

4 – Ben Hogan (1942, 1946, 1954 & 1955)
4 – Jack Nicklaus (1964, 1971, 1977 & 1981)
4 – Tom Weiskopf (1969, 1972, 1974 & 1975)

❋ US MASTERS LONGEVITY CHAMPION ❋

Arnold Palmer holds the record for the highest number of consecutive Masters participations with 50 from 1955 to 2004. Palmer won four green jackets (1958, 1960, 1962 and 1964).

❋ WIT AND WISDOM OF GOLF (6) ❋

"I don't know if I'll ever do it again or not, but frankly I don't really care."
Jack Nicklaus, after claiming his sixth Masters title

❋ BABY CUB ❋

In 1997 Tiger Woods became the youngest player to win the coveted Masters title, aged just 21 years, 3 months and 14 days.

Did You Know That?
Tiger Woods's 1997 final score of 270 is the lowest score after 72 holes in the history of The Masters.

❋ GETTING BETTER WITH AGE ❋

Kermit Dannehl of the USA holds the record for the highest number of 18-hole rounds completed in which the total number of shots played did not exceed his age. Between 1992 and 2005, Kermit, who was born on 31 August 1919, completed 930 of them.

❋ 11 BELOW AGE ❋

In 1983 a 71-year-old Sam Snead carded a round of 60 (12 under par) at the Homestead in Hot Springs, Arkansas, USA.

❋ OUT FRONT IN THE BRITISH OPEN ❋

Only five players in the 146-year history of the Open Championship have led the competition after every single round including ties:

Harry Vardon, 1899 and 1903 ❖ J. H. Taylor, 1900
Lee Trevino, 1971 ❖ Gary Player, 1974 ❖ Tiger Woods, 2005

❋ THE END OF THE GUTTY ❋

When Walter Travis, originally from Australia, won the 1901 United States Amateur Championship using the Haskell ball, and then Alex Herd won the 1902 Open Championship at Royal Liverpool Golf Club, also using the new ball, it was the beginning of the end of the gutta-percha ball's 55-year dominance of the sport. Almost every golfer ceased using the gutty in favour of the Haskell.

❋ MARK HURRIES BACK ❋

In 1992 Mark Calcavecchia recorded the lowest ever score in The Masters fourth-round back nine when he completed it in 29 shots. His record was subsequently equalled in 1998 by David Toms.

❋ SOUTH AFRICA'S LION KING ❋

In 1994 Nick Price won two Majors back-to-back, the Open Championship and the US PGA Championship, to add to his first Major, the US PGA Championship in 1992. Price, born in Durban, South Africa, but a Zimbabwean citizen, topped the US PGA Tour money list in 1993 and 1994, setting a new earnings record each time, and spent a total of 43 weeks at number one in the official world golf rankings. In 2003 Price was inducted into the PGA World Golf Hall of Fame, and in 2005 he won the Bobby Jones Award, the highest honour given by the USGA in recognition of distinguished sportsmanship in golf.

❋ BEST MASTERS ROUND ❋

In 1986 Nick Price broke the record for the lowest score for any round in the US Masters when he hit 63 in the third round. His feat was equalled in 1996 when Greg Norman scored 63 in the first round.

❋ FOUR-IN-A-ROW IN THE SUN ❋

In 1930 Gene Sarazen won the Miami Open for the fourth consecutive year to equal Walter Hagen's record for the most successive wins in a single event. Tiger Woods would also later equal the record.

❋ KING OF THE SENIORS ❋

In 1996 Jack Nicklaus became the first person in the history of the PGA to win the same Senior PGA Tour (now the Champions Tour) event four times, when he captured the Tradition tournament. Nicklaus is also the only person in the history of the PGA to win all of the major championships on both the PGA Tour and the Champions Tour. Nicklaus never won the Senior British Open but the tournament was not recognized as a Senior Major in the US until 2003, after the Golden Bear had packed his clubs away for good.

WALTER HAGEN (1892–1969)

Walter Charles Hagen was born in Rochester, New York, on 21 December 1892. Hagen took golf up in his teens, and in 1912, aged 19, he participated in the Canadian Open, where he finished 11th. When he returned to his home golf club, Oakland Hills CC in Michigan, and was asked how he had done, the young Hagen replied: "I lost." The following year he entered the US Open and finished one stroke behind Harry Vardon, Ted Ray and the young American, Francis Ouimet, who sensationally won the 1913 US Open in a play-off.

In 1914 Hagen won the US Open at the Midlothian Country Club, Illinois, the first of his 11 Majors. In 1916 he took victory in the Metropolitan Open, followed by two more wins the same year, in the Shawneee Open and the Western Open. After the First World War, he claimed his second Major, and his second US Open title, in 1919 at the Brae Burn Country Club, Massachusetts. Wins in the Florida West Coast Open, the Metropolitan Open (his third in four years) and the Bellevue Country Club Open all came in 1920. Always looking to improve his game and test himself against the best the sport had to offer, Hagen crossed the Atlantic in 1920 to play in his first British Open Championship. However, because he was a professional he was not permitted to enter the clubhouse at Royal Cinque Ports Golf Club, Deal. The flamboyant Hagen responded by hiring a Rolls-Royce, which he had his chauffeur park outside the entrance to the clubhouse, and ate lunch from a hamper. In 1921 he claimed victory in the 1921 PGA Championship and sixth in the Open. His PGA win in 1921 proved to be the first of five, including four consecutive PGA titles from 1924 to 1927. (In 1922 he did not play, and in 1923 he was second.)

Then in 1922, he did it: he became the first American golfer to win the British Open Championship when he took victory at Royal St Georges. Over the decade Hagen dominated the event, finishing runner-up in 1923, winner in 1924, tied for third in 1926, winner in 1928 and winner again in 1929. (He did not play in the Open Championships of 1925 and 1927.) By the end of the 1920s Hagen had won 11 Major Championships, which puts him in third place overall in the table of Major winners.

During his career the World Golf Hall of Famer won 44 PGA Tour events and captained the US team in the first six Ryder Cups, playing in the first five of them. At his funeral in 1969 the pallbearers included some legendary figures from sport, including George Morris and Arnold Palmer.

❋ WIT AND WISDOM OF GOLF (7) ❋

"The best is always good enough for me."
Sir Henry Cotton

❋ OPENED UP TO TELEVISION ❋

In 1954 the golf course hosting the US Open (Baltusrol GC) was roped from tee to green for the first time in the event's 60-year history. The same year also marked the first national television coverage of the US Open, won by Ed Furgol. Then, in 1965, the present format of four 18-hole daily rounds was implemented for the first time. National television coverage of the US Open was expanded by ABC Sports in 1977, so that all 18 holes of the final two rounds were broadcast live. Then in 1982, on the ESPN cable network, the first two rounds were broadcast live for the first time in the tournament's history (Tom Watson the victor at Pebble Beach GL). It was not until 1995 that NBC began televising the US Open for the first time (won by Corey Pavin at Shinnecock Hills GC.

❋ MEXICAN RICHES ❋

In 1930 the largest golf purse to date, a total of $25,000 with $10,000 going to the winner, was offered by the Agua Caliente Open in Tijuana, Mexico. Gene Sarazen was the winner.

❋ TIGER CLUB LOST ❋

As Tiger Woods eyed up a putt on the 7th green in his singles match against Robert Karlsson on the final day of the 2006 Ryder Cup, his caddy dropped his nine-iron into the River Liffey. Steve Williams had the club in his hand along with a towel, and when he reached down to wet the towel in order to clean the club, the nine-iron fell from his grasp into the water.

❋ THE SHOT HEARD 'ROUND THE WORLD ❋

Gene Sarazen holed a four-wood second shot at the 525-yard par-five 15th to earn a very rare double-eagle two. This enabled him to tie with Craig Wood after 72 holes of the 1935 Augusta National Invitational tournament (now known as The Masters). It is known as "the shot heard 'round the world". The following day Sarazen went on to claim a famous victory in a 36-hole play-off.

❋ WORST ROUND BY AN OPEN CHAMPION ❋

Fred Daly of Northern Ireland holds the Open Golf Championship record for the worst round by a player who would go on to win that year's tournament. At Hoylake (Royal Liverpool Golf Club) in 1947 Fred carded a third-round score of 78 on his way to a final 72-hole score of 293 and the famous old Claret Jug.

Did You Know That?
On his way to winning the Open in 1999, Scotland's Paul Lawrie carded a 76 in the third round at Carnoustie, a score that remains the second worst round in the tournament by a Champion.

❋ NEW BALLS, PLEASE ❋

The "Spalding Kro-Flite" became the first liquid-centre golf ball covered with wound rubber and a balata surface in 1930. The sports equipment manufacturer also produced one of the first sets of matched clubs featuring hickory shafts the same year.

❋ SMARTY PANTS ❋

Bobby Jones was as successful away from the golf course as he was on it. In 1922 he was made a Bachelor of Science in Mechanical Engineering at Georgia Institute of Technology and in 1924 a Bachelor of Arts in English Literature at Harvard University. Amazingly, after just one year in law school (1926–27) at Emory University, he passed the bar exam. When he retired from golf, aged 28, having won 13 Majors, he concentrated on his Atlanta law practice.

Did You Know That?
During his lifetime Jones made 18 instructional films, 12 entitled *How I Play Golf, by Bobby Jones*, and 6 entitled *How to Break 90*, and worked with A. G. Spalding & Co. in developing the first set of matched clubs.

❋ JACK OVER AND OUT ❋

Jack Nicklaus ended his career at the 2005 British Open at St Andrews, but the last competitive tournament in which he played in the US was the "Bayer Advantage Classic" in Overland Park, Kansas, on 13 June 2005.

❋ WIE IN A RUSH TO MAKE HISTORY ❋

On Monday 15 May 2006, Michelle Wie became the first woman to be invited to play on the men's European Tour. The following day, the Hawaiian became the first female to progress through the qualification stages for the men's US Open Championship. Her level-par round of 72 on her home course in the Turtle Bay Resort on the island of Oaha was the best score posted by any of the 40 players competing and means that technically she could lay claim to being the first female to win a men's professional tournament. Wie had yet to notch up her first victory in the ladies' professional ranks. However, she failed to make it on the big stage with the men.

❋ PRAYERS AT THE 18TH ❋

Tom Lehman, the captain of the 2006 USA Ryder Cup team, held a prayer meeting at the side of the 18th green at Medinah CC prior to the start of the 2006 US PGA Championship, just as family and friends were gathering in Portrush for the funeral of Darren Clarke's wife, Heather, who died a few days earlier from breast cancer.

❋ LPGA GRAND SLAM ❋

No woman has ever won the LPGA's Grand Slam of all four women's Majors in the same year. However, Babe Zaharias won all three Majors contested in 1950, and Sandra Haynie won both of the Majors that were played in 1974. Meanwhile six ladies have completed a "Career Grand Slam" by winning all four Majors at least once: Pat Bradley, Juli Inkster, Annika Sörenstam, Louise Suggs, Karrie Webb and Mickey Wright.

❋ DOUBLE CINK ❋

In 2004 Stewart Cink was a captain's choice by the US Ryder Cup team captain, Hal Sutton, and two years later Tom Lehman, captain of the 2006 Ryder Cup team, also named Cink as one of his two wild-card choices.

❋ IT NEVER LEAVES YOU ❋

In 1997 an 85-year-old Sam Snead fired a round of 78 at the Old White course of the Greenbrier in White Sulphur Springs, West Virginia. Not bad going for an octogenarian.

❋ GREAT GOLF COURSES OF THE WORLD (4) ❋

Royal Melbourne (Composite Course), Australia
Opened: 1891
Designer: Tom Finlay
Yardage: 6,566 Par: 71
Major events: Australian Open 1905, 1907, 1909, 1912, 1913, 1921, 1924, 1927, 1933, 1939, 1953, 1963, 1984, 1985, 1987, 1991. World Amateur Championship 1968. World Cup 1988. President's Cup 1998, 2011

The formation of the Royal Melbourne Club owes a debt mainly to Scotland, in the shape of men such as John Bruce, Tom Finlay and Hugh Playfair from St Andrews and William Knox and Tom Brentnall who played golf at Musselburgh. On 22 May 1891, a meeting was held at Scott's Hotel in Melbourne, Victoria, and the Melbourne Golf Club was duly constituted. By the end of June a suitable area for an 18-hole course was found close to the Caulfield Railway Station, and Tom Finlay designed a course of 4,750 yards. The founding Captain was John Munro Bruce (father of later Australian Prime Minister Viscount Stanley Melbourne Bruce). In 1895, Royal patronage was granted by Queen Victoria. Royal Melbourne was selected by the US PGA Tour to hold the President's Cup for the first time outside the USA in December 1998, and it is due to return there in 2011.

❋ THE HOGAN SLAM SEASON ❋

In golf "the Hogan Slam Season" is a reference to 1953, when Ben Hogan captured three of the four Majors: The Masters, the Open Championship and the US Open Championship. Having already won the PGA Championship in 1946 and again in 1948, his Open triumph at Carnoustie, Scotland, meant that he had now won all four of golf's glittering prizes. It still stands as one of the greatest single seasons in the history of professional golf. Unluckily for Hogan he was denied the opportunity of claiming all four Majors in the same year, the Grand Slam, because the PGA Championship (1–7 July) overlapped the British Open (6–10 July). His nine Major championships leave him tied fourth with Gary Player in the all-time list, trailing only Jack Nicklaus (18), Tiger Woods (12) and Walter Hagen (11).

Did You Know That?
Although he won it twice (1946 & 1948), Hogan very often declined to play in the PGA Championship.

❋ WIT AND WISDOM OF GOLF (8) ❋

"By the time you get to your ball, if you don't know what to do with it, try another sport."
Julius Boros

❋ THE EISENHOWER CABIN ❋

There are 10 cabins around the grounds of Augusta National Golf Club, the most famous being the Eisenhower Cabin. It is named in honour of President Dwight D. Eisenhower, who became a member at the Augusta National Golf Club in 1948, when he was a US Army General. Because Ike so very much enjoyed visiting Augusta (according to the official Masters site, Ike visited five times prior to becoming president, 29 times while in office and 11 times after leaving office), the club built the cabin for the President and Mrs Eisenhower in 1953. The cabin was built to security specifications stipulated by the US Secret Service. The arrangement was that when the Eisenhowers visited Augusta, the cabin was theirs, and at other times it could be used by other members of the club.

❋ WOODS CELEBRATES 10TH ANNIVERSARY ❋

Ten years to the day after turning pro on 27 August 1996, Tiger Woods celebrated by winning the 2006 World Golf Championships Bridgestone Invitational. It was Woods's 52nd PGA Tour triumph and his fourth successive win on the PGA Tour, a sequence which began with victory in the 2006 British Open. Woods made an eight-foot birdie putt on the fourth play-off hole against Stewart Cink in Akron, Ohio. Woods's victory was his fifth in the seven years Firestone has hosted this World Golf Championship tournament, and this win meant that he had now won more PGA Tour events on this golf course than on any other; he has won four times each at Augusta National and Torrey Pines.

❋ SOLID AS A ROCK ❋

Englishman Robert Rock turned professional aged 21 in 1998, but he did not make his European PGA Tour entry until 2003. He made little impact until 2009, when he had three second-place finishes, including losing a playoff in the Irish Open (won by Irish amateur Shane Lowrie). His best Major finish was seventh in the 2010 Open Championship, and he won his first event at the 2011 Italian Open.

❋ WIT AND WISDOM OF GOLF (9) ❋

"For five hundred thousand pounds, you'd play on a runway."
Colin Montgomerie

❋ VARDON TROPHY WINNERS ❋

Every year the PGA of America awards the "Vardon Trophy". The award is in honour of the legendary British golfer Harry Vardon, who won six Open Championships and one US Open Championship. When the inaugural award was presented in 1937 it was awarded on the basis of a points system. However, in 1947 the PGA commenced awarding it for the lowest scoring average, and in 1988 another rule change occurred, with the trophy going to the golfer with the lowest adjusted scoring average over a minimum of 60 rounds of golf.

❋ BRITISH OPEN YOUNGEST WINNERS ❋

Young Tom Morris, 1868 – 17 years, 5 months, 8 days
Willie Auchterlonie, 1893 – 21 years, 24 days
Seve Ballesteros, 1979 – 22 years, 3 months, 12 days

❋ SEVENTH HEAVEN FOR TIGER ❋

In 2005 Tiger Woods won a record-breaking seventh PGA Player of the Year Award despite the fact that six PGA Tour events still had to be played. His seventh players' crown moved him one ahead of Tom Watson, who won consecutive titles from 1977 to 1980 and also won in 1982 and 1984. Tiger's previous wins came in 1997, 1999, 2000, 2001, 2002 and 2003.

❋ LARA CLAIMS FIRST TOUR WIN ❋

On 19 November 2006, Spain's Jose Manuel Lara won the Hong Kong Open, finishing with a 15-under-par total of 265. Lara, who led the tournament from start to finish, beat Juvic Pagunsan of the Philippines by a stroke to claim his first ever European Tour victory. Lara became the third Spanish player to win it in the past six years (Jose-Maria Olazabel in 2001 and Miguel Angel Jiminez in 2004). The $2 million tournament is sanctioned by both the European and Asian tours. "You can't believe how many people say to me every week, when are you going to win? Now I win and everything is good," said an ecstatic Lara.

❋ HIGH FIVES FOR TIGER ❋

Tiger Woods's victory in the 2006 Deutsche Bank Championship, played in Boston, was his fifth straight victory on the PGA Tour. It was also Woods's seventh PGA Tour victory of 2006 from 14 tournament starts.

❋ THE PGA GRAND SLAM OF GOLF ❋

The PGA Grand Slam of Golf is the most prestigious tournament the sport has to offer. The tournament is held annually and since 2009 has been held at the Port Royal Golf Course in Bermuda and is contested by the winners of the year's four Majors (The Masters, the British Open, the US Open and the USPGA Championship). It is contested at the end of the year after both the European Tour and the PGA Tour events have been concluded. The PGA Grand Slam of Golf is organized by the PGA of America, but the prize money on offer does not count towards the PGA Tour money list. The inaugural competition took place in 1979 and ended in a tie between Andy North (USA) and Gary Player (South Africa). The tournament is a 36-hole stroke-play competition which takes place over two days. If a golfer wins more than one Major in a calendar year, the PGA of America reserve the right to invite former Major winners with the best overall finishes in that particular year's four Majors to complete the four-man field. Between 1979 and 1993 the competition was hosted at a different golf course each year, but since 1994 the Poipu Bay Golf Course in Koloa, Hawaii, has played host on a permanent basis. The winner takes home a pay cheque worth $600,000.

Did You Know That?
The 2010 PGA Grand Slam of Golf contained only the winners of the US Open (Graeme McDowell) and the US PGA Championship (Martin Kaymer) and they finished tied for third behind winner Ernie Els and second-placed David Toms, who took part as alternates. It was Els's second win – his first came back in 1997.

❋ JACK DISLIKES SAWGRASS ❋

Jack Nicklaus won the prestigious Players Championship three times, but failed to capture the prestigious tournament at its current home, the TPC at Sawgrass. Nicklaus was a fierce critic of the Sawgrass course and disliked its set-up so much he once described playing on it as "like stopping a five-iron on the hood of a car".

❋ HOIST WITH HIS OWN PETARD ❋

At the Merion Open in 1934, Bobby Cruickshank looked to be on course for victory, especially when a wayward shot from the Scot hit a rock and bounced on to the green instead of sinking into a water hazard. A delighted Cruickshank, who had reached the semi-finals of the 1922 and 1923 PGA Championship before losing both times to the eventual champion Gene Sarazen, threw his club in the air and when it came down it hit him on the head. A dazed Cruickshank finished in third place.

❋ THE MAN OF STEEL ❋

On 28 November 2006 Darren Clarke released his autobiography. During an interview with *Sky Sports News* Clarke admitted that he was so nervous on the first tee at the K Club during the 2006 Ryder Cup that he thought he might swing and miss. The Irishman, a wild-card pick by the European team captain Ian Woosnam, missed much of the season to care for his wife Heather, who died of breast cancer just six weeks before the competition began. Walking to the first tee his close friend and partner for the opening day's four-balls, Lee Westwood, sprinted ahead of Clarke so that Clarke's fellow Irishmen could cheer him all the way up to the first tee. "It was a very pressurized situation for me, because it's the Ryder Cup and because of what I had gone through prior to that. You are never quite sure what way things are going to go, but I managed to get through it, tee it up and make pretty solid contact with it," said the 38-year-old, who managed to find the fairway with his drive and went on to secure a one-hole victory with Westwood over the American pair of Chris DiMarco and Phil Mickelson. Amazingly, Clarke is the only European player to have won a World Golf Championship event (he has two to his name), but he has yet to open his Major championship account despite enduring several near misses. However, Clarke feels that his opening drive of the 2006 Ryder Cup might just be the turning-point in his career in his pursuit of a Major. "Hopefully that shot will stand me in good stead for the future. I'm sure there is no situation that I am ever going to face again where there is going to be more pressure on me than there, so if and when I do get into position to challenge for Majors, then hopefully that is going to give me a little bit of extra back-up," he added.

Did You Know That?
Darren Clarke played in five consecutive Ryder Cups for Europe (1997–2006) and was on the winning team on four occasions.

NAMES OF THE HOLES AT MUSSELBURGH

Musselburgh Links in East Lothian in Scotland has claims to be the oldest playing golf course in the world. The nine holes of the Old Links are named as follows:

1 .... The Short Hole
2 .... The Graves
3 .... Barracks Entry
4 .... Mrs Foreman's
5 .... The Sea Hole
6 .... The Table
7 .... The Bathing Coach
8 .... Hole Across
9 .... The Gas

THE OLD MAN OF GOLF

Walter Travis won the US Amateur Championship in 1900, 1901 and 1903, and in 1904 he became the first non-British player to win the British Amateur Championship. Travis, nicknamed "the Old Man of Golf", because he only took up playing golf in October 1896, aged 34, was inducted into the World Golf Hall of Fame in 1979. In 1999 *Golf World* magazine ranked Travis second in its Top 10 List of "Underrated Golf Course Architects". Four golf courses either designed or remodelled by Travis feature in *Golfweek*'s rankings of America's Top 100 Classic courses on a regular basis: namely Ekwanok Country Club, Westchester CC's West Course, Hollywood Golf Club and Garden City Golf Club.

THE GREATEST GAME EVER PLAYED

The Greatest Game Ever Played is a 2005 Walt Disney biographical sports movie about Francis Ouimet, an amateur golfer who was not expected to do very well when he entered the 1913 US Open Championship. Francis, who previously gave his father his word that he would not play golf again after critics said he froze when he was up against professionals, went back on his word and not only participated in the 1913 US Open Championship but won it in a dramatic play-off against Harry Vardon and Ted Ray, two of the best golfers in the world at the time. The movie's screenplay was adapted by Mark Frost from his novel, *The Greatest Game Ever Played: Harry Vardon, Francis Ouimet, and the Birth of Modern Golf.*

❋ WIT AND WISDOM OF GOLF (10) ❋

"You build a golf game like you build a wall, one brick at a time."
Tony Lema

❋ NEVER MEANT TO BE ❋

Dai Rees holds the unenviable record of having played in the highest number of Opens, 29, without ever winning the old Claret Jug. Despite winning four British PGA Championships and playing the final round of the Open on 23 occasions, he could only manage three runner-up places. Many golf writers consider Rees "the best golfer never to have won the Open". However, all of Wales was proud of Rees when he captained the 1957 Ryder Cup team that brought the trophy back to Europe after an absence of 22 years. Rees, a veteran of nine Ryder Cups, became a national celebrity.

Did You Know That?
Dai Rees was a big fan of Arsenal FC and in 1983 crashed his car on the way back from a game. Although he survived he never fully recovered from the trauma and died a few months later.

❋ THE WORLD CUP OF GOLF ❋

The inaugural World Cup of Golf was first competed for in 1953 and was won by the Argentinian duo of Roberto De Vicenzo and Antonio Cerda. Sometimes referred to "Golf's Olympic Games", it is the sport's oldest world-wide team competition. In 1953 the format for the competition was 36 holes of stroke play with the combined score of the two-man team determining the winner. The following year and up to 1999, the format was 72 holes of stroke play. Then, in 2000, the format alternated between stroke-play rounds of fourballs and foursomes. In 2000 the event became part of the World Golf Championships organized by the International Golf Federation of PGA Tours. The United States of America has dominated the tournament with 23 wins, their last in 2000. Eight different countries won the World Cup of Golf 2002–09: Japan, South Africa, England, Wales, Germany, Scotland, Sweden and Italy. Early in 2010, it was announced that the tournament would played only in odd number of years starting from 2011, mainly to accommodate the addition of golf in the Olympic Games (from Rio de Janeiro 2016). Held at Shenzen, China, since 2007, the event will be played at Haikou, Hainan province, China, from 2011.

❃ BEN HOGAN (1912–97) ❃

William Ben Hogan was born in Dublin, Texas, on 12 August 1912. He began caddying aged 11, and in 1931 he turned professional. In his early years on the golf course Hogan struggled to make a living from the sport, and it wasn't until 1938 that he won his first Tour event, the Hershey Four-Ball (with Vic Ghezzi). Many at the time said that Hogan was too mechanical, a supreme driver of the ball but lacking the delicacy of touch required to dominate events. However, what Hogan did possess was an unerring accuracy from within six feet of the hole.

In 1940 he won the North and South Open played at Pinehurst No. 2 Course, followed by three more Tour events the same year. In 1941 Hogan played in 39 Tour events, winning five of them (the Asheville Open, the Chicago Open, the Hershey Open, the Miami Biltmore International Four-Ball, with Gene Sarazen, and the Inverness Four-Ball, with Jimmy Demaret), and remarkably was only out of the top five money places just once. Hogan's years of patience with his style of game paid off in 1946 when he captured 13 Tour wins including his first Major, the PGA Championship. Seven more Tour wins came in 1947 for the man nicknamed "The Hawk", and over the winter of 1947 Hogan concentrated on altering his low drawing hook into a slice.

In 1948, Hogan won 10 Tour events, including two Majors: a second PGA Championship and the first of three US Open titles (his first at the Riviera Country Club, which subsequently became known as "Hogan's Alley" because of his success there). Early in 1949 Hogan and his wife, Valerie, crashed head-on into a bus on a fog-bound highway east of Van Horn, Texas. Hogan suffered a double fracture of his pelvis, a fractured collarbone, a fracture to his left ankle, a chipped rib and almost fatal blood clots. At the hospital he was told by doctors that he might never walk again, let alone play golf. However, Hogan was a fighter and a player who practised more than any other golfer; indeed it is claimed that Hogan "invented practice". He was also one of the first players to match particular clubs to yardages in order to improve his distance control. One year on from his accident, Hogan won his fourth Major and his second US Open Championship. In 1951 Hogan won three Tour events and took his Majors tally to six after snaring the first of his two Masters titles and claiming his third US Open in four years when he won at Oakland Hills. His greatest year was 1953, when he won The Masters, the US Open and the British Open. The man regarded by many as the greatest ever golfer won 64 Tour events.

❋ GREAT GOLF COURSES OF THE WORLD (5) ❋

ROYAL ST GEORGE'S, ENGLAND
Opened: 1887
Designer: Dr William Laidlaw Purves
Yardage: 7,102 Par: 70
Majors: British Open Championship 1894, 1899, 1904, 1911, 1922, 1928, 1934, 1938, 1949, 1981, 1985, 1993, 2003, 2011

Royal St George's Golf Club, Sandwich, has hosted many Major tournaments for both amateur and professional golfers including: the Walker Cup, the Curtis Cup, the Amateur Championship, the English Amateur Championship, the PGA Championship, the Home Internationals and the Brabazon Trophy. In 1894 Royal St George's hosted the first Open Championship to be played outside Scotland. Amazingly, the 1894 Open also produced the first English winner of golf's most coveted Major, J. H. Taylor. Royal patronage was granted in 1902, and the Prince of Wales (later King Edward VIII) became club captain. Arnold Palmer, nicknamed "The King", won the PGA in 1975 at Royal St George's and will forever be remembered for his memorable play on the 14th hole, reaching the green with two mammoth blows from his driver on a stormy day when no other player managed to get closer than 40 yards from the green in two.

❋ WIT AND WISDOM OF GOLF (11) ❋

"The only thing that scares me is the Americans' dress sense."
Mark James prior to the 1993 Ryder Cup

❋ EUROPE'S ROYAL KINGS ❋

Europe sealed victory in the inaugural Royal Trophy in 2006 after holding off Asia by a score of 9–7 at the Amata Spring Country Club in Bangkok, Thailand. After trailing Europe 6–2 following Saturday's foursomes and fourballs the hosts fought back before Sweden's Henrik Stenson beat Thailand's Thongchai Jaidee 5 & 4 to win the final singles match. "I am really happy with the final score. It has been a great two days of competition and the team played fantastically," said a beaming Seve Ballesteros, the Europe captain. Masahiro Kuramoto, the captain of the Asian team, said: "For a moment it looked possible that we could upset Europe as our players grew in confidence. I was happy to see the boys fight back."

❋ THE BANTAM GOLFER ❋

During the early years of his pro career Ben Hogan was known, because of his slight build, as "Bantam", a nickname he detested.

❋ CAPTAIN HOGAN ❋

Ben Hogan played on two US Ryder Cup teams (1947 & 1951) and captained the team three times (1947, 1949 & 1967), famously claiming on the latter occasion to have brought "the 12 best golfers in the world" to play in the competition. They did not let him down.

❋ THE YEARS OF OCHOA ❋

Lorena Ochoa not only won the 2006 LPGA Player of the Year Award and was ranked the number one lady golfer on the ADT official money list, she dominated the LPGA for three more years. The 2003 Rookie of the Year also won the Vare Trophy, awarded to the player with the lowest average round score on the LPGA Tour, every year from 2006 to 2009. The 2010 LPGA Player of the Year was Yani Tseng, aged 21, from Taiwan, who won two of the four women's Majors.

❋ EUROPEAN RYDER CUP POINTS WINNERS ❋

Rank	*Name*	*Points*
1	Nick Faldo	25
2	Bernhard Langer	24
3	Colin Montgomerie	23.5
4	Seve Ballesteros	22.5
5	Jose-Maria Olazabal	20.5
6	Lee Westwood	19
7	Tony Jacklin	17
8	Ian Woosnam	16.5
9	Bernard Gallacher	15.5
	Peter Oosterhuis	15.5
	Neil Coles	15.5
12	Sergio Garcia	15
13	Christy O'Connor Snr	13
14	Peter Alliss	12.5
15	Brian Huggett	11
16	Brian Barnes	10.5
17	Sam Torrance	10

Up to and including the 2010 Ryder Cup

✽ US OPEN PAST WINNERS ✽

Year	*Player*	*Venue*
2011	Rory McIlroy	Congressional CC
2010	Graeme McDowell	Pebble Beach GL
2009	Lucas Glover	Bethpage State Park (Black Course)
2008*	Tiger Woods	Torrey Pines GC (South Course)
2007	Angel Cabrera	Oakmont CC
2006	Geoff Ogilvy	Winged Foot GC
2005	Michael Campbell	No. 2 Course at Pinehurst R & CC
2004	Retief Goosen	Shinnecock Hills GC
2003	Jim Furyk	Olympia Fields CC
2002	Tiger Woods	Bethpage State Park (Black Course)
2001*	Retief Goosen	Southern Hills CC
2000	Tiger Woods	Pebble Beach GL
1999	Payne Stewart	No. 2 Course at Pinehurst R & CC
1998	Lee Janzen	The Olympic Club
1997	Ernie Els	Congressional CC
1996	Steve Jones	Oakland Hills CC
1995	Corey Pavin	Shinnecock Hills GC
1994*	Ernie Els	Oakmont CC
1993	Lee Janzen	Baltusrol GC
1992	Tom Kite	Pebble Beach GL
1991*	Payne Stewart	Hazeltine National GC
1990*	Hale Irwin	Medinah CC
1989	Curtis Strange	Oak Hill CC
1988*	Curtis Strange	The Country Club
1987	Scott Simpson	The Olympic Club
1986	Raymond Floyd	Shinnecock Hills GC
1985	Andy North	Oakland Hills CC
1984*	Fuzzy Zoeller	Winged Foot GC
1983	Larry Nelson	Oakmont C.
1982	Tom Watson	Pebble Beach GL
1981	David Graham	Merion GC
1980	Jack Nicklaus	Baltusrol GC
1979	Hale Irwin	Inverness Club
1978	Andy North	Cherry Hills
1977	Hubert Green	Southern Hills
1976	Jerry Pate	Atlanta Athletic Club
1975*	Lou Graham	Medinah CC
1974	Hale Irwin	Winged Foot GC
1973	Johnny Miller	Oakmont CC
1972	Jack Nicklaus	Pebble Beach GL

1971*	Lee Trevino	Merion GC
1970	Tony Jacklin	Hazeltine National GC
1969	Orville Moody	Champions GC
1968	Lee Trevino	Oak Hill CC
1967	Jack Nicklaus	Baltusrol GC
1966*	Billi Casper	Olympic Club
1965*	Gary Player	Bellerive CC
1964	Ken Venturi	Congressional CC
1963*	Julius Boros	The Country Club
1962*	Jack Nicklaus	Oakmont CC
1961	Gene Littler	Oakland Hills CC
1960	Arnold Palmer	Cherry Hills CC
1959	Billy Casper	Winged Foot GC
1958	Tommy Bolt	Southern Hills CC
1957*	Dick Mayer	Inverness Club
1956	Cary Middlecoff	Oak Hill CC
1955*	Jack Fleck	Olympic Club
1954	Ed Furgol	Baltusrol GC
1953	Ben Hogan	Oakmont CC
1952	Julius Boros	Northwood Club
1951	Ben Hogan	Oakland Hills CC
1950*	Ben Hogan	Merion GC
1949	Cary Middlecoff	Medinah CC
1948	Ben Hogan	Riviera CC
1947*	Lew Worsham	St. Louis CC
1946*	Lloyd Mangrum	Canterbury GC
1942–45: No Championships due to Second World War		
1941	Craig Wood	Colonial CC
1940*	Lawson Little	Canterbury GC
1939*	Byron Nelson	Philadelphia CC
1938	Ralph Guldahl	Cherry Hills Club
1937	Ralph Guldahl	Oakland Hills CC
1936	Tony Manero	Baltusrol GC
1935	Sam Parks Jr.	Oakmont CC
1934	Olin Dutra	Merion Cricket Club
1933	John Goodman (Am)	North Shore CC
1932	Gene Sarazen	Fresh Meadow CC
1931*	Billy Burke	Inverness Club
1930	Bobby Jones (Am)	Interlachen CC
1929	Bobby Jones (Am)	Winged Foot GC
1928*	Johnny Farrell	Olympia Fields CC
1927*	Tommy Armour	Oakmont CC
1926	Bobby Jones (Am)	Scioto CC

1925*	William Macfarlane	Worcester CC
1924	Cyril Walker	Oakland Hills CC
1923	Bobby Jones (Am)	Inwood CC
1922	Gene Sarazen	Skokie CC
1921	James M. Barnes	Columbia CC
1920	Ted Ray	Inverness Club
1919*	Walter Hagen	Brae Burn CC
1917–18: *No championships due to First World War*		
1916	Charles Evans Jr (Am)	Minikahda Club
1915	Jerome D. Travers (Am)	Baltusrol GC
1914	Walter Hagen	Midlothian CC
1913	Francis Ouimet (Am)	The Country Club
1912	John J. McDermott	CC of Buffalo
1911*	John J. McDermott	Chicago GC
1910*	Alex Smith	Philadelphia Cricket Club
1909	George Sargent	Englewood GC
1908*	Fred McLeod	Myopia Hunt Club
1907	Alex Ross	Philadelphia Cricket Club
1906	Alex Smith	Onwentsia Club
1905	Willie Anderson	Myopia Hunt Club
1904	Willie Anderson	Glen View Club
1903*	Willie Anderson	Baltusrol GC
1902	Laurence Auchterlonie	Garden City GC
1901*	Willie Anderson	Myopia Hunt Club
1900	Harry Vardon	Chicago GC
1899	Willie Smith	Baltimore CC
1898	Fred Herd	Myopia Hunt Club
1897	Joe Lloyd	Chicago GC
1896	James Foulis	Shinnecock Hills GC
1895	Horace Rawlins	Newport GC

*NOTES: * – Won in a play-off   Am – Amateur*

❋ GOLDEN BEAR CLAWS HIS WAY BACK ❋

In 1963 a 23-year-old Jack Nicklaus arrived at Dallas Athletic Club for the US PGA Championship following his run in the British Open Championship, where he finished third, one shot away from a play-off (in which Bob Charles beat Phil Rodgers). But the trip to Dallas paid off as Nicklaus clawed back Bruce Crampton's three-stroke lead in the final round (with a 68) to win his first US PGA title (by two strokes from Dave Ragan). Nicklaus's win meant that he now joined Ben Hogan, Byron Nelson and Gene Sarazen as the only men to date to win the US PGA, US Open and Masters Championships.

❋ BLUES ON THE GREENS ❋

The first Oxbridge university golf match was played at Wimbledon in 1878, with Oxford beating the light blues of Cambridge. As the British Amateur Championship was only contested for the first time in 1885, the Varsity Match can claim to be the oldest amateur fixture in world golf. The 118th Varsity Golf Match was held on 23–24 March 2007 at Aldeburgh Golf Course in Suffolk, and resulted in a win for Cambridge by 8 ½ to 6 ½.

❋ SARAZEN HONOURED ❋

In 1992, Gene Sarazen was presented with the Bob Jones Award, the highest honour given by the United States Golf Association in recognition of distinguished sportsmanship in golf.

❋ AUGUSTA ARCHITECT ❋

Alister Mackenzie, the golf course architect who designed The Masters' course, was born in England in 1870 and worked with Harry Colt on courses in Great Britain before emigrating to the US in the early 1920s. Bobby Jones selected and hired Mackenzie as the course architect for Augusta National, and Jones and Mackenzie worked closely together on the design. Indeed, Jones would hit test shots from different spots to help Mackenzie calibrate the holes. Augusta is one of Mackenzie's three masterpieces, the others being Cypress Point in California and Royal Melbourne in Australia. All three are considered to be among the world's very best golf courses. Other famous Mackenzie designs include Pasatiempo in California, and the Scarlet Course at Ohio State University. Alister Mackenzie died in 1934, the year of the first Masters tournament.

❋ THE WOMEN'S WORLD CUP OF GOLF ❋

The Women's World Cup of Golf took place every year between 2005 and 2008 in South Africa.

Year	*Winners*	*Players*	*Host/Venue*
2005	Japan	Rui Kitada, Ai Miyazato	South Africa
2006	Sweden	Liselotte Neumann, Annika Sorenstam	South Africa
2007	Paraguay	Julieta Granada, Celeste Troche	South Africa
2008	Philippines	Jennifer Rosales, Dorothy Delasin	South Africa

❋ WIT AND WISDOM OF GOLF (12) ❋

"If I had cleared the trees and drove the green, it would've been a great shot."
Sam Snead

❋ BOBBY JONES ON THE SILVER SCREEN ❋

Bobby Jones was the subject of the biographical 2004 feature film entitled *Bobby Jones: A Stroke of Genius*, in which he was portrayed by James Caviezel. Jones was also used as a supporting character in the 2000 movie *The Legend of Bagger Vance*, and the time he called his own penalty in the US Open is used for the main character, Rannulph Junuh.

Did You Know That?
Jones authored several books on golf including *Down the Fairway* with O. B. Keeler (1927), *The Rights and Wrongs of Golf* (1933), *Golf is My Game* (1959), *Bobby Jones on Golf* (1966), and *Bobby Jones on the Basic Golf Swing* (1968) with illustrator Anthony Ravielli.

❋ THE HOME OF THE OPEN CHAMPIONSHIP ❋

St Andrews has hosted the British Open Golf Championship a record 28 times up to and including the 2010 tournament: 1873, 1876, 1879, 1882, 1885, 1888, 1891, 1895, 1900, 1905, 1910, 1921, 1927, 1933, 1939, 1946, 1955, 1957, 1960, 1964, 1970, 1978, 1984, 1990, 1995, 2000, 2005 and 2010.

❋ TIGER CHASES THE GOLDEN BEAR ❋

Tiger Woods was voted the 2009 PGA Tour Player of the Year by his peers for the 10th time in 12 years. He won six times on the Tour and finished with 14 Majors, four shy of Jack Nicklaus's record of 18. After being voted PGA Tour Player of the Year in 2006, Woods said, "It's always an honour to get the respect of your peers – this year has been interesting to say the least, on and off the golf course. I played as bad as I did at the US Open [he missed the cut] and to get it going after that was nice, because I was playing well early in the year and then in the springtime got a little bit more. I went back to the same things I was working on at the beginning of the year and they started clicking in and I won a few [eight] tournaments," said the world number one. Sadly for Tiger he lost his father Earl to cancer that year.

❋ BOBBY JONES (1902–1971) ❋

Robert Tyre "Bobby" Jones was born on St Patrick's Day in 1902 in Atlanta, Georgia. Jones was in such poor health as a child that he was unable to eat solid food until he was five years old. Jones took up golf a year later, around the time his family moved to a summer home near the East Lake Country Club, where Bobby grew stronger. He won his first tournament when he was only six and won the Atlanta Athletic Club junior title aged nine. When he was 14 he made it to the third round of the 1916 US Amateur Championship, losing out to the defending champion, Bob Gardner. This made him the youngest ever player to both qualify for and play in the tournament. Jones learned how to play golf by following East Lake's Scottish professional, Stewart Maiden, around the course. During his early career Jones struggled with a volatile temper. The legendary sportswriter Grantland Rice once said that Jones had "the face of an angel and the temper of a timber wolf". In 1921 he crossed the Atlantic and played for an American team against their British counterparts in an event that would become the Walker Cup the following year. He also participated in two competitions, the British Amateur and British Open Championships. He played very poorly at St Andrews in the Open before withdrawing after 11 holes in the third round.

In 1923 he won the first of his 13 Majors and his first US Open title. Amazingly, Jones won 13 Majors from only 20 attempts, to place him second overall in Major Championship wins, behind Jack Nicklaus on 18 (Amateur Championships were considered to be Majors during Jones's era). Jones won the US Amateur Championship five times between 1924 and 1930. In 1926 he became the first golfer, and to date the only amateur, to win the "Double", netting both US Open and British Open in the same year. A second British Open title followed in 1927, and in 1929 he won his third US Open, his ninth Major. It is unlikely that anyone will ever again achieve what Jones did in 1930, when he became the first and, to date, only player to win golf's Grand Slam of all four Majors in the same year by winning the US Amateur, British Amateur, US Open and British Open titles.

Throughout his career he participated as an amateur and represented the US in five Walker Cups, winning nine of his 10 matches. Jones also won two other tournaments against professionals: the 1927 Southern Open and the 1930 Southeastern Open. Amazingly, Jones only played golf on a part-time basis and retired aged just 28.

❋ WIT AND WISDOM OF GOLF (13) ❋

"Jack is playing an entirely different game, and one which I'm not even familiar with."
Bobby Jones, watching Jack Nicklaus win the 1965 Masters

❋ GREAT GOLF COURSES OF THE WORLD (6) ❋

ROYAL COUNTY DOWN, NORTHERN IRELAND
Opened: 1895
Designer: Tom Morris Snr
Yardage: 6,968 Par: 72
Major events: British Amateur 1970. British Women's Amateur 1899, 1907, 1920, 1927, 1935, 1950, 1963, 2006.
Curtis Cup 1968, Walker Cup 2007

Royal County Down is one of Ireland's oldest golf clubs, with traditions dating back to the 1890s. The links course is situated in Newcastle, County Down, where "The Mountains of Mourne sweep down to the sea", to use the immortal words of local bard Percy French. It hosted the Senior British Open in 2000, 2001 and 2002 and the 2007 Walker Cup only the second club in Ireland, after Portmarnock, to provide the venue for the biennial contest.

❋ A VERY LONG WALK ❋

The longest ever golf course to host an Open Championship was the 7,361-yard Carnoustie golf course in 1999 and again in 2007. The winners were Paul Lawrie and Padraig Harrington respectively.

❋ McGINLEY FORFEITS RECORD CHANCE ❋

At the 2006 Ryder Cup, Ireland's Paul McGinley conceded a putt that quite possibly denied the 2006 European Ryder Cup team a record-breaking feat. With victory already in the bag for the Europeans, McGinley gave J. J. Henry a 25-footer on the last after a streaker ran on to the green, and thus agreed a half even though McGinley was strongly placed to hole out and win the match. If Henry had missed and McGinley had sunk his putt from less than five feet, Europe would have set a new record-winning margin of victory of 19–9. "Yes, it's crossed my mind," said McGinley later. "I've been told on several occasions. But, you know, it was a gesture that was done in the right spirit."

❋ US MEN'S AMATEUR CHAMPIONSHIP ❋

Ten years after the inaugural Amateur Championship, the United States Men's Amateur Golf Championship was inaugurated in 1895. The tournament is organized by the United States Golf Association and is the country's leading annual tournament for male amateur golfers. In 1894 there were two tournaments called the "National Amateur Championship". One of them was played at Newport Country Club and was won by William G. Lawrence, while the other was won by Laurence B. Stottard at St Andrew's Golf Club. This led Charles B. Macdonald (Chicago Golf Club) to call for the creation of a national governing body to authorize an official national championship for amateur golfers, and thus the Amateur Golf Association of the United States (subsequently renamed the United States Golf Association) was formed on 22 December 1894. The following year the AGAUS organized both the inaugural US Amateur Championship and the inaugural US Open Championship, with both tournaments hosted by the Newport Country Club. Although there is no minimum age for entry, all players must possess a handicap index of 2.4 or less. The tournament is made up of two days of stroke play followed by a knockout competition in which the leading 64 competitors play under match-play rules to decide the champion. All knockout matches are over 18 holes except for the final, which consists of 36 holes, separated into morning and afternoon 18-hole rounds.

Did You Know That?
Before the modern professional game became so dominant, the US Amateur Championship was regarded as one of the Majors. The winner still receives an automatic invitation to play in all of the Majors except the US PGA Championship, while the runner-up is invited to play in the US Open.

❋ TIGER HONOURED ❋

In 1996 Tiger Woods was named 1996's "Sportsman of the Year" by *Sports Illustrated* magazine and "PGA Rookie of the Year" by the PGA Tour. In 1997 he became the first, and only, golfer to win the "PGA Player of the Year" award in the year following his rookie season.

Did You Know That?
Woods is the only active golfer currently in the top 10 in either career Major wins or career PGA Tour wins.

❋ THE AMATEUR CHAMPIONSHIP ❋

The Amateur Championship is a UK-based tournament, although around the world it is commonly referred to as the "British Amateur Championship". The inaugural tournament was held at the Royal Liverpool Golf Club's Hoylake course in 1885, with England's Allen MacFie defeating fellow countryman Horace Hutchinson 7 & 6. It has been organized by the Royal & Ancient Golf Club of St Andrews for almost all of its history. The tournament is open to golfers of any nationality and is played in June each year, with the winner receiving invitations to play in the following month's British Open Championship and the following year's Masters. Prior to the Second World War it was considered to be one of golf's Majors.

Did You Know That?
Bobby Jones won the 1930 Amateur Championship, which formed part of his Grand Slam.

❋ PARNEVIK ERUPTS ❋

Jesper Parnevik is famous on the PGA Tour for wearing an upturned peak on his baseball cap, and when he represented Europe in the Ryder Cup (1997, 1999 & 2002) the team's outfitters made him a customized team cap with the Ryder Cup logo on the bottom of the peak instead of the front, so that it could be seen when he turned the peak up. Parnevik has now dispensed with the baseball cap and sports a necktie worn under his golf shirt.

Did You Know That?
Parnevik eats volcanic dust as a dietary supplement.

❋ BIRDIE KIM ❋

Birdie Kim was born Ju-Yun Kim in Ik-San, South Korea, on 26 August 1981. In 2004 she changed her first name to "Birdie" in an attempt to distinguish herself from the numerous other Korean golfers named Kim on the women's LPGA Tour. Up to the end of 2010, she won her only Major to date, the US Women's Open, at Cherry Hills Country Club in 2005.

Did You Know That?
Six different Kims, including Birdie but as yet no Eagle, currently play on the LPGA Tour.

❋ WIT AND WISDOM OF GOLF (14) ❋

"Hold up a one-iron and walk. Not even God can hit a one-iron."
Lee Trevino, on how to play golf during a lightning storm

❋ PGA PLAYER OF THE YEAR WINNERS ❋

In 1948, the PGA of America presented the first "PGA Player of the Year Award". Since 1982 the award has been based on a points system with points awarded for accomplishments throughout the year (i.e. victories, top 10 finishes, bonus points for winning a Major, a player's ranking on the PGA money list and his scoring average).

❋ LIFETIME ACHIEVEMENT AWARD ❋

In 1996 the PGA created the "PGA Tour Lifetime Achievement Award" to honour individuals who have made an outstanding contribution to the PGA Tour by their actions both on and off the greens.

Year	*Winners*	*Country*
2009	George H.W. Bush	USA
2008	Jack Nicklaus	USA
2007	Deane Beman	USA
2005	Pete Dye	USA
2003	Jack Burke	USA
1998	Arnold Palmer	USA
1998	Sam Snead	USA
1997	Byron Nelson	USA
1996	Gene Sarazen	USA

❋ THE LEXUS CUP ❋

On 11 December 2005, Annika Sorenstam captained the International Team to a 16–8 win over Team Asia in the inaugural Lexus Cup. Sorenstam's team led 8–4 going into the final day and singles points from Sorenstam, Paula Creamer, Natalie Gulbis, Karen Stupples and Erica Blasberg ensured victory. The Lexus Cup was sanctioned by the US Ladies' Professional Golf Association and lasted four years. The format was similar to the Ryder Cup: 12 players per team, selected mainly from the respective orders of merit, and a mixture of fourballs and foursomes (six each) and singles (12) were played. The series was hosted by Singapore in 2005, 2007 and 2008, and by Perth, Western Australia in 2006. Both teams won the Lexus Cup on two occasions.

❋ WIT AND WISDOM OF GOLF (15) ❋

"Here, Eddie, hold the flag while I putt out."
Walter Hagen to the Prince of Wales

❋ PING JUNIOR SOLHEIM CUP ❋

The inaugural PING Junior Solheim Cup, the only girls' team event of its kind at junior level, was played at Oak Ridge Country Club in Hopkins, Minnesota, in 2002 and was won by Team USA. The PING Junior Solheim Cup follows the same format as the Solheim Cup and features the top 12 European girls pitched against their American peers. In 2003 Team Europe beat Team USA in Sweden, but the Team USA regained the trophy in 2005 in Indianapolis. Home advantage has continued to to apparently decide the outcome as Europe won in Sweden in 2007 and the USA in Illinois in 2009.

❋ 11 FROM 9 NETS SECOND US OPEN ❋

Retief Goosen needed just 11 putts over the final 9 holes to withstand the challenge of Phil Mickelson to win his second US Open title, by two strokes, with a four-under-par 276 at Shinnecock Hills GC in 2004.

❋ THE HOGAN FADE ❋

Ben Hogan was known for his famous "Hogan fade" ball flight, lower than usual for a great player and from left to right. This ball flight was the result of Hogan using a "draw" type swing in association with a "weak" grip, a combination that effectively negated the chances of him hitting a hook-shot. Hogan's "secret fade", a special wrist movement, known as "cupping under", was revealed by the golf legend in an interview with *Life* magazine in 1955.

❋ FALDO REPLACES LANNY ❋

On 3 October 2006, CBS announced that they had signed Nick Faldo to replace Lanny Wadkins as the television network's lead golf analyst. "I view this as a fabulous opportunity for me, which may come once every 10 years," said Faldo. "But it will seriously curtail my playing career. My playing days aren't completely over, but my priority now is given to CBS." Because of his work commitments with CBS, the six-times Major winner will miss the opportunity of winning a fourth green jacket at the 2007 Masters.

❋ AUGUSTA ARCHITECT ❋

Alister Mackenzie, the golf course architect who designed the Masters course, was born in England in 1870 and worked with Harry Colt on courses in Great Britain before emigrating to the US in the early 1920s. Bobby Jones selected and hired Mackenzie as the course architect for Augusta National, and Jones and Mackenzie worked closely together on the design. Indeed, Jones would hit test shots from different spots to help Mackenzie calibrate the holes. Augusta is one of Mackenzie's three masterpieces, the others being Cypress Point in California and Royal Melbourne in Australia. All three are considered to be among the world's very best golf courses. Other famous Mackenzie designs include Pasatiempo in California, Crystal Downs in Michigan and the Scarlet Course at Ohio State University. Alister Mackenzie died in 1934, the year of the first Masters tournament.

❋ THE FIVE LESSONS ❋

Ben Hogan's book, *Five Lessons: The Modern Fundamentals of Golf*, is one of the most widely-read golf tutorials ever written.

Did You Know That?
In 2000, the famous golf instructor, David Leadbetter, wrote a book entitled *The Fundamentals of Hogan*.

❋ CHEWING THE CUD AT AUGUSTA ❋

Bobby Jones co-designed the Augusta National golf course with Alister Mackenzie and was one of the founders of the tournament which became known as The Masters, first played at Augusta National in 1934. During the Second World War Jones served as an officer in the US Army Air Forces and permitted the US Army to graze cattle on the grounds at Augusta National.

❋ NO ONE IS A MATCH FOR ERNIE ❋

The World Matchplay Championship at Wentworth has been dominated by South African golfers. From 1965 to 1973, Gary Player won the trophy on a record five occasions, a mark that lasted until 2004 when compatriot Ernie Els completed his second hat-trick of World Matchplay Championships. He added a seventh in 2007, but there were no tournaments in 2008 or 2010. English golfers Ross Fisher (2009) and Ian Poulter (2011) were the most recent winners.

❋ BYRON NELSON (1912–2006) ❋

John Byron Nelson Jnr was born on 4 February 1912 near Waxahachie, Texas. As a child he nearly died from typhoid fever after losing almost half of his body weight. At the age of 12 he began caddying at the Glen Garden Country Club, where caddies were not permitted to play the course. Undeterred, the young Nelson used to play it in the dark, placing a white handkerchief over each hole as a marker. Soon, however, the club altered its policy and even sponsored the Glen Garden Caddie Tournament, where a 14-year-old Nelson beat fellow caddy and future golf legend Ben Hogan by a single stroke after a nine-hole play-off.

Nelson entered the PGA Tour in 1935 and won his first senior event the same year, the New Jersey State Open. The following year he won the Metropolitan Open, and then in 1937 he captured the first of his five Majors, The Masters, adding the Belmont Country Club Match Play tournament the same year. Two more PGA wins followed in 1938 before he won his second Major, the US Open in 1939. He won four times in 1939, adding the Phoenix Open, the North and South Open and the Western Open to his US Open title. Nelson won his first PGA Championship in 1940, as well as two other titles, giving him a total of seven PGA Tour wins in two years. A blood disorder meant that Nelson was exempt from military service during the Second World War.

In 1942 he added his second US Masters to his first Majors triumph in Augusta five years earlier, and in 1944 he captured eight PGA Tour titles: including the San Francisco Victory Open, the Knoxville War Bond Tournament and the Minneapolis Four-Ball (with Harold "Jug" McSpadden).

Even more success followed in 1945, when Nelson claimed no fewer than 18 PGA Tour events, a record that still stands today, plus his fifth and final Major, a second PGA Championship. His 18 victories also included a record 11 consecutive victories on the Tour. After winning six more Tour events in 1946 he effectively ended his career, although he did play in, and win, the Bing Crosby Pro-Am in 1951 and the French Open in 1955.

Up until Tiger Woods passed him, Nelson held the record for making the most consecutive cuts on the PGA Tour. Nelson's total was 113, whereas Tiger notched up 142 (although in Nelson's day "making the cut" meant a top 20 finish). Nelson won the Vardon Trophy in 1939, played on the US Ryder Cup teams in 1937 and 1947, and was the non-playing captain of the team in 1965. Nelson died on 26 September 2006, aged 94, at home in Roanoke, Texas.

❋ SUPER SEVE ❋

Severiano Ballesteros was the inspirational non-playing captain of the winning European side in the Ryder Cup held at Valderrama Golf Club in Sotogrande, Spain in 1997. This was the first ever Ryder Cup held in continental Europe. Seve retired in 2007, after only one Champions Tour event, and sadly died from a brain tumour in 2011.

❋ RYDER CUP HOLES-IN-ONE ❋

Up to and including the 2010 Ryder Cup there have only ever been six holes-in-one, with Europe claiming five of them. Casey's in 2006 is the only one to have decided a match.

❋ THE COMEBACK MASTER ❋

Gary Player's ninth and final Major win came in 1978 when he won The Masters. Amazingly, after starting his final round seven strokes behind the leaders, he won his third green jacket by one shot with birdies at seven of the last 10 holes for a back-nine score of 30 and a final-round total of 64. One week later, Player came from seven strokes back in the final round to win the Tournament of Champions.

❋ THE KING OF OZ ❋

Only Gary Player has won more Australian Open titles than Jack Nicklaus. Player has seven Stonehaven Cups to Nicklaus's six.

❋ ARNIE CALLS IT A DAY ❋

Arnold Palmer finally retired from tournament golf on 13 October 2006, during the Champions Tour's Administaff Small Business Classic. After completing just four holes he withdrew from the event, because of his total dissatisfaction with his own play. He played the remaining holes but did not keep score.

❋ EIGHT FOR TIGER ❋

In 2009 Tiger Woods won a record-breaking eighth Vardon Trophy for Adjusted Scoring Average, having ended the year with an average of 68.05. He had previously won the trophy in 1999, 2000, 2001, 2002, 2003, 2005 and 2007.

❋ WIT AND WISDOM OF GOLF (16) ❋

"I miss. I miss. I miss. I make."
Seve Ballestero, describing his four-putt at Augusta's 16th hole in 1988

❋ TRUNK SLAMMING ❋

"Slammin' his trunk on a Friday" is a term used mainly by American golfers to describe a player who has failed to make the cut of a tournament after 36 holes of play.

❋ PASSING ON THE CROWN ❋

Tiger Woods won each Major in the same year that Jack Nicklaus last appeared in it as a player.

US Open Championship: 2000
US PGA Championship: 2000
US Masters: 2005
British Open Championship: 2005

❋ RAKING IT IN ❋

Women's professional golf is not as lucrative as it is for the men and the first time a woman earned $1 million in a Ladies Professional Golf Association (LPGA) tour season was in 1996, when Karrie Webb of Australia won $1,002,000. the all-time single season earnings record was set in 2007, when Lorena Ochoa of Mexico won eight tournaments and collected $4,364,994. The second most successful season belongs to Sweden's Annika Sorenstam, who amassed $2,863,904 in 2002. In fact, only Sorenstam (five times) and Ochoa (three) have won more than $2 million in a single season, and they were all achieved between 2001 and 2008. Ochoa ended Sorenstam's reign as the LPGA Tour No.1 by winning the Mitchell Company Tournament of Champions at the RTJ Golf Trail in Mobile, Alabama, with a tournament record 21 under par.

❋ NUMBER ONE WITHOUT A MAJOR ❋

In October 2010, English golfer Lee Westwood became the first world No 1 without ever having won a Major. He had been runner-up in both the Masters and British Open Championship in 2010.

❋ GREAT GOLF COURSES OF THE WORLD (7) ❋

BALTUSROL (LOWER COURSE), NEW JERSEY
Opened: 1895
Designer: Albert W. Tillinghast
Yardage: 7,022 Par: 70
Majors: US Open Championship 1903, 1915, 1936, 1954, 1967, 1980, 1993. US PGA Championship 2005

The Baltusrol Golf Club is a 36-hole country club located in the Springfield Township, Union County, New Jersey. In 2005 Baltusrol hosted the 87th US PGA Championship, won by Phil Mickelson. Normally the course is a par 72, but for Major Championships it plays to a par 70. The course is named in honour of Baltus Roll, the son of Abraham Roll and Mary Brooks, who was murdered at his home on 22 February 1831. In 1909 the original clubhouse burned down and its replacement became the first venue to host an American President, William Howard Taft. The course was redesigned in 1952 by the legendary golf course architect Robert Trent Jones and then reworked again in 1992 by Rees Jones. Baltusrol has also hosted 15 USGA National Championships in its prestigious history.

❋ SARAZEN'S LAST WIN ❋

Gene Sarazen won the last of his 39 PGA Tour events in 1941, when he claimed victory in the Miami Biltmore International Four-Ball (with Ben Hogan).

❋ MR GRAND SLAMMER ❋

Jack Nicklaus won five US PGA Championships (1963, 1971, 1973, 1975 and 1980), a record for the tournament shared with the legendary Walter Hagen. He made the cut 27 times in 37 finishes and was runner-up on four occasions. His 1971 US PGA Championship triumph made him the first player to win the Grand Slam twice, an achievement that was matched by Tiger Woods at the 2005 British Open.

❋ SAM THE LEGEND OF GOLF ❋

In 1978 Sam Snead won the inaugural "Legends of Golf" event, which two years later became the Senior PGA Tour, now known as the Champions Tour.

❋ WIT AND WISDOM OF GOLF (17) ❋

"Golf is a good walk spoiled."
Mark Twain

❋ JACK LEADS THE MAGNIFICENT SEVEN ❋

On 8 December 2006, the PGA Golf Professional Hall of Fame inducted seven new entrants: 18-times Major winner Jack Nicklaus, the PGA of America President Roger Warren, the 1986 PGA Teacher of the Year Manuel de la Torre, Dow Finsterwald, the 2005 PGA Golf Professional of the Year Bill Eschenbrenner, the PGA Master Professional William Heald and the 1987 PGA Teacher of the Year Gary Wiren. The seven inductees were honoured in a ceremony that ran in conjunction with the 10th PGA Teaching & Coaching Summit held at the PGA Learning Center at PGA Village in Port St Lucie, Florida, USA.

❋ THE MASTERS' HONORARY TRIUMVIRATE ❋

From 1984 to 2002, Sam Snead had the honour of hitting the honorary starting tee shot at The Masters; until 1999 Snead was joined by Gene Sarazen, and until 2001 he was joined by Byron Nelson.

❋ LITTLE POISON ❋

During his career Paul Runyan won 29 times on the PGA Tour, including two Majors, with his first victory coming in the North and South Open in 1930 and his final victory coming in the 1941 Goodall Round Robin. Amazingly, 16 of his 29 Tour wins came in 1933 and 1934 (9 & 7) while 1937 was the only year during the 1930s in which he failed to capture a PGA win.

Did You Know That?
Runyan was nicknamed "Little Poison" because he was unable to drive the ball a great distance but compensated with a superb short game.

❋ THE OLD FOX ❋

At the Hanover Westchester Classic in 1979, Sam Snead became the oldest golfer to make a cut on the PGA Tour. He was 67 years, 2 months and 21 days old at the time. In 1987, Sam's nephew, Jesse Carlyle "J. C." Snead, won the Westchester Classic.

❋ THE YEAR OF LORD BYRON ❋

In 1945 Byron Nelson won a record 18 PGA Tour events, including a record 11 in succession. His record-breaking year saw him win: the Phoenix Open, the Corpus Christi Open, the New Orleans Open, the Charlotte Open, the Greater Greensboro Open, the Durham Open, the Atlanta Open, the Montreal Open, the Philadelphia Inquirer, the Chicago Victory National Open, the Tom O'Shanter Open, the Canadian Open, the Knoxville Invitational, the Esmeralda Open, the Seattle Open, the Glen Garden Open, the PGA Championship (his fifth and final Major) and the Miami Four-Ball (with Harold "Jug" McSpadden).

Did You Know That?
Byron Nelson officially retired when he was just 34 to become a rancher. His stroke average for 1945 was 68.33.

❋ MARKING HIS CARD ❋

In the final round of the 1968 Masters at Augusta, Roberto de Vicenzo signed his scorecard for a score higher than his actual score on the 17th hole. The reigning British Open Championship holder signed for a par four instead of the birdie he had actually made. Under the Rules of Golf, the higher score stands as soon as a player has signed his scorecard. Had it not been for his blunder the Argentinian would have tied for first place with Bob Goalby forcing an 18-hole play-off for the coveted green jacket. DeVicenzo's quote afterwards summed up his feelings: "What a stupid I am!" In 1970 he was presented with the Bob Jones Award, and in 1989 he was inducted into the World Golf Hall of Fame.

❋ THE CHALLENGE BELT ❋

The Claret Jug, presented to each year's winner of the Open Championship, is not the original prize. In 1860 Willie Park Snr, the winner of the inaugural Open at Prestwick, was presented with the Challenge Belt, made of rich morocco leather and embellished with a silver buckle and emblems. In 1870, Tom Morris Jnr won his third consecutive Open and became the outright owner of the belt. In the absence of a decision as to the venue for the 1871 Open or the champion's prize, the Open Championship was not played in 1871. It resumed in 1872, again played at Prestwick and was again won by Tom Morris Jnr, for the fourth time in succession.

❋ THE JACK NICKLAUS TROPHY ❋

The Jack Nicklaus Trophy is awarded to the Player of the Year on the Champions Tour and is determined by a vote of the players at the end of the year. Here is a list of past recipients:

1990	Lee Trevino	2000	Larry Nelson
1991	Mike Hill, George Archer	2001	Allen Doyle
1992	Lee Trevino	2002	Hale Irwin
1993	Dave Stockton	2003	Tom Watson
1994	Lee Trevino	2004	Craig Stadler
1995	Jim Colbert	2005	Dana Quigley
1996	Jim Colbert	2006	Jay Haas
1997	Hale Irwin	2007	Jay Haas
1998	Hale Irwin	2008	Bernhard Langer
1999	Bruce Fleisher	2009	Bernhard Langer
		2010	Bernhard Langer

❋ PAR-THREE MASTERS ❋

No golfer has ever won the par-three contest at the Augusta National Golf Club and then gone on to win The Masters in the same year. However, a number of par-three tournament winners have won The Masters in other years. Masters champions such as Ben Crenshaw, Arnold Palmer, Vijay Singh, Sam Snead and Tom Watson have all triumphed at the tournament's traditional curtain-raiser, but the six-times Masters champion, Jack Nicklaus, never won it.

❋ SPORT'S FIRST MILLIONAIRE ❋

Walter Hagen, an 11-time Major Championship winner (including five US PGA Championships) is generally believed have been the first sportsman in history to earn $1 million in his career. Hagen once famously said: "I never wanted to be a millionaire, just to live like one." He was the first golfer to realize the commercial opportunities of golf merchandise endorsement and carried 22 clubs in his bag instead of 14 because he was paid $500 per year for every club he carried. At the height of his stardom (1920s & 1930s), he charged considerable appearance fees for exhibition matches, and as a professional at his base in Florida he charged $40 per lesson. Hagen is reported to have once spent $10,000 on a party, which at the time was equivalent to the lifetime earnings of a working man.

❋ RECORD LEADS IN THE OPEN – POST-1892 ❋

After 18 holes of play
4 strokes – James Braid 1908, Bobby Jones 1927,
Henry Cotton 1934, Christy O'Connor Jnr, 1985
After 36 holes of play
9 strokes – Henry Cotton 1934
After 54 holes of play
10 strokes – Henry Cotton 1934

❋ COURSE PROLIFERATION ❋

In 2005 *Golf Digest* magazine calculated that there were nearly 32,000 golf courses around the world, with approximately 50 per cent of them located in the USA.

❋ A MAN OF PROPERTY ❋

Three-time Major Championship winner Vijay Singh purchased an island on the Worlds' Islands archipelago in Dubai. The Fijian intends to build a water golf course on his property.

❋ BEN HONOURED ❋

Ben Hogan won the Vardon Trophy for the lowest scoring average three times: 1940, 1941 and 1948. In 1953 he won the Hickok Belt as the top professional athlete of the year in the USA. He was inducted into the World Golf Hall of Fame in 1974 and received the Bob Jones Award in 1976.

❋ LUCKY 13 FOR SAM ❋

Sam Snead won 13 tournaments on the Seniors/Champions Tour:

1963 PGA Seniors' Championship
1964 World Seniors
1965 PGA Seniors' Championship, World Seniors
1967 PGA Seniors' Championship
1970 PGA Seniors' Championship, World Seniors
1972 PGA Seniors' Championship, World Seniors
1973 PGA Seniors' Championship, World Seniors
1980 Golf Digest Commemorative Pro-Am
1982 Legends of Golf (with Don January)

❋ WIT AND WISDOM OF GOLF (18) ❋

"You can talk to a fade, but a hook won't listen."
Lee Trevino

❋ MULTIPLE AMATEUR WINS ❋

In the 125-year history of the British Amateur Championship, including 2010, only 16 players have won the title on more than one occasion:

8 wins:	John Ball
5 wins:	Michael Bonallack
4 wins:	Harold Hilton
3 wins:	Joseph Carr
2 wins:	Horace Hutchinson, Johnny Laidley, Freddie Tait, Robert Maxwell, Ernest Holderness, Cyril Tolley, Lawson Little, Frank Stranahan, Trevor Homer, Dick Siderowf, Peter McEvoy, Gary Wolstenholme

❋ TIGER ON TOP OF THE WORLD ❋

In late 1999 Tiger Woods topped the official world rankings and went on to set a record of 264 consecutive weeks as the world's number one ranked player. During this remarkable streak Woods won seven out of the 11 Majors on offer, beginning with the 1999 US PGA Championship at Medinah CC and ending with the 2002 US Open Championship at Bethpage Black. Woods also broke the record for the biggest winning margin in a Major, set by Old Tom Morris in the 1862 Open Championship, with his 15-stroke win in the 2000 US Open at Pebble Beach.

❋ TIGER'S RECORD NO MATCH FOR NELSON ❋

Byron Nelson's record of 113 consecutive cuts made is second only to the 142 set by Tiger Woods in 2004. However, it is worth noting that the PGA Tour defines "making a cut" as receiving a monetary sum even if an event has no actual cut in the modern sense. In Nelson's era, only the top 20 players in a tournament received prize money. Therefore, the "113 consecutive cuts made" by Nelson mean that he actually made 113 consecutive top 20 tournament finishes. On the other hand the best sequence Woods has ever produced is 21 consecutive top 20 finishes.

❋ THE CHARLES SCHWAB CUP ❋

The Charles Schwab Cup is awarded to the player with the most consistent top 10 finishes on the Champions Tour. Allen Doyle of the USA won the inaugural award in 2001. Points are earned per thousands of dollars earned in each top 10 finish in Champions Tour tournaments. In 2006 points were doubled for Majors and the Charles Schwab Cup Championship.

❋ JUST TOO GOOD ❋

Bobby Jones only played in a total of 52 tournaments, both amateur and professional, and won an amazing 23 of them, including 13 Majors – four US Opens, three British Opens, five US Amateur Championships and one British Amateur Championship. He retired from the game, aged only 28, shortly after winning the probably never to be repeated Grand Slam of golf in 1930. Francis Ouimet, winner of the 1913 US Open, once said of Jones: "I'd run with Bobby, and he would absolutely annihilate me. You have no idea how good Bobby was."

❋ HOGAN'S ALLEY ❋

In 1948 Ben Hogan won 10 Tour events, including the US Open at the Riviera County Club, a course that subsequently became known as "Hogan's Alley" because of his success there. The Colonial Country Club, Fort Worth, Texas, a modern-day PGA tournament venue, is also known as "Hogan's Alley". In addition, the name has been given to the par-five 6th hole at Carnoustie, in Scotland. Here Hogan took a famously difficult line off the tee during each of his rounds on his way to winning the 1953 British Open.

❋ FUTURE BRITISH AMATEUR VENUES ❋

Year	*Venue*
2013	Royal Cinque Ports
2012	Royal Troon
2011	Hillside Golf Club

❋ MOST RUNNERS-UP AT BRITISH OPEN ❋

7 – Jack Nicklaus, 1964, 1967, 1968, 1972, 1976, 1977, 1979
6 – J. H. Taylor, 1896, 1904, 1905, 1906, 1907, 1914

❋ JACK NICKLAUS (1940–) ❋

Jack William Nicklaus was born on 21 January 1940 in Columbus, Ohio. Jack grew up in, and attended public schools in, the suburb of Upper Arlington, Ohio, where he earned his famous "Golden Bear" nickname as an Upper Arlington Golden Bear, the popular name of the local high school's sports teams. When he was a very young child Nicklaus overcame a mild case of polio and began to play golf when he was 10 years old. Even at such an early age the evidence was there that Jack was going to be a top golfer. In 1952 he won the first of six Ohio State Junior titles, and aged 13 he shot under 70. While at college he won the US Amateur title twice (1959 & 1961) and added an NCA Championship (1961).

At the 1960 US Open Championship played at Cherry Hills CC the 20-year old almost bagged his first Major by carding a 282 only to finish runner-up to Arnold Palmer. Indeed, Nicklaus's US Open debut was so impressive that his 282 remains the lowest total ever carded by an amateur in the US Open Championship. He played for the US Walker Cup teams of 1959 and 1961, wining both his matches. Following his success as an amateur Nicklaus turned professional in 1962, and the rest as they say is history. Over the next two decades Nicklaus, like Bobby Jones before him, totally dominated the game, winning a record 18 Majors that included six Masters, five US PGA Championships, four US Opens and three British Opens. At the height of his game Nicklaus was almost invincible. In total, the Golden Bear notched up 46 top-three finishes in Majors (including 19 second-place finishes and nine third places), 56 top-five finishes and 73 top-10 finishes. He was so dominant at The Masters that he finished in the top ten at Augusta every year throughout the 1970s.

In 1962 he won the first of his record haul of Majors when he defeated Arnold Palmer in a play-off for the US Open played at Oakmount CC. The following year he took his first Masters and his first US PGA back to the Nicklaus trophy cave. He is one of only five golfers to win all four current Majors, the "Grand Slam", the first of only two to have won all four Majors at least once (with Tiger Woods) and the only golfer in the history of the sport to win all four Majors at least three times. Nicklaus stands second only to one man on the all-time list of players with the most PGA Tour wins: Nicklaus snared 73, while the legendary Sam Snead took 82 PGA titles. Amazingly, during 17 consecutive seasons from 1962 to 1978 he won at least two PGA Tour titles and was never outside the top four on the money list. He played on six Ryder Cup teams.

❋ GREAT GOLF COURSES OF THE WORLD (8) ❋

PINE VALLEY, NEW JERSEY
Opened: 1919
Designer: George Crump
Yardage: 6,656 Par: 70
Majors: None

Pine Valley Golf Club was founded in 1912 by a group of amateur golfers from the Philadelphia Country Club, led by George Crump. Crump managed to persuade 18 of his friends to donate $1,000 each to purchase land situated in Clementon, New Jersey. The course took seven years to complete, and during that time Crump lived in a small bungalow on the site. Sadly, Crump died in January 1918 with only 14 holes completed, but thankfully there was enough money in his estate to see his dream come to fruition. In 2005 Pine Valley was named the No. 1 golf course in *Golfweek Magazine*'s America's Top 100 Classic Courses (it was No. 2 in 2006). Although it is regarded as one of the greatest courses in the world, Pine Valley has not played host to a Major simply because there is not enough room on the course to accommodate tens of thousands of spectators. However, it has hosted the Walker Cup twice in 1936 and 1985.

❋ WIT AND WISDOM OF GOLF (19) ❋

"It took me seventeen years to get three thousand hits in baseball. I did it in one afternoon on the golf course."
Hank Aaron

❋ SHADOW PUTTING ❋

"These greens are so fast I have to hold my putter over the ball and hit it with the shadow."
Sam Snead

❋ JACK ON THE MONEY ❋

Jack Nicklaus won the Open Championship three times (1966, 1970 & 1978) and was runner-up a record seven times. The Golden Bear made the cut in 32 out of 38 appearances, and between 1966 and 1980 he never finished below sixth. Nicklaus is held in such high esteem by British golf fans that the Royal Bank of Scotland printed Nicklaus's image on a special issue of two million £5 bank notes.

❋ AUGUSTA'S CLUBHOUSE ❋

The Clubhouse at the Augusta National Golf Club was built in 1854 by Dennis Redmond, the owner of the Indigo Plantation at the time.

❋ THE SEVE TROPHY ❋

The Seve Trophy is a biennial tournament between male teams from Great Britain & Ireland and Continental Europe. It was founded in 2000 and is named in honour of the five-times Major winner, Severiano Ballesteros. It is similar to the Ryder Cup in that it is played over three days, with two days of pairs matches and a final set of singles matches on the third day. It differs from the Ryder Cup in that each team comprises 10 players rather than 12, and prize money is on offer. The event is played in September in a non-Ryder Cup year and is played in the same week that Europe's Ryder Cup opponents, Team USA, take on an "International Team" in the Presidents Cup. At first the Seve Trophy was contested in even-numbered years, but as a result of the postponement of the 2001 Ryder Cup following the 9/11 attacks in the US, it is now played in odd-numbered years.

Year	*Venue*	*Winners*		*Losers*	
2009	Golf de Saint-Nom-la-Bretèche, France	GB & Ire	16½	Continental Europe	11½
2007	The Heritage Golf & Spa Resort, Ireland	GB & Ire	16½	Continental Europe	11½
2005	Wynyard Golf Club, England	GB & Ire	16½	Continental Europe	11½
2003	Paradores, Spain	GB & Ire	15	Continental Europe	13
2002	Druids Glen, Republic of Ireland	GB & Ire	14½	Continental Europe	11½
2000	Sunningdale Old Course, England	Continental Europe	13½	GB & Ire	12½

❋ BRITISH OPEN BIGGEST WINS ❋

Margin	***Winner, Year***
13 strokes –	Old Tom Morris, 1862
12 strokes –	Young Tom Morris, 1870
8 strokes –	J. H. Taylor, 1900, 1913; James Braid, 1908; Tiger Woods 2000
7 strokes –	Louis Oosthuizen 2010

❋ ELDERLY STATESMEN ❋

For many years after his retirement, Gene Sarazen was a familiar figure as an honorary starter at The Masters. For nearly 20 years he used to join Byron Nelson and Sam Snead in hitting the ceremonial tee shot before each Masters tournament.

❋ THE ST ANDREWS TROPHY ❋

In November 1955 the Championship Committee of the Royal and Ancient Golf Club of St Andrews suggested to the European Golf Association that there should be an international amateur men's team event between Great Britain & Ireland and Europe. The inaugural tournament was held in 1956 at Wentworth, and the series has continued on a biennial basis in non-Walker Cup years ever since. Victory in the first event went to Great Britain & Ireland, captained by Gerald Micklem, by a score of 12½ to 2½. In recent years the event has been staged alternately on a home and away basis. The tournament was known as the match between the British Isles and the Continent of Europe up until 1963, when the St Andrews Trophy was presented to the winners by the R&A. The tournament comprises four morning foursomes followed by eight afternoon singles over two consecutive days.

❋ TOM THE DESIGNER ❋

Tom Watson designed the National Golf Club of Kansas City golf course. In 1987 he was awarded the Bob Jones Award in recognition of distinguished sportsmanship in golf, and in 1988 he was inducted into the World Golf Hall of Fame.

❋ SENIOR SKINS ❋

Arnold Palmer won three Senior Skins: 1990, 1992 and 1993.

❋ GOLF'S FIRST MASTER OF PSYCHOLOGY ❋

Walter Hagen is widely believed to be the first golfer to have used psychology in order to exploit any weakness in his opponent. On one occasion he invited his main competitor out of the clubhouse to watch him sink a putt on the 18th green and then told his opponent that he would beat him the next day. And he did! Hagen possessed the ability to make his opponents lose concentration.

❋ WIT AND WISDOM OF GOLF (20) ❋

"A buoyant, positive approach to the game is as basic as a sound swing."
Tony Lema

❋ BRITISH OPEN YOUNG AND OLD ❋

The following golfers are the youngest/oldest competitors in the Open Championship:

Young Tom Morris, 1865 – 14 years, 25 days
Gene Sarazen, 1976 – 74 years, 4 months, 9 days

❋ FUTURE US AMATEUR VENUES ❋

Year	*Venue*
2013	The Country Club, Brookline, Massachusetts
2012	Cherry Hills Country Club, Colorado
2011	Erin Hills Golf Course, Wisconsin

❋ TICKER-TAPE WELCOME ❋

Upon his return to the United States after winning the 1953 Open Championship at Carnoustie, Scotland, Ben Hogan received a ticker-tape parade in New York City. It was the only time he played the British Open.

❋ THE MONEY MAN ❋

Jack Nicklaus topped the PGA Tour money list eight times: in 1964, 1965, 1967, 1971, 1972, 1973, 1975 and 1976.

❋ KIWI RULES US OPEN ❋

New Zealand's Michael Campbell won the 2005 US Open Championship played at Pinehurst No. 2, North Carolina. The Kiwi's superb one-under-par score of 69 gave him a two-stroke victory over Tiger Woods, a winner's cheque worth $1.17 million and the accolade of becoming the first New Zealand golfer to win the US Open. What was all the more amazing about his victory was that Campbell had failed to survive the weekend in his previous four US Open appearances and had not even finished in the top ten in a Major since the 1995 British Open at St Andrews.

❋ AN HONEST PLAYER ❋

Bobby Jones was not only one of the greatest players that golf has ever witnessed but he also exemplified the principles of fair play and true sportsmanship. At the beginning of his career he was in the final play-off for the US Open Championship. During his match one of his shots landed in the rough adjacent to the fairway and just as he was setting up to play his next shot his iron caused the ball to move very slightly. Jones, being the honest player he was, instantly turned to the nearby marshals and called a foul on himself. The marshals discussed Jones's request among themselves and even questioned some of the gallery to ascertain if anyone had seen the foul. With only Jones witnessing the foul, the marshals decided that it was up to Jones himself, and so Jones called the foul shot. When a marshal complimented Jones for possessing an extremely high level of integrity, an angry Jones retorted: "Do you commend a bank robber for not robbing a bank? No you don't. This is how the game of golf should be played at all times." Jones lost the US Open by one stroke. Appropriately, the United States Golf Association's sportsmanship award is named the Bob Jones Award.

❋ AN OUTSTANDING CUB ❋

Tiger Woods won the US Amateur Championship on three consecutive occasions (1994, 1995 & 1996), the only player to win three in a row. Tiger was only 18 when he won his first, making him the youngest winner of the tournament, and bettering the previous record of Nathaniel Crosby (son of Bing Crosby).

❋ THE BEAR'S POWER FADE ❋

Jack Nicklaus popularized the "power fade" which was the Golden Bear's characteristic ball flight.

❋ LOW-SCORING BRITISH OPEN CHAMPIONS ❋

Only three players have won the Open Championship by carding all four rounds under 70 (and three non-champions have also managed to achieve the same impressive feat):

Greg Norman	1993	Royal St George's	(66, 68, 69, 64)
Nick Price	1994	Turnberry	(69, 66, 67, 66)
Tiger Woods	2000	St Andrews	(67, 66, 67, 69)

❋ WIT AND WISDOM OF GOLF (21) ❋

"It is nothing new or original to say that golf is played one stroke at a time. But it took me many years to realize it."
Bobby Jones

❋ THE SOLHEIM CUP ❋

The Solheim Cup is a biennial transatlantic team match-play competition generally regarded as the most prestigious team event in women's golf. The tournament was founded in 1990 by Karsten Manufacturing Corporation (KMC), the company that makes the PING golf equipment. The Solheim Cup features 12 of the leading European-born players from the Ladies European Tour (LET) and 12 of the leading American-born players from the Ladies Professional Golf Association (LPGA). As with the men's equivalent competition, the Ryder Cup, players on both sides of the Atlantic earn points in their respective tour events to secure places on the team. The tournament is played over three days and comprises 28 matches: 8 foursome matches, 8 four-ball matches and, on the final day, 12 singles. Up to and including the 2009 tournament, Team USA leads Europe by eight wins to three. The 2011 Solheim Cup will be played at Killeen Castle Golf Resort in County Meath, Ireland.

Year	*Venue*	*Winner*
1990	Lake Nona G & CC	US
1992	Dalmahoy CC	Europe
1994	The Greenbrier	US
1996	St Pierre G & CC	US
1998	Muirfield Village	US
2000	Loch Lomond GC	Europe
2002	Interlachen CC	US
2003	Barsebäck G & CC	Europe
2005	Crooked Stick GC	US
2007	Rich Harvest Farms	US
2009	Halmstad GK	US

❋ STRUCK BY LIGHTNING ❋

John White, a Scottish international footballer who played for Tottenham Hotspur, was struck and killed by lightning when playing a round of golf at Crews Hill Golf Course, Enfield, on 24 July 1964.

❋ POSTHUMOUS HONOURS FOR NELSON ❋

Following Byron Nelson's death on 26 September 2006, a number of posthumous honours were bestowed on one of the true giants of the sport. State Highway 114 Business through Roanoke, where he died, was named "Byron Nelson Boulevard", while the street he lived on was changed to "Eleven Straight Lane" in honour of his record of 11 consecutive PGA Tour victories in 1945. "Byron Nelson Parkway" in Southlake, Texas, was named in his honour, and on 16 October 2006, President George W. Bush approved the award of the Congressional Gold Medal, the highest award that can be bestowed by the Legislative Branch of the US government.

❋ THE MIRACLE AT OAKLAND HILLS ❋

Gary Player bogeyed the 14th and 15th holes during the final round of the 1972 US PGA Championship, played at Oakland Hills Country Club, and at the next he sliced his tee shot. From his lie on the 16th he couldn't see the flagstick, so he borrowed a chair from the gallery and stood on it to line up his approach shot. Few in attendance gave Player any chance of winning, but he proceeded to hit one of the most spectacular recovery shots in the history of Championship golf, a nine-iron that barely cleared the trees and a lake before finally rolling to within four feet of the cup. Player then sank the birdie putt and went on to win his second US PGA Championship with pars on the final two holes.

❋ A SAD LOSS ❋

On 18 June 2006, when she was driving from a tournament in Decatur, Illinois, to her next tournament in Lima, Ohio, Gaelle Truett, a player on the Futures Tour, died following a car accident, aged just 27. Gaelle was the first Tour player to be killed in a traffic incident in the 26-year history of the Futures Tour and the 56-year history of the LPGA Tour.

❋ GOLF'S 21-GUN SALUTE ❋

Payne Stewart died in a plane crash shortly after winning the 1999 US Open Championship. The 2000 US Open Championship played at Pebble Beach Golf Links began with 21 of Stewart's fellow professionals simultaneously hitting balls into the Pacific Ocean in a golf version of the 21-gun salute.

❋ GREAT GOLF COURSES OF THE WORLD (9) ❋

Turnberry, Scotland
Opened: 1906
Designers: Willie Fernie, Mackenzie Ross
Yardage: 7,204 Par: 70
Majors: Open Championship 1977, 1986, 1994, 2009

Turnberry is the youngest of Scotland's Open Championship courses. The first 13 holes were laid out by Willie Fernie, the winner of the 1883 Open Championship, in 1903, and three years later Turnberry became the world's first hotel and golf complex. It did not host the Open until 1977, when Tom Watson won. Turnberry's trademark is the 9th hole with its remote tee perched on a promontory of cliff at the sea's edge, with a sheer drop of 50 feet. The locals say that if you can't see Ailsa Craig, the 1,208-foot-high granite rock situated off the coast, it's raining; if you can see it, then it's about to rain. Colin Montgomerie has described the course as "the finest links course in the world". The 2009 Open Championship at Turnberry nearly had one of the greatest romance stories in golf history, but 59-year-old Watson bogied the 72nd hole, then lost a play-off to Stewart Cink.

❋ JACK'S THE MASTER ❋

Jack Nicklaus's record six wins in The Masters came in 1963, 1965, 1966, 1972, 1975 and 1986. Not only does he hold the record for the most green jackets won, but he also finished as runner-up a record four times. In 1998, aged 58, Nicklaus finished an impressive sixth. Over his career he appeared in the event 45 times and made the cut 37 times.

❋ A REMARKABLE OPEN CHAMPIONSHIP ❋

The 2010 British Open Championship was played at St Andrews and was won by Louis Oosthuizen. The South African won with a 16-under par total of 272, scoring better than par (72) in all four rounds he played (65-67-69-71=272) and finishing seven strokes clear of Lee Westwood. It was Oosthuizen's first Major Championship victory and remarkably he had only made the cut once from his eight previous appearances in a major, the 2008 PGA Championship. On the opening day of the championship, Northern Ireland's Rory McIlroy became the eighth player in British Open history (and the 22nd in majors) to shoot a 63.

❋ A FITTING OPEN TRIBUTE ❋

Jack Nicklaus turned 65 on 21 January 2005, the year that his exemption ran out on the PGA Tour, as he won his last Major, The Masters, in 1986. When he announced that he would retire from professional golf following the 2005 British Open, the Royal & Ancient Golf Club of St Andrews scheduled the Open for the Old Course at St Andrews in honour of the Golden Bear. Several years earlier the R&A had actually nominated St Andrews as host to the 2006 Open, but when Nicklaus decided to call it a day they promptly altered the schedule to give him an opportunity to play his last Open there.

❋ TEAM ASIA WIN 2006 LEXUS CUP ❋

Team Asia won the Lexus Cup on 17 December 2006, defeating the International Team 12½–11½ in Singapore. Lee Seon-hwa from South Korea secured the winning point for the hosts when she beat Paraguay's Julieta Granada 2 & 1. The International Team was captained by the ladies' number one player, Annika Sorenstam, who beat the Asia captain Grace Park 4 & 3 in the opening singles. England's Laura Davies suffered her third straight defeat, losing 4 & 3 to Sakura Yokomine. It was the second time the tournament had been played following the International Team's 16–8 inaugural victory in Singapore in December 2005.

❋ GUSTY PERFORMANCE ❋

In gusty Augusta winds at the 1998 Masters, aged 63 years and five months, Gary Player became the oldest golfer to make to the cut, breaking the 25-year-old record set by the legendary Sam Snead.

❋ ARNOLD PALMER AIRPORT ❋

Arnold Palmer was born in Latrobe, Pittsburgh, and had an airport named in his honour, the Arnold Palmer Airport. Palmer himself is an aircraft pilot and bought the first Cessna Citation X, a plane in which he set a speed record on a 5,000km closed course.

Did You Know That?
Arnold Palmer also had a drink named in his honour, the Arnold Palmer, which consists of half iced tea (either sweetened or unsweetened) and half lemonade.

❋ ARNOLD PALMER (1929–) ❋

Arnold Daniel Palmer was born on 20 September 1929 in Latrobe, Pittsburgh, Pennsylvania. The young Arnie was taught how to play golf by his father, who was a professional at Latrobe Country Club. When he was just seven years old he broke 70 at Bent Creek Country Club. After winning the 1954 US Amateur title he turned professional in 1954, and won his first PGA Tour event, the Canadian Open, in 1955. Two PGA Tour victories followed in 1956 (the Insurance City Open & the Eastern Open), and 1957 proved even more successful for Palmer, with four wins on the Tour: in the Houston Open, the Azalea Open Invitational, the Rubber City Open Invitational and the San Diego Open Invitational.

In 1958 Palmer won the first of his seven Majors and the first of his four Masters titles. He also claimed the St Petersburg Open Invitational and the Pepsi Championship in 1958. Palmer ended the decade with three more PGA Tour wins before he exerted his dominance of the sport during the 1960s. Between 1960 and 1963 he won a staggering 29 PGA Tour events in four years, including eight titles in both 1960 and 1962. In 1960, he won the Hickok Belt, awarded to the top professional athlete of the year, and was named by *Sports Illustrated* magazine as their "Sportsman of the Year". Golfers are assessed on the number of Majors they win and in 1960 Arnie won his second green jacket and the first of two US Open Championships, bringing his Majors' total to three. Then in 1961 he won the British Open Golf Championship, which he retained the following year along with his third green jacket at Augusta. His seventh and final Major arrived in 1964 in the shape of a fourth US Masters victory.

Palmer won the coveted Vardon Trophy four times and played on six US Ryder Cup teams. In 1963 he was the last playing captain in the Ryder Cup, and he captained the team again in 1975. He was the PGA Tour's top money-winner on four occasions and twice voted the PGA Player of the Year. During his career Arnie won 62 PGA Tour events, plus 189 other tournaments. After winning his first PGA Tour event in 1955 he went on to win a PGA Tour event every year up until 1971.

In 1967 he became the first man to reach $1 million in career earnings on the PGA Tour and during his career he built up a wide fan base, often referred to as "Arnie's Army". In 1980 he was eligible for the inaugural Senior PGA Tour and took the prestigous inaugural Seniors PGA Championship the same year. In total he won 10 events on the Seniors Tour from 1980 to 1988.

❋ WIT AND WISDOM OF GOLF (22) ❋

"A rough should have high grass. When you go bowling they don't give you anything for landing in the gutter, do they?"
Lee Trevino

❋ JACK NICKLAUS AWARD WINNERS ❋

In 1990 the PGA Tour inaugurated the "PGA Tour Player of the Year Award (Jack Nicklaus Award)" in direct competition with the "PGA Player of the Year Award", which is presented by the PGA of America. However, unlike the PGA of America's award, the Jack Nicklaus Award is based on a vote by PGA Tour members. Tiger Woods won the award for a tenth time in 2009.

❋ DOTTING THE "I" ❋

A Jack Nicklaus Museum stands proudly on the campus of Ohio State University in Columbus, Ohio, where Jack Nicklaus was born. On 28 October 2006, the Golden Bear was afforded the unique privilege of dotting the "i" of "Ohio" in "Script Ohio" which is the signature formation of the Ohio State University Marching Band at the Ohio State (Buckeyes) homecoming game. This is considered the greatest honour that can be bestowed on a non-band member.

❋ GOLF GOES TO HOLLYWOOD ❋

The following movies have all been made about golf:

A Gentlemen's Game ❖ *Banning* ❖ *Bobby Jones: Stroke of a Genius* ❖ *Caddyshack* ❖ *Caddyshack II* ❖ *Dead Solid Perfect* ❖ *Follow the Sun* ❖ *Happy Gilmore* ❖ *The Greatest Game Ever Played* ❖ *The Legend of Bagger Vance* ❖ *The Story of Golf* ❖ *Tin Cup*

❋ WIE BACKS KOREAN OLYMPIC BID ❋

On 20 December 2006, Michelle Wie was invited to become an honorary ambassador for the 2014 Winter Olympics bid of South Korean ski resort Pyeongchang. The 17-year-old star of the LPGA grew up in Hawaii but has Korean parents. Pyeongchang narrowly lost out to Vancouver in the race to host the 2010 Winter Olympics and Paralympics. On 4 July 2007, the International Olympic Committee chose Sochi, Russia, to host the 2010 Winter Olympic Games.

❋ A STRONG FAMILY TRADITION ❋

Ramon Sota was a four-time Spanish professional champion who also won the 1965 French Open, the 1969 Madrid Open and the 1971 Italian Open. In 1965 Sota finished sixth in The Masters and in 1971 he took 10th place on the European Tour Order of Merit. His nephew, Severiano Ballesteros, won six European Tour Order of Merit titles, and Manuel, Seve's older brother, finished in the top 100 on the European Tour Order of Merit every year from 1972 to 1983. Seve's other brothers, Vicente and Baldomero, were also professional golfers and his nephew, Raul, has played the European Tour since the turn of the millennium but with little success.

❋ USGA FOUNDED ❋

The United States Golf Association (USGA) was founded on 22 December 1884 and officially marked the formal organization of golf in the USA. The USGA became the sport's governing body in the USA and assumed full responsibility for writing the Rules, organizing National Championships and establishing a national system of handicapping. The USGA also plays a prominent role as the game's historian, collecting and displaying golf artefacts and memorabilia at its museum and archives in Far Hills, New Jersey.

❋ THE TIGER'S HAUL ❋

Up to the end of 2010, Tiger Woods has won 14 Majors:

Year	*Championship*
1997	The Masters
1999	PGA Championship
2000	US Open
2000	The Open Championship
2000	PGA Championship *(2)*
2001	The Masters *(2)*
2002	The Masters *(3)*
2002	US Open *(2)*
2005	The Masters *(4)*
2005	The Open Championship *(2)*
2006	The Open Championship *(3)*
2006	PGA Championship (3)
2007	PGA Championship (4)
2008	US Open (3)

❋ WIT AND WISDOM OF GOLF (23) ❋

"You know it's truly amazing. The more I practise, the luckier I get."
Gary Player, in response to a heckler's claim that he was "lucky"

❋ MARRIED ON AND OFF THE COURSE ❋

In 2001 Nick Faldo married Valerie Bercher on the very same day that his former caddie, Fanny Sunesson, got married. Prior to meeting Valerie Bercher, Faldo had begun a relationship with a 20-year-old golf student named Brenna Cepelak in 1995. When Faldo ended his relationship with Brenna she famously battered his Porsche 959 with a golf club, causing £10,000 worth of damage.

❋ BRITISH OPEN LOWEST ROUNDS ❋

63 – Mark Hayes, 2nd round Turnberry, 1977; Isao Aoki, 3rd round Muirfield, 1980; Greg Norman, 2nd round Turnberry, 1986; Paul Broadhurst, 3rd round St Andrews, 1990; Jodie Mudd, 4th round Royal Birkdale, 1991; Nick Faldo, 2nd round and Payne Stewart, 4th round Royal St George's, 1993; and Rory McIlroy, 1st round St Andrews, 2010

❋ THE TEN-MINUTE STANDING OVATION ❋

Jack Nicklaus played his last round of professional golf at the British Open at St Andrews on 15 July 2005. During the second round Nicklaus hit the final tee shot of his legendary career on the 18th, strolled to the Swilcan bridge waving to the appreciative crowd and received a 10-minute standing ovation. He played alongside Luke Donald and Tom Watson, and his son, Steve, was his caddy. He was certain to miss the cut, but in typical Nicklaus style he brought the curtain down on his career by sinking a 15-foot birdie putt and extending his putter and left arm in the air, just as he had done so many times in his career to celebrate crucial putts.

❋ AGAINST ALL ODDS ❋

In the 1920 British Open Golf Championship held at Royal Cinque Ports Golf Club, George Duncan trailed the tournament leader, Abe Mitchell, by 13 shots, was level with him after 54 holes of play and eventually overhauled Mitchell's lead in the final round to win the Open Championship.

❋ BUFFALO GOLFER SHOT ❋

In 1972 John Mosley got into an argument with a guard at Delaware Park Golf Course in Buffalo, New York, over green fees. The heated dispute ended when the guard drew his gun and shot Mosley in the chest. Mosley was pronounced "dead on arrival" when he reached the hospital. Mosley's wife was paid over $100,00 in compensation while the guard was convicted of second-degree manslaughter and sentenced to prison for 7½ years.

❋ THE SATURDAY SANDWICH ❋

Arnold Palmer's favourite sandwich is a peanut butter and jelly sandwich which he calls "the Saturday". The jelly half of the sandwich is refrigerated, and the side with the peanut butter is toasted. The toasted bread is usually wheat bread, while the refrigerated piece of bread is typically potato bread.

❋ PHILATELICALLY SPEAKING ❋

Gary Player has been featured on a South African postage stamp – surely the only time the Black Knight found himself licked!

❋ CAPTAIN SEVE ❋

In 2006 and again in 2007, Seve Ballesteros successfully captained (non-playing) the European Team to Royal Trophy success against Team Asia at the Amata Spring Country Club in Bangkok. In 1997 Seve was the non-playing captain of Europe's winning Ryder Cup team at Valderrama, Spain. Seve also won the Ryder Cup in 1985, 1987, 1989 and 1995.

❋ THE SHOT OF 2006 ❋

Paul Casey's remarkable hole-in-one in the Ryder Cup at the K Club, his first in a professional tournament, was voted the Royal Bank of Scotland Shot of the Year for 2006. Casey, and his Europe team partner David Howell, were leading the US pair of Stewart Cink and Zach Johnson 4 & 5 as they stood on the tee at the par-three 14th. Casey then holed with a four-iron from 213 yards to seal a 5 & 4 win over their opponents. Casey's ace was the first Ryder Cup hole-in-one since Howard Clark's effort at Oak Hill in 1995. It was also the first time anyone had aced a hole to close out a Ryder Cup match.

✻ RYDER CUP CHANGES FORMAT ✻

From the inaugural Ryder Cup in 1927 up until 1959, the competition comprised four foursomes (alternate shot) matches on the first day and eight singles matches on the second day, each of 36 holes. In 1961 a change to the format meant that four 18-hole foursomes matches were played on the morning of the first day, four more foursomes that afternoon, eight 18-hole singles on the morning of the second day and eight more singles that same afternoon. Consequently the total number of points to be won doubled to 24. In 1963 fourball (better-ball) matches were added for the first time, thereby increasing the total number of points to 32. Then, in 1977, five foursomes were played on the first day, five fourball matches on the second day and 10 singles matches on the final day. The new format reduced the total points available to 20. Perhaps the most significant change to the Ryder Cup format came in 1979, when the Great Britain & Ireland team was expanded to include players from Continental Europe. The same year the format was revised to provide four fourball and four foursomes matches on each of the first two days and 12 singles matches on the third and final day. This raised the total number of points available to 28, and the format has remained unchanged to this day.

✻ DEPICTING VARDON ✻

In 2004 the Irish-American actor Aidan Quinn played Harry Vardon in the movie *Bobby Jones: A Stroke of Genius*. Then, in 2005, the English actor Stephen Dillane played Vardon in director Bill Paxton's movie entitled *The Greatest Game Ever Played*.

✻ WOOSIE STICKS TO HIS GUNS ✻

Ian Woosnam, captain of the winning European team at the 2006 Ryder Cup, revealed in an interview with the *Independent* newspaper in December 2006 that he was on the verge of quitting as skipper after Denmark's Thomas Bjorn criticized his two wild-card picks and his style of captaincy. Bjorn was upset when Woosnam chose Lee Westwood instead of him and launched a blistering verbal attack on Woosnam, for which he later apologized – and received a £10,000 fine. However, history will show that Woosnam's wild-card choices were completely vindicated, as Westwood and Darren Clarke made significant contributions to Europe's 18½–9½ victory over Team USA.

❋ ARNIE'S FIVE ATTRIBUTES ❋

During the late 1950s Arnold Palmer was the first client signed up to the pioneering sports agent Mark McCormack. In later interviews McCormack listed five attributes that made Palmer particularly marketable: his good looks; his relatively modest background (his father was a greenkeeper at Latrobe CC prior to becoming the club professional; the way he played golf, taking risks and wearing his emotions on his sleeve; his involvement in a string of exciting finishes in early televised tournaments, and his affability.

Did You Know That?
Palmer won the inaugural World Matchplay Tournament when it was played in England in 1964 (not a European Tour event at the time).

❋ SEPARATE TEES ❋

The year 1870 is generally recognized as the date when separate teeing grounds began to be introduced. Up until this time players had teed off for the next hole from the green of the preceding hole.

❋ THE GREAT TRIUMVIRATE ❋

James Henry Taylor won his third Open Championship in 1900, followed home by Harry Vardon and James Braid. Before their careers were over the three players known as the "Great Triumvirate" would win 16 British Open titles between them. Later the same year Harry Vardon won the US Open Championship to become the first golfer to win both the British and US Open titles. Harry was on an exhibition tour at the time and won using his own "Vardon Flyer" golf ball.

❋ PENNILESS OPEN CHAMPION ❋

Robert Ferguson lost the 1883 British Open Championship to Willie Fernie in extra holes, falling one short of equalling Young Tom Morris's record of four consecutive titles. Later in life Ferguson ended up penniless, working out of the Musselburgh caddy-shack.

❋ OUT OF AFRICA ❋

When the Royal Cape Golf Club opened at Wynberg, in South Africa, it was the first golf club to be built in Africa.

❋ WIT AND WISDOM OF GOLF (24) ❋

"Got more dirt than ball. Here we go again."
Alan Shepard, Apollo 14 commander and amateur golfer, preparing to take another swing during his famous moon walk in 1971

❋ GOLFERS' NICKNAMES ❋

All Day Gay	Brian Gay
The Angry Ant	Gavin Coles
Big Easy	Ernie Els
The Black Knight	Gary Player
BMW	Rory McIlroy
Boom Boom	Fred Couples
Boss of the Moss	Loren Roberts
The Bulldog	Corey Pavin
Chachi	Billy Andrade
Champagne Tony	Tony Lema
Chi-Chi	Juan Rodriguez
The Chief	Dennis Paulson
Chippy	Paul Lawrie
Double D	David Duval
The Duck	Angel Cabrera
El Nino	Sergio Garcia
Fuzzy	Frank Zoeller
GMac	Graeme McDowell
The Golden Bear	Jack Nicklaus
The Goose	Retief Goosen
Grand Master Funk	Fred Funk
The Great Shark	Greg Norman
Italian Bandit	Constantino Rocca
Jumbo	Masashi Ozaki
The King	Arnold Palmer
Lefty	Phil Mickelson
Long Jim	Jim Barnes
Louis	Lodewicus Oosthuizen
Lumpy	Tim Herron
Mechanic	Miguel Angel Jimenez
The Merry Mex (also Super Mex)	Lee Trevino
Monty	Colin Montgomerie
The Pink Panther	Jesper Parnevik
Popeye	Craig Parry
Radar	Mike Reid
Seve	Severiano Ballesteros
Shoulders	David Lynn
The Silver Scot	Tommy Armour
Slammin' Sammy	Sam Snead
The Smiling Assassin	Shigeki Maruyama
The Squire	Gene Sarazen
Sunshine	Paul Goydos
Tank	K. J. Choi
Tiger	Eldrick Woods
Trigger	Mark Roe
Van Helsing	Thomas Bjorn
Volcano	Steve Pate
The Walrus	Craig Stadler
Westy	Lee Westwood
Wild Thing	John Daly
Yogi	Steve Lowery
Zinger	Paul Azinger

❋ PUT YOUR MONEY ON IT ❋

In 1898 Freddie Tait bet a friend that he could reach the clubhouse of the Royal Cinque Ports Golf Club from the clubhouse at Royal St George's, a distance of three miles, in 40 shots or fewer. He put his 32nd shot straight through a window at the Royal Cinque Ports club.

❋ WIT AND WISDOM OF GOLF (25) ❋

"You're only here for a short visit. Don't hurry. Don't worry. And be sure to smell the flowers along the way."
Walter Hagen

❋ GREAT GOLF COURSES OF THE WORLD (10) ❋

WINGED FOOT (WEST COURSE), NEW YORK
Opened: 1923
Designer: Albert W. Tillinghast
Yardage: 6,980 Par: 70
Majors: US Open Championship 1929, 1959, 1974, 1984, 2006.
US PGA Championship 1997

In 1920 a small group of men sitting in the New York Athletic Club agreed that another world-class golf course was needed in the metropolitan area. Golf was already being enjoyed by New Yorkers at Shinnecock Hills, at the National on Long Island and at Baltusrol in New Jersey. The men found the land they were looking for to build a new course at Mamaroneck, NY. In 2006 Winged Foot played host to its fifth US Open Championship, the 106th edition of the event, which was won by Australia's Geoff Ogilvy. Previous Open Champions at Winged Foot include Bobby Jones, Billy Casper, Hale Irwin and Fuzzy Zoeller.

❋ GOLF IN THE EMERALD ISLE ❋

In 1856 the Royal Curragh Golf Club was founded in Kildare to become the first golf club in Ireland. In France the Pau Golf Club was founded to become the first golf club on the Continent. A rule change to the game was enacted in 1856, stating that in match play the ball must be played as it lies or the player must concede the hole.

❋ A SPLENDID VINTAGE ❋

The following famous births occurred in 1870:

Harry Vardon – six-times British Open champion
J. H. Taylor – five-times British Open champion
James Braid – five-times British Open champion
Vardon, Taylor and Braid are known as the "Great Triumvirate" of British golf.

❋ A MULTI-NATIONAL OPEN ❋

The first 29 British Opens (1860–89) were all won by Scottish golfers (there was no Open in 1871), and it was not until 1890 that an Englishman, John Ball Jnr, won the Claret Jug. In 1907 France's Arnaud Massy became the first non-British player to win the event, and it was not until 1920, a full 60 years after the inaugural Open, that an American, Jock Hutchinson, took the trophy across the Atlantic for the first time. Since Hutchinson's victory, the first Open to be played after the First World War, only eight other nationalities, making 12 in total, have won the coveted prize (the following list details only the first winner from each country):

1860	Willie Park	Scotland
1890	John Ball Jnr	England
1907	Arnaud Massy	France
1920	Jock Hutchison	USA
1947	Fred Daly	Northern Ireland
1949	Bobby Locke	South Africa *(he won the Open four times)*
1954	Peter Thomson	Australia *(he won the Open five times)*
1963	Bob Charles	New Zealand
1967	Roberto de Vicenzo	Argentina
1979	Severiano Ballesteros	Spain *(he won the Open three times)*
1994	Nick Price	Zimbabwe
2007	Padraig Harrington	Ireland *(he won the Open twice)*

❋ PASS ME THE MASHIE NIBLICK ❋

The following lists the arcane names of clubs and their modern equivalents:

Driver	1 wood
Brassie	2 wood
Spoon	3 wood
Baffie	4 wood
Cleek	1 iron
Mid-Iron	2 iron
Mid-Mashie	3 iron
Mashie Iron	4 iron
Mashie	5 iron
Spade Mashie	6 iron
Mashie Niblick	7 iron
Pitching Niblick	8 iron
Niblick	9 iron

Did You Know That?

In 1895 the USGA banned the use of a pool cue as a putter, and Spalding, the sports equipment manufacturer, became the first American company to manufacture golf balls.

❋ GARY PLAYER (1935–) ❋

Gary Player was born on 1 November 1935 in Johannesburg, South Africa. Gary's mum died of cancer when he was just eight years old, and it was his father who encouraged the young Player to take up golf and later took out a loan to pay for him to travel overseas and compete. Player first played golf at the nearby Virginia Park golf course in Johannesburg aged 14 and parred the first three holes. When he was 16 he boldly predicted that one day he would become the world's number one player, and in 1953 he embarked on a life as a professional golfer. In 1957 Player joined the PGA Tour in America, and the very next year he won the first of his 24 PGA Tour victories, in the Kentucky Derby Open. But the young South African really hit the big time when he captured the 1959 Open Championship, the first of what would prove to be a haul of nine Major trophies out of a worldwide career total of 163 tournament victories.

More success followed Player following his 1959 Open victory at Muirfield, Scotland. Three PGA Tour victories in 1961 included his second Major, The Masters. Then, in 1962, he bagged a third different Major by winning the US PGA Championship. Over the following two years he claimed two wins on the Tour before completing a "Grand Slam" by winning the only Major he had not won to date, the US Open Championship in 1965. He now had four Majors under his belt, one of each of the sport's most coveted prizes. In 1968 he won his second Claret Jug, but had to wait a further four years before he won his sixth Major, the US PGA Championship. In 1974 he had what was probably his greatest year as a professional, winning both The Masters and the Open along with nine other victories around the world. Player won his 24th PGA Tour event in 1978 when he claimed victory in the Shell Houston Open after winning The Masters, his ninth Major, and the Tournament of Champions the same year. But his success over the last five decades stretched far beyond the borders of the US PGA Tour.

In the course of his career Player achieved 73 victories on the South African Sunshine Tour (1955–81), and on the PGA Tour of Australasia he won 18 times (1956–81), including seven Australian Opens. He also won other prestigious tournaments during his career: the individual World Cup (twice), the World Matchplay Championship (five times) and the World Series of Golf (three times). He won 23 Champions Tour events (including nine Senior Major Championships), and amassed a further 13 senior wins. Player has travelled in excess of 14 million miles by air and is generally considered to be "the world's most travelled athlete".

❋ BRITISH OPEN VENUES ❋

St Andrews has hosted the greatest number of British Open Championships, 28, since the inaugural tournament in 1860, while only five other courses are in double figures:

Prestwick	– 24
Muirfield	– 15
Royal St George's *(Sandwich)*	– 13
Royal Liverpool Golf Club *(Hoylake)*	– 11
Royal Lytham	– 10
Royal Birkdale	– 9
Royal Troon	– 8
Musselburgh	– 6
Carnoustie	– 7
Turnberry	– 4
Deal	– 2
Royal Portrush	– 1
Prince's *(Sandwich)*	– 1

❋ BORN IN THE USA ❋

John Reid, a Scotsman living in New York, built three golf holes and promoted the game to his companions in 1888. Reid and a few others formed St Andrew's Golf Club at Yonkers in New York, which is generally considered to be the first club specifically established for golf in the United States. Today it is the country's oldest surviving golf club.

Did You Know That?
In 1888 a golf club opened in Antwerp which was the first in Belgium and only the second in continental Europe.

❋ GOING DUTCH ❋

The word "golf" is derived from the Dutch word "kolf", meaning club. Many historians are of the opinion that golf actually originated in Holland and not in Scotland. It is believed that Dutch colonial officers brought the game to Sri Lanka before the game was first played in Scotland around 1457. Today kolven (singular golf) is a Dutch game played by a few individuals with klieks (heavy curved bats) and a ball between two poles on an indoor court (kolven course). The course is 17.5 metres long and 5 metres wide.

❋ SEVEN LEAN YEARS, SEVEN FAT YEARS ❋

From 1916 to 1923 Bobby Jones never won a Major. Then, from 1923 to 1930, he won 13 of the 21 Majors he entered. During this period Jones was so dominant that his two main rivals, Walter Hagen and Gene Sarazen, never won any US or British Open Championships in which Jones played.

❋ KINGS OF OZ ❋

South Africa's Gary Player, with seven wins, has been the king of the Australian Open.

7 wins

Gary Player: 1958, 1962, 1963, 1965, 1969, 1970, 1974

6 wins

Jack Nicklaus: 1964, 1968, 1971, 1975, 1976, 1978

5 wins

Greg Norman: 1980, 1985, 1987, 1995, 1996

I. H. Whitton *(amateur)*: 1912, 1913, 1926, 1929, 1931

❋ GOLF BALL HIT INTO SPACE ❋

Michael Tyurin, a Russian cosmonaut, made golfing history by firing a tee shot from a precarious perch outside the International Space Station on 23 November 2006. Tyurin, Commander of Soyuz-13 (TMA-9)/ Expedition 14 that launched on 18 September 2006 from Baikonour, stood on a ladder by the docking port and hit a lightweight golf ball with a gold-plated six-iron club. Tyurin hit the tee shot into space as a publicity stunt for the Canadian golf company, Element 21 Golf, who in turn paid the Russian Space Agency an undisclosed sum. Space experts disagreed on how far the ball would travel in space. Element 21 Golf claimed the ball would fly through space for three years, while NASA said it would probably fall into the Earth's atmosphere and burn up within three days. However, Tyurin's drive was estimated to have travelled 460,000,000 miles. The plan was stalled for several months while NASA carried out an investigation to ensure the ball would not come back and hit the space station.

Did You Know That?

In 1971 US astronaut Alan Shepard, commander of Apollo 14, took a golf shot while on the surface of the Moon (*see* pages 79 and 164).

❋ GREAT GOLF COURSES OF THE WORLD (11) ❋

Muirfield, Scotland
Opened: 1899
Designers: Harry Colt and Tom Morris Snr
Yardage: 6,980 Par: 71
Majors: Open Championship 1892, 1896, 1901, 1906, 1912, 1929, 1935, 1948, 1959, 1966, 1972, 1980, 1987, 1992, 2002
Ryder Cup: 1973

Muirfield is the home of the Honourable Company of Edinburgh Golfers and holds the distinction of being the oldest golf club in the world, although the game of golf is several centuries older. The club's records date back to 1744, when it produced 13 "Rules of Golf" for its inaugural competition, the "Silver Club". In the beginning the club played on the five holes at Leith Links, where it stayed for almost a century before moving in 1836 to Musselburgh's nine-hole Old Course. The present course has played host to 15 Open Championships, most recently in 2002 when the winner was Ernie Els. In addition to the Open, Muirfield has also played host to the Amateur Championship on numerous occasions, as well as Curtis Cup, Walker Cup and Ryder Cup matches. A superb links course, it was so much to the liking of Jack Nicklaus, who won his first Open there in 1966, that he gave the name Muirfield Village to his golf complex in Ohio. Muirfield is considered by many of the greatest players of all time to be the toughest examination of championship golf among the many historic courses of the British Isles.

❋ WIT AND WISDOM OF GOLF (26) ❋

"I look into their eyes, shake their hand, pat their back, and wish them luck, but I am thinking, 'I am going to bury you'."
Seve Ballesteros

❋ FUTURE RYDER CUP VENUES ❋

2012 .... Medinah CC, Medinah, Illinois
2014 .... Gleneagles, Auchterarder, Scotland
2016 .... Hazeltine National GC, Chaska, Minnesota
2018 .... Le Golf National, France
2020 .... Whistling Straits, Sheboygan, Wisconsin

❋ WIT AND WISDOM OF GOLF (27) ❋

"When a man misses his drive, and then misses his second shot, and then wins the hole with a birdie, it gets my goat."
Bobby Jones, after losing a 72-hole "World Championship" match to Walter Hagen

❋ TREVINO NOT SHOWING HIS AGE ❋

In 1984 Lee Trevino, Gary Player and Lanny Wadkins starred in one of the most exciting finishes in the history of the US PGA Championship. The tournament was played at Shoal Creek Country Club, Birmingham, Alabama. However, it was the 44-year-old Trevino who won through in the end with a superb 15-under-par performance which gave him a comfortable four-stroke victory over his rivals. Before the tournament, Trevino revealed, his wife had said to him: "Even though you're 44, your clubs don't know your age." Trevino played so well over the four days of competition that he also earned the distinction of becoming the first US PGA Champion to win with four rounds in the 60s. It was Trevino's second US PGA Championship victory after winning the 1974 PGA at Tanglewood, Winston-Salem, North Carolina.

❋ THE FIELD WIDENS ❋

A total of only 11 players participated in the inaugural US Open Championship played at Newport GC in 1895. It was won by Horace Rawlins. The 100-mark was passed with 131 entrants in 1912; the 200-mark (265) in 1920; the 500-mark (696) in 1926; the 1,000-mark (1,064) in 1928, and the 5,000-mark (5,255) in 1982.

❋ HISTORY OF THE GOLF BALL ❋

The Feathery

In 1618 a leather-covered golf ball was made that contained chicken or goose feathers tightly packed into the sphere. The feathers and leather (horse or cow hide) were boiled and softened and then fashioned into a ball while wet. A small opening was left in the outer casing through which to stuff the feathers in before applying the final stitches. As the "feathery" dried out, the leather shrank and the feathers expanded to create a hardened ball. The ball was then hammered, to make it round, and painted with several layers of white paint. Because of the difficulty and amount of time involved in hand-crafting featheries, they were quite an expensive product, often more expensive than the clubs. Notable ball-makers of the 1600s were Andrew Dickson, of Leith, and Henry Mills, of St Andrews. Although quite fragile in nature, the feathery was used for almost four centuries.

The Gutty

The gutta-percha ball, or "gutty", was introduced in 1848 by Revd Dr Adam Paterson of St Andrews and was made from gutta-percha packing material.

Gutta-percha is the evaporated milky juice or rubber-like sap produced from the gutta tree found in Malaysia. When heated to the temperature of boiling water the rubber softened and could easily be made into a sphere and used as a golf ball. Unlike the feathery, the gutty was inexpensive to produce and it could also be easily repaired by reheating and then reshaping the rubber. Initially gutties had a smooth surface, which meant that they didn't travel as far as the featheries. This led to varieties in the gutta including the hand-hammered gutta and the bramble. The balls were usually stamped with the ball-maker's stamp, most notably the hand-marked private brands of the Scottish club-makers, such as Morris, Allan Robertson, Gourlay and the Auchterlonies.

The Rubber Ball

In 1898 Coburn Haskell, a golfer from Cleveland, Ohio, introduced the one-piece rubber-cored ball in association with Bertram Work of the B. F. Goodrich Company. The ball featured rubber thread wound around a solid rubber core encased in a gutta-percha sphere. After James Braid won the 1901 Open using it, the Haskell ball became the number-one choice for golfers. The rubber balls looked quite similar to the gutties but gave the average golfer an extra 20 yards from the tee. When W. Millison invented a thread-winding machine, Haskell balls were mass-produced and became easily affordable. In 1905 William Taylor applied the dimple pattern to a Haskell ball, which maximized lift while minimizing drag, and this design has remained more or less unchanged today. Goodrich introduced the pneumatic golf ball, a Haskell ball filled with a compressed-air core, but unfortunately it was prone to expansion with heat and often exploded when it was struck by the club.

Did You Know That?

A dimple-patterned gutty in good condition is worth about $500 today. Feathery balls have sold at auction for over $20,000.

❋ US PGA PAST WINNERS ❋

Year	*Player*	*Venue*
2010*	Martin Kaymer	Whistling Straits, Sheboygan, WI
2009	Yang Yong-eun	Hazeltine National GC, Chaska, MN
2008	Padraig Harrington	Oakland Hills CC, Bloomfield, MI
2007	Tiger Woods	Southern Hills CC, Tulsa, OK
2006	Tiger Woods	Medinah CC, Medinah, IL
2005	Phil Mickelson	Baltusrol GC, Springfield, NY
2004*	Vijay Singh	Whistling Straits, Sheboygan, WI
2003	Shaun Micheel	Oak Hill CC, Rochester, NY
2002	Rich Beem	Hazeltine National GC, Chaska, MN
2001	David Toms	Atlanta Athletic Club, Duluth, GA
2000*	Tiger Woods	Valhalla GC, Louisville, KY
1999	Tiger Woods	Medinah CC, Medinah, IL
1998	Vijay Singh	Sahalee CC, Sammamish, WA
1997	Davis Love III	Winged Foot GC, Mamaroneck, NY
1996*	Mark Brooks	Valhalla GC, Louisville, KY
1995*	Steve Elkington	Riviera CC, Pacific Palisades, CA
1994	Nick Price	Southern Hills CC, Tulsa, OK
1993*	Paul Azinger	Inverness Club, Toledo, OH
1992	Nick Price	Bellerive CC, St Louis, MO
1991	John Daly	Crooked Stick GC, Carmel, IN
1990	Wayne Grady	Shoal Creek G&CC, Birmingham, AL
1989	Payne Stewart	Kemper Lakes GC, Long Grove, IL
1988	Jeff Sluman	Oak Tree GC, Edmond, OK
1987*	Larry Nelson	PGA National, Palm Beach Gardens, FL
1986	Bob Tway	Inverness Club, Toledo, OH
1985	Hubert Green	Cherry Hills CC, Cherry Hills Village, CO
1984	Lee Trevino	Shoal Creek G&CC, Birmingham, AL
1983	Hal Sutton	Riviera CC, Pacific Palisades, CA
1982	Raymond Floyd	Southern Hills, Tulsa, OK
1981	Larry Nelson	Atlantic Athletic Club, Duluth, GA
1980	Jack Nicklaus	Oak Hill CC, Rochester, NY
1979*	David Graham	Oakland Hills CC, Bloomfield Hills, MI
1978*	John Mahaffey	Oakmont CC, Oakmont, PA
1977*	Lanny Wadkins	Pebble Beach, CA
1976	Dave Stockton	Congressional CC, Bethesda, MD
1975	Jack Nicklaus	Firestone CC, Akron, OH
1974	Lee Trevino	Tanglewood Park, Clemmons, NC
1973	Jack Nicklaus	Canterbury GC, Beachwood, OH
1972	Gary Player	Oakland Hills CC, Bloomfield Hills, MI
1971	Jack Nicklaus	PGA National, Palm Beach Gardens, FL
1970	Dave Stockton	Southern Hills CC, Tulsa, OK
1969	Ray Floyd	NCR Country Club, Dayton, OH
1968	Julius Boros	Pecan Valley, San Antonio, TX
1967*	Don January	Columbine CC, Denver, CO
1966	Al Geiberger	Firestone CC, Akron, OH
1965	Dave Marr	Laurel Valley GC, Ligonier, PA
1964	Bobby Nichols	Columbus CC, Columbus, OH

1963 Jack Nicklaus ... Dallas Athletic Club, Dallas, TX
1962 Gary Player ... Aronimink GC, Newtown Square, PA
1961* Jerry Barber ... Olympia Fields CC, Olympia Fields, IL
1960 Jay Hebert ... Firestone CC, Akron, OH
1959 Bob Rosburg ... Minneapolis GC, Minneapolis, MI
1958 Dow Finsterwald ... Llanerch CC, Havertown, PA
1957 Lionel Hebert ... Miami Valley CC, Dayton, OH
1956 Jack Burke ... Blue Hill CC, Canton, MA
1955 Doug Ford ... Meadowbrook CC, Detroit, MI
1954 Chick Harbert ... Keller GC, St Paul, MI
1953 Walter Burkemo ... Birmingham CC, Birmingham, MI
1952 Jim Turnesa ... Big Spring CC, Louisville, KY
1951 Sam Snead ... Oakmont CC, Oakmont, PA
1950 Chandler Harper ... Scioto CC, Columbus, OH
1949 Sam Snead ... Hermitage CC, Richmond, VA
1948 Ben Hogan ... Norwood Hills CC, St Louis, MO
1947 Jim Ferrier ... Plum Hollow CC, Detroit, MI
1946 Ben Hogan ... Portland GC, Portland, OR
1945 Byron Nelson ... Moraine CC, Dayton, OH
1944 Bob Hamilton ... Manita G&CC, Spokane, WA
1943 *No championship (Second World War)*
1942 Sam Snead ... Seaview CC, Atlantic City, NJ
1941 Vic Ghezzi ... Cherry Hills CC, Cherry Hills Village, CO
1940 Byron Nelson ... Hershey CC, Heshey, PA
1939 Henry Picard ... Pomonok CC, Flushing, NY
1938 Paul Runyan ... Shawnee Inn, Smithfield Township, PA
1937 Denny Shute ... Pittsburgh Field Club, O'Hara, PA
1936 Denny Shute ... Pinehurst Resort, Pinehurst, NC
1935 Johnny Revolta ... Twin Hills G&CC, Oklahoma City, OK
1934 Paul Runyan ... The Park CC, Williamsville, NY
1933 Gene Sarazen ... Blue Mound GC, Wauwatosa, WI
1932 Olin Dutra ... Keller GC, St Paul, MN
1931 Tom Creavy ... Wannamoisett CC, Rumford, RI
1930 Tommy Armour ... Fresh Meadow CC, Great Neck, NY
1929 Leo Diegel ... Hillcrest CC, Los Angeles, CA
1928 Leo Diegel ... Baltimore CC, Timonium, MD
1927 Walter Hagen ... Cedar Crest CC, Dallas, TX
1926 Walter Hagen ... Salisbury GC, East Meadow, NY
1925 Walter Hagen ... Olympia Fields CC, Olympia Fields, IL
1924 Walter Hagen ... French Lick Springs, French Lick, IN
1923 Gene Sarazen ... Pelham CC, Pelham Manor, NY
1922 Gene Sarazen ... Oakmont CC, Oakmont, PA
1921 Walter Hagen ... Inwood CC, Inwood, NY
1920 Jock Hutchison ... Flossmoor CC, Flossmoor, IL
1919 James Barnes ... Engineers CC, Roslyn Harbor, NY
1917–18 – *suspended (First World War)*
1916 James Barnes ... Siwanoy CC, Bronxville, NY

* *won in a playoff*. **Note:** Match-play event 1916–1957

❋ POINTS VICTORY ❋

D.A. Points won his first PGA Tour event at the 2011 Pebble Beach National Pro-Am. His amateur partner was comedian Bill Murray.

❋ THE LANGUAGE OF GOLF ❋

Ace .... A hole-in-one.
Albatross .... Three strokes under par for a hole; also double eagle.
Apron .... The short area located around the green which separates it from the fairway; also called the fringe.
Birdie .... One stroke under par for the hole.
Bogey .... One stroke over par for the hole.
Cup .... The hole in the green where the ball is to be putted.
Dormie .... A match play term when the lead is the same number of holes as those remaining. For instance, dormie two is two up with two holes to play.
Dunk .... A ball landing in a water hazard.
Eagle .... Two strokes under par for the hole.
Featherie .... Early golf balls made of compressed feathers inside a leather outer casing.
Fore .... A warning to other players and spectators that your ball may hit them.
Fried Egg .... A term used to describe a ball that remains in its own pitch mark after it has landed in a bunker.
Gimmie .... When your opponent decides that it is not necessary to play the next shot because he thinks you will putt-out anyway.
Green Jacket .... Awarded to the winner of The Masters.
Haskell .... The first modern golf balls, made with rubber straps wound around a core and encased in gutta-percha.
Jigger .... Another name given to a four-iron.
Jungle .... Term used to describe heavy rough.
Kitty Litter .... A term used to describe a sand bunker.
Links .... A golf course located within four miles of the coast.
Medal .... A stroke-play competition where every shot is recorded and the winner is the one with the lowest number of shots in total.
Nineteenth Hole .. The clubhouse bar.
Stableford .... Point scoring competition in which points are awarded as follows: 1 point for a bogey, 2 for a par, 3 for a birdie, 4 for an eagle and 5 for an albatross.
Yips .... Nervous twitch causing players to miss short putts.

❋ WIT AND WISDOM OF GOLF (28) ❋

"Hit it hard. It will land somewhere."
Mark Calcavecchia

❋ ANY OLD IRONS ❋

When golf was first played on the eastern coast of Scotland in 1457, the players used their own carved clubs and balls made from wood. However, it was not long before golf enthusiasts of the fifteenth century approached skilled craftsmen to make them a set of clubs. Indeed, the earliest reference to a set of specially made clubs is when King James IV of Scotland commissioned a bow-maker in Perth, Scotland to make him a set in 1502.

A set of clubs in the fifteenth century comprised a set of play clubs (longnoses) for driving, fairway clubs (or grassed drivers) for medium-range shots, spoons for short-range shots, niblicks (similar to today's wedges) and a putting cleek. The clubheads were made from tough woods like beech or holly, while ash or hazel were used for the shaft. Club-makers joined the clubhead to the shaft using a splint and then bound them tightly together using leather straps. Because of their somewhat brittle nature, it was not unusual for a player to break a club during a round of golf. Consequently in its early years the game of golf tended to be an upper-class sport.

Over the years the clubs changed, and some club-makers experimented with the implanting of metal and bone fragments into the club-face in an effort to prevent it from shattering. Around 1750, some club-makers used forged metal heads for niblicks. In 1819 Hugh Philp was appointed club-maker at St Andrews, while his family was linked by marriage to that of another club-maker, Robert Forgan of Fife, Scotland. In 1826 Forgan began to use hickory imported from America to manufacture shafts, and this was quickly adopted as the wood of choice, but because it was expensive the other woods continued to be used. Wooden and iron-headed clubs with hickory, ash or bamboo shafts remained the adopted norm until the late 1920s, when steel shafts and a matched set of golf clubs first appeared. Today the steel shaft has been replaced by graphite.

Did You Know That?
Ely Callaway named his drivers "Big Bertha", after the German cannon that fired shells many miles further than those of the Americans or British during the Second World War.

❋ GENE SARAZEN (1902–99) ❋

Eugeno Saraceni was born in Harrison, New York on 27 February 1902, the son of Italian immigrants. When he embarked on his golf career, aged 17, he changed his name to Gene Sarazen. His early years on the greens were unspectacular, but in 1922 he arrived. Early in the year he won his first PGA event, the Southern (Spring) Open, and later he captured the first two of his seven Majors by winning the US Open Championship at Stokie followed by the PGA Championship at Oakmont. To win the US Open Sarazen carded a 68, at the time the lowest ever final-round score to win a Major. Things got even better for the 20-year-old Sarazen when he defeated Walter Hagen for the 1922 "World Championship".

In 1923 Sarazen retained the PGA Championship, at the time a match-play tournament, by defeating Hagen again. It proved to be Sarazen's sole PGA win of 1923, and the following year was barren. In 1925 he claimed the Metropolitan Open, and in 1926 the Miami Open. He had three PGA victories in 1927, including the retention of his Miami Open title. These were followed in 1928 by wins in the Miami Beach Open, the Miami Open, the Nassau Bahamas Open and the Metropolitan PGA. A fourth consecutive Miami Open title came in 1929, along with his second successive Miami Beach Open.

In 1930 Sarazen won eight times on the PGA Tour and narrowly missed out on winning the PGA Championship, losing one-down to Tommy Armour at Flushing Meadow, New York. However, it was performances in the Majors on which a player was assessed, and Sarazen knew it, having not won one of golf's glittering prizes in seven years. His fiercest rivals, Hagen, Ben Hogan and Bobby Jones, were practically sweeping all before them. Sarazen had a very successful 1932, winning two Majors, the Open Championship by five shots at Prince's, Sandwich, and then two weeks later the US Open Championship, in addition to the True Temper Open and the Coral Gables Open Invitational events. His third PGA Championship success came in 1933, and two years later he claimed victory in his first Masters – and only the second ever – at Augusta, Georgia. Craig Wood looked to be on his way to winning the 1935 Masters when suddenly Sarazen holed a four-wood second shot at the par-five 15th to draw level, and the following day Sarazen won the play-off. In total Sarazen won 39 times on the PGA Tour and played in six USA Ryder Cup teams (1927, 1929, 1931, 1933, 1935 & 1937). He died in Naples, Florida, on 13 May 1999.

❋ GREAT GOLF COURSES OF THE WORLD (12) ❋

Oakmont Country Club (West Course), Pennsylvania

Opened: 1904

Designer: Henry C. Fownes

Yardage: 6,921 Par: 71

Majors: US Open Championship 1927, 1935, 1953, 1962, 1973, 1983, 1994, 2007. US PGA Championship 1922, 1951, 1978. US Women's Open Championship 2010

One of America's most prestigious golf courses, Oakmont Country Club is in Pennsylvania, 15 miles northeast of downtown Pittsburgh. It has played host to eight US Open Championships, three US PGA Championships, five US Amateur Championships. and, most recently (in 2010, when American Paula Creamer won), the US Women's Open. Oakmont's Church Pews bunker is one of the most famous hazards in golf. Measuring 60 yards long and 40 yards wide, it has seven grass-covered ridges running across it and comes into play on the 3rd and 4th holes. The Oakmont course is forever remembered for Johnny Miller's unforgettable eight-under-par round of 63 at the 1973 US Open, a tournament record that he still holds today.

❋ WIT AND WISDOM OF GOLF (29) ❋

"If I'm on the course and lightning starts, I get inside fast. If God wants to play through, let him."
Bob Hope

❋ MASTERS SUDDEN DEATH ❋

In 1979 The Masters witnessed its first ever sudden-death play-off. Masters rookie Fuzzy Zoeller was involved in a three-way play-off to decide the championship. All three players had finished eight under after 72 holes, and at the first extra hole, the 10th, all four made birdie. Then Zoeller birdied the 11th hole to become the first player since Gene Sarazen in 1935 to win the tournament at his first attempt.

❋ GOLF IN THE CLOUDS ❋

La Paz Golf Club, a 72-hole golf course situated in Bolivia, is reputed to be the highest golf club in the world, at 10,800 feet above sea level.

❋ PGA TOUR CAREER VICTORIES ❋

Sam Snead heads the list for the most PGA Tour victories with 82, while Jack Nicklaus is nine behind him in second place. In 2008, Tiger Woods claimed his 71st PGA Tour title to move into third place on the overall list. In 1995 the PGA Tour commenced counting British Open Championship victories as PGA Tour wins, and then in September 2002 the PGA Tour Policy Board officially recognized British Open wins prior to 1995 as official victories on the PGA Tour.

❋ QUEEN OF CLUBS ❋

Mary Queen of Scots was born on 8 December 1542, and at the time of her birth the game of golf became firmly established on the east coast of Scotland. Her father, James V of Scotland, died within a week of Mary's birth, which made her the Queen of Scotland. However, her mother, Mary of Guise, ruled as regent while the young Mary was sent to France for her formal education. During her time in France Mary played golf and helped to popularize the sport on the Continent. So fond was Mary of the game that she was seen playing golf in the fields beside Sefton just a few days after the murder of her second husband, Lord Darnley. This led to her being openly criticized by the Church for her lack of respect in not affording her husband a proper time of mourning.

❋ BRITAIN'S MICHELLE WIE ❋

Kiran Matharu has been described by golf writers as Britain's Michelle Wie, young, female and Asian. She won the 2006 English Ladies' Amateur Championship to qualify for the 2007 Ladies' European Tour, the youngest female golfer to do so. She was also selected to represent Great Britain & Ireland in the Curtis Cup to play against the United States at Bandon Dunes GC, Oregon (the youngest player of either team). Her best finish on the Ladies' European Tour of Merit was second in the 2007 Nykredit Masters in Denmark.

❋ GOLF GIVES WAY TO SAIL ❋

The inaugural US Open and the inaugural US Amateur Golf Championships had originally been scheduled for September, but were postponed because of a conflict with a more established Newport, Rhode Island sports spectacle, the America's Cup yacht races.

❋ WOODS IN PGA SEVENTH HEAVEN ❋

Tiger Woods won his seventh consecutive PGA Tour title by claiming the Buick Invitational in San Diego on 28 January 2007. Woods's victory means that he now holds the second longest winning streak in PGA history behind Byron Nelson, who holds the record with 11 consecutive PGA victories.

❋ WAY TO GO, MR PRESIDENT ❋

Soon after golf came to America in the late nineteenth century, the Royal & Ancient game quickly established a powerful allure for occupants of the Oval Office. The first golfer in the White House was William Howard Taft. He was also a renowned gambler and drinker – so he certainly knew how to enjoy himself. Franklin D. Roosevelt was generally considered to be the most accomplished player and Dwight Eisenhower was arguably the most obsessed golfer – Ike got a putting green created on the South Lawn on the White House. John F. Kennedy, who was a pretty good golfer himself, waspishly said his Republican rival Richard Nixon was a bit of a duffer. Gerald Ford was a college golfer in his youth, and a great enthusiast for the sport. Bill Clinton is reputed to be an incredibly slow player, while George W. Bush hacks his way round at great speed. By all accounts, 15 of the last 19 US presidents have been staunch devotees of the game Barack Obama played more than 70 times during his presidency, and received criticism in some circles when he played a round during the Memorial Day holiday in May 2011. The 15 golfing presidents are:

William Howard Taft ❖ Herbert Hoover ❖ Franklin D. Roosevelt
Harry Truman ❖ Dwight Eisenhower ❖ John F. Kennedy
Lyndon Johnson ❖ Richard Nixon ❖ Gerald Ford ❖ Jimmy Carter
Ronald Reagan ❖ George Bush Snr ❖ Bill Clinton
George W. Bush ❖ Barack Obama

❋ BORDER CROSSING ❋

The 1894 British Open was played on an English course, Royal St George's, for the first time and was won by a professional English golfer for the first time, John Henry Taylor. Royal St George's went on to host 12 more Open Championships, with wins by Ben Curtis, Greg Norman, Sandy Lyle, Bill Rogers, Bobby Locke, Reg Whitcombe, Henry Cotton (twice) and Jack White.

❋ WIT AND WISDOM OF GOLF (30) ❋

"If I'm going to putt and miss, I want to look good doing it."
Chi-Chi Rodriguez, on his refusal to use a long-handled putter

❋ THE OLD CLARET JUG ❋

In 1872 the R&A, Prestwick Golf Club and the Honourable Company of Edinburgh Golfers were given responsibility for the organization of the British Open Golf Championship and offered a new prize for the winner, a claret jug. The Claret Jug was first presented to Young Tom Morris, who won his fourth consecutive Open Championship (1868, 1869, 1870, 1872 – no contest in 1871). A "Championship Belt" had been presented to winners from 1860 to 1870, with each winner retaining it for a year. However, the rules stipulated that anyone who won three Championships in a row would be permitted to keep the belt permanently. Following Young Tom Morris's British Open Championship victory in 1870 the belt was his to keep.

Did You Know That?
Young Tom Morris's winning streak included an 11-stroke victory in 1869 and a 12-stroke victory in 1870 (over a 36-hole format), while his score of 149 over 36 holes in the 1870 Open represents a stroke average that would not be equalled until the rubber-cored ball was invented in 1898.

❋ THE BOGEY MAN ❋

In 1890, Mr Hugh Rotherham, Secretary of the Coventry Golf Club, invented the idea of standardizing the number of shots at each hole that a reasonable golfer should take and he called this total the "ground score". Dr Browne, Secretary of the Great Yarmouth Golf Club, adopted Rotherham's scoring technique and introduced it in match-play games. During one particular match-play competition at Great Yarmouth GC, Mr C. A. Wellman (possibly Major Charles Wellman), is believed to have said to Dr Browne: "This player of yours is a regular Bogey Man." Towards the end of the nineteenth century, music halls were popular throughout England and Wellman may well have been likening the golfer to the eponymous subject of an Edwardian music hall song "Hush! Hush! Hush! Here Comes the Bogey Man". Following Wellman's joking remark Rotherham's "ground score" became known as the "bogey score" at Great Yarmouth GC and the term is universally used today by golfers.

❋ FATAL PLANE CRASH ❋

In 1966 Tony Lema, winner of the British Open in 1964, was flying to an exhibition match in Chicago, Illinois, accompanied by his wife Betty, when their chartered aircraft ran out of fuel and crashed. All four people on board were killed. Ironically the twin-engined Beechcraft Bonanza crashed on the 7th hole of a golf course in Lansing, Illinois.

❋ DR FRANK STABLEFORD ❋

Wallasey Golf Club is known as the "Home of Stableford" as the eponymous scoring system was devised by Dr Frank Barney Gorton Stableford, a member of Wallasey Golf Club who during his early career had served as a surgeon in the Royal Army Medical Corps, and spent some years in South Africa. Stableford was an excellent golfer possessing a handicap of +1 and in 1907 he won the Royal Porthcawl Club Championship. In 1914, his medical career brought him to Wallasey and he joined the golf club. Stableford's scoring system was born out of frustration with the bogey system of scoring used at the time which made it almost impossible for a golfer to go round Wallasey Golf Club in a score of par or better as a result of the strong winds around the course. Very few players managed to reach the long par-4s in regulation. The upshot was the now famous Stableford scoring system, and club golfers around the world are forever indebted to their inventor.

The Stableford Scoring System

Under the Stableford scoring system each player or side plays against the par of each hole and receives points according to how he/she scores in relation to par. The scoring system is as follows:

2 or more over par........0 points
1 over par........1 point
par........2 points
1 under par........3 points
2 under par........4 points
3 under par........5 points
and so on

Did You Know That?

Wallasey was used as a final qualifying course for the British Open when it returned to Royal Liverpool (Hoylake) in 2006.

⁂ BY ROYAL APPOINTMENT ⁂

The Royal and Ancient Golf Club was founded on 14 May 1754, when 22 noblemen and gentlemen of Fife presented a silver club to be played for annually over the links of St Andrews. The winner became captain for the year. The Society of St Andrews Golfers, as the club was originally known, soon evolved from this competition, meeting regularly to take part in the "healthful exercise of golf", usually followed by a dinner. In 1806 the club began playing for the gold medal at the autumn meeting, and it is likely that the captaincy became an elected office at that time. In 1834 King William IV agreed to become patron of the club and the Society of St Andrews Golfers became the Royal and Ancient Golf Club of St Andrews. As at January 2011, 62 golf clubs around the world enjoyed the accreditation of "royal" prefixing their name.

Golf club	*Year of royal patronage*	*Year golf club founded*
Royal Aberdeen	1903	1780
Royal Adelaide	1923	1892
Royal & Ancient	1834	1754
Royal Ascot	1887	1887
Royal Ashdown	1893	1888
Royal Belfast	1885	1881
Royal Birkdale	1951	1889
Royal Blackheath	1857	1766
Royal Burgess	1929	1773
Royal Calcutta	1911	1829
Royal Canberra	1934	1926
Royal Cape	1910	1885
Royal Cinque Ports	1910	1892
Royal Colombo	1928	1879
Royal Colwood	1931	1913
Royal County Down	1908	1889
Royal Cromer	1887	1888
Royal Dornoch	1906	1877
Royal Dublin	1891	1885
Duff House Royal	1925	1909
Royal Durban	1932	1892
Royal Eastbourne	1887	1887
Royal Epping Forest	1888	1888
Royal Fremantle	1930	1905
Royal Guernsey	1891	1890

Royal Harare	1929	1898
Royal Hobart	1925	1896 *
Royal Jersey	1879	1878
Royal Johannesburg & Kensington	1931	1890
Royal Liverpool	1871	1869
Royal Lytham & St Annes	1926	1886
Royal Malta	1888	1888
Royal Marianske Lazne	2003	1905
Royal Mayfair	2006	1922
Royal Melbourne	1895	1891
Royal Mid-Surrey	1926	1892
Royal Montreal	1884	1873
Royal Montrose	1845	1810
Royal Musselburgh	1876	1774
Royal Nairobi	1935	1906
Royal North Devon	1865	1864
Royal Norwich	1893	1893
Royal Ottawa	1912	1891
Royal Perth	1937	1895 **
Royal Perth Golfing Society	1833	1824
Royal Port Alfred	1924	1907
Royal Porthcawl	1909	1891
Royal Portrush	1892	1888
Royal Quebec	1934	1874
Royal Queensland	1921	1920
Royal Regina	1999	1899
Royal St David's	1908	1894
Royal St George's	1902	1887
Royal Sydney	1897	1893
Royal Tarlair	1926	1925
Royal Troon	1978	1870
Royal Wellington	2004	1878
Royal West Norfolk	1892	1865
Royal Wimbledon	1882	1878
Royal Winchester	1913	1888
Royal Worlington & Newmarket	1895	1893

**The forerunner to Hobart Golf Club (later Royal Hobart Golf Club) was formed in 1896 and known as the Newlands Golf Club. The Hobart Golf Club was actually formed in 1901.*

***The club was founded in 1895 on the Burswood Island site as a 9-holes course before moving to Wattle Grove Farm, Belmont in 1900, again another 9-holes course. On 2 August 1908, the Governor of Western Australia, Sir Frederick Bedford, officially opened the new course on its present site (9-holes).*

❋ GREAT GOLF COURSES OF THE WORLD (13) ❋

VALDERRAMA, SPAIN
Opened: 1975
Designer: Robert Trent Jones
Yardage: 6,819 Par: 72
Majors: None

The Valderrama Golf Club (Club de Golf Valderrama) is situated in Sotogrande, Andalucia, Spain and is one of the most famous golf courses in Europe. The course layout was designed by the famous Robert Trent Jones, and its 4th hole, La Cascada, is the course's signature hole, a par five with a pond to the right of a two-tiered green. Valderrama hosted the inaugural Volvo Masters in 1988, but its greatest moment came in 1997, when it played host to the Ryder Cup and all of Spain rejoiced as Seve Ballesteros led his European team to a famous 14½–13½ victory over the United States.

❋ GOLF BANNED IN SCOTLAND ❋

In 1457, the Scottish Parliament of King James II issued a decree banning golf and football to preserve the skills of archery which was an essential aspect of Scotland's military training for the wars against the English. The decree denounced them as "unprofitable sports". Forty-five years later, in 1502, King James IV, the grandson of King James II, lifted the ban following the signing of the Treaty of Glasgow between England and Scotland. Then on 21 September 1502, King James IV made what is considered by historians to be the first recorded purchase of golf equipment, a set of clubs from a bow-maker in Perth for 14 shillings.

❋ EUROPEAN TREBLE ❋

Europe's victory over the US in the 2006 Ryder Cup was their third consecutive victory in the competition, and the first time the US had lost three consecutive Ryder Cups.

❋ WHAT'S IN A NAME – "FORE!" ❋

The Shorter Oxford Dictionary records the first use of the word "fore!" in 1878, describing it as a warning cry to people in front of a golf stroke, perhaps an abbreviation of the word "before". However, no certain etymology for the golf word "fore!" has ever been agreed.

❋ WIT AND WISDOM OF GOLF (31) ❋

"In choosing a partner, always pick the optimist."
Tony Lema

❋ THE SKINS GAME ❋

The inaugural Skins Game was held in 1983 and was devised by Don Ohlmeyer and Gary Frank. Four of the world's greatest golfers participated in the 1983 tournament – Jack Nicklaus, Arnold Palmer, Gary Player and Tom Watson. Gary Player was the inaugural champion with the event becoming an instant television hit with golf fans. The format for the Skins Game is an 18-hole match-play format competition that is televised over two days and contested by a select invited four golfers only. Every hole a player wins outright he wins money for that hole and if a hole is halved then the prize money for that hole is added to the prize total for the next hole.

Did You Know That?

At the 2005 Skins Game Annika Sorenstam hit a longer drive on the third hole than Fred Funk that then caused Funk to remove a pink shirt from his bag which he wore all the way to the green. Funk's three competitors laughed at Funk but Funk had the last laugh, cleaning up both days, taking the 2005 Skins Game title with a total of 15 Skins and $925,000.00. Funk also became the oldest Skins Game winner in the history of the event, surpassing Gary Player, the 48-year-old winner of the inaugural tournament.

❋ CADDIE SACK ❋

Two weeks after Ian Woosnam lost two strokes at the 2001 British Open for having the wrong number of clubs in his bag, the former US Masters Champion sacked his caddie for failing to show up for the final round of the 2001 Scandinavian Masters. David Byrne failed to count the clubs in Woosnam's bag before the first tee on the final round of the British Open and then at the Scandinavian Masters Byrne turned up late on the course after Woosnam, the 1991 US Masters winner had already teed off with caddie master Tommy Strand carrying his clubs.

Did You Know That?

Club officials also had to help the Welshman break into his locker to get his golf shoes as Byrne had the locker key.

❋ SAM SNEAD (1912–2002) ❋

Samuel Jackson "Sam" Snead was born on 27 May 1912 in Ashwood, Virginia, USA. In 1937 Sam embarked on his first year as a professional and signed up for the PGA Tour having won his first PGA Tour event the previous year, the West Virginia Closed Pro. He won five tournaments in his maiden year, including the Oakland Open at the Claremont County Club, California, and the Miami Open. In 1938 Sam won the first of a record eight Greater Greensboro Open titles, his eighth victory coming at the age of 52 in 1965. He also captured the first of four Vardon Trophy wins in 1938 for the lowest scoring average on the Tour (the others coming in 1949, 1950 & 1955). Further tournament successes followed in 1940 with three wins, including the Canadian Open, and in 1941 with six Tour wins, including the Bing Crosby Pro-Am and a second successive Canadian Open.

In 1942 Slammin' Sammy won the first of his seven Majors, the PGA Championship, but a trophyless 1943 followed. In 1944 Sam bounced back with two Tour wins, the Portland Open and the Richmond Open, and then in 1945, Sam snared six Tour victories, including the Los Angeles Open, the Pensacola Open and the Dallas Open. In 1946 Sam crossed the Atlantic and walked away with the Open Championship at the home of golf, St Andrews. (This was not counted as a PGA Tour win at the time, although it was designated as such in 2002.) In the same year he also captured the World Championship of Golf. Snead was famous for his folksy image, playing barefoot wearing a straw hat, but in 1949 he added a green jacket to his dress code when he won the first of his three Masters titles at Augusta, and later the same year he won his second PGA Championship.

Sam emblazoned his name in golf history in 1950, when he won an incredible 11 Tour events, a record which still stands today. That year he won the Los Angeles Open, the Bing Crosby Pro-Am (tied with Jack Burke Jnr, Smiley Quick and Dave Douglas), the Texas Open, the Miami Beach Open, the Greater Greensboro Open, the Western Open, the Colonial National Invitational, the Inverness Four-Ball Invitational (with Jim Ferrier), the Reading Open, the North and South Open and the Miami Open. Snead went on to win a further 22 PGA Tour events, including three more Majors: his third PGA Championship in 1951 and two more green jackets in 1952 and 1954. In total Snead won 82 PGA Tour events during his career, a record that still stands today, although Tiger Woods, on 54 wins to the end of 2006, is hot on Slammin' Sam's tail.

❋ WIT AND WISDOM OF GOLF (32) ❋

"Perhaps if I dyed my hair peroxide blonde, and called myself 'the Great White Tadpole', people would take more notice of me."
Ian Woosnam

❋ AMATEURS BECOMING OPEN CHAMPIONS ❋

3 – Bobby Jones, 1926, 1927 and 1930
2 – Harold Hilton, 1892, 1897 ❖ 1 – John Ball, 1890

Did You Know That?
Only one amateur has ever finished as the runner-up in the Open, Roger Wethered, who lost a play-off to Jock Hutchison in 1921 at St Andrews. It was Hutchison's maiden Open Championship.

❋ A GOLF DAY AT THE RACES ❋

Royal Ascot Golf Club, founded in 1887, was in the centre of Royal Ascot Racecourse for 117 years surrounded by Ascot Heath. It was given Royal status in 1887 by Queen Victoria, who it is known had a large family. The Prince of Wales, later to become Edward VII, was a member and played the course with at least four of his sisters. It is recorded that four of the princesses had lessons with the first club professional, Joseph George Longhurst, a position he held for 25 years. Due to the expansion of Royal Ascot racecourse a new golf course and clubhouse started construction in January 2004 approximately half a mile from the old course and within the confines of Windsor Forest.

❋ THE HOLES AT GLENEAGLES ❋

The White Tees King's Course at Gleneagles has its 18 holes whimsically named in Scottish dialect.

1	Dun Whinny	10	Cauty Lye
2	East Neuk	11	Deil's Creek
3	Silver Tassie	12	Tappit Hen
4	Broomy Law	13	Braid's Brawest
5	Het Girdie	14	Denty Den
6	Blink Bonnie	15	Howe o'Hope
7	Kittle Kink	16	Wee Bogle
8	Whaup's Nest	17	Warshin' Lea
9	Heich o'Fash	18	King's Hame

WIT AND WISDOM OF GOLF (33)

"It's good sportsmanship not to pick up lost golf balls, while they are still rolling."
Mark Twain

ROYAL ULSTER GOLF CLUB

Royal Belfast Golf Club was founded on 9 November 1881. The Royal Belfast Golf Club is the oldest club in Ireland and its formation proved to be the inspiration for the growth of the game in Ireland. The founding of the club is primarily due to Mr Thomas Sinclair who, having played golf with friends at St Andrews while visiting Scotland in the summer of 1881, was smitten by the game. The Royal Belfast Golf Club is one of only four golf clubs in Ireland that have been honoured with the title "royal", having been visited in 1885 by the Prince of Wales, who became the club's first patron. This patronage has continued through the history of the club, the position currently being held by Prince Andrew, Duke of York.

US MASTERS MOST WINS

6............Jack Nicklaus (1963, 1965, 1966, 1972, 1975, 1986)
4............Arnold Palmer (1958, 1960, 1962, 1964)
4............Tiger Woods (1997, 2001, 2002, 2005)
3............Jimmy Demaret (1940, 1947, 1950)
3............Sam Snead (1949, 1952, 1954)
3............Gary Player (1961, 1974, 1978)
3............Nick Faldo (1989, 1990, 1996)
3............Phil Mickelson (2004, 2006, 2010)
2............Horton Smith, Byron Nelson, Ben Hogan, Tom Watson, Seve Ballesteros, Bernhard Langer, Ben Crenshaw, Jose-Maria Olazabal

AMATEUR VENTURI

In 1956 Ken Venturi, an amateur, finished second in The Masters after leading the tournament from the first round. A final-round 80, played in difficult conditions, prevented the 24-year-old from becoming the first amateur to win the coveted green jacket. Later Venturi won the 1964 US Open Championship at the Congressional Country Golf Club, Maryland and with his victory he won *Sports Illustrated* magazine's "Sportsman of the Year" award.

❋ BEASTLY INTERFERENCE ❋

"Beware: Dangerous Animals. Enter at Your Own Risk" is the warning on a sign to golfers as they enter the 9-hole (18 tees) Skukuza Golf Course in South Africa. And before they are permitted to tee off all players are required to sign a compulsory indemnity form. In addition to warthogs grazing on the fairways hippopatami can be found in the lake that wraps itself around Skukuza, while golfers never know what type of animal they are likely to encounter during their round as the course is situated beside Kruger Park without a fence separating the two. Kruger Park is home to a variety of animals including capé buffalos, elephants, leopards, lions, puff adders and rhinos. A woman on a golf course in nearby Hazyview was killed by a hippopotamus when she got between the animal and the water while golfers at Skukuza are advised in literature handed to them prior to playing their round: "Do not run away! ... If you run, the animal will believe that it has gained the advantage and it will be more likely to give chase."

The Golfer's Handbook has had a number of unusual instances involving animals interrupting a round of golf. Such cases have involved incidents with alligators that have either been in sand traps or on the verge of water hazards during tournaments held in Florida, USA. At Wilmslow Golf Club in Cheshire, England a bird used to steal golf balls before someone eventually shot it. Other reported "hazards" include cases where golf balls have killed animals and fish including on one occasion a cow being killed after being struck on the head by a wayward golf ball. At Royal Troon a golfer is reported to have killed two seagulls at successive holes with his tee shot while also in Scotland, an 11-year-old schoolboy apparently killed the first grouse of the season with his tee shot on a local golf course. However, the most frequently offending animal of all is the dog, believed to be responsible for the most golf ball thefts from courses.

❋ AMATEUR DAYS ❋

The format of the US Open changed in 1898, when the tournament was extended to 72 holes, with 36 holes played on each of two days. The winner, at Myopia Hunt Club, was Fred Herd. During the first 10 years of the tournament the US Open was conducted for amateurs and the largely British wave of immigrant golf professionals coming to the USA. However, it was not until 1911 that the US Open savoured a native-born American winner, when John J. McDermott claimed the first prize, a feat he repeated as champion in 1912.

❋ WIT AND WISDOM OF GOLF (34) ❋

"To be a champion, you must act like one."
Sir Henry Cotton

❋ THE HOLES AT THE NGLA ❋

The National Golf Links of America (Long Island, New York) has its 18 holes named in tribute to some of the great holes of world golf:

1	Valley	10	Shinnecock
2	Sahara	11	Plateau
3	Alps	12	Sebonac
4	Redan	13	Eden
5	Hog's Back	14	Cape
6	Short	15	Narrows
7	St Andrews	16	Punchbowl
8	Bottle	17	Peconic
9	Long	18	Home

❋ US MASTERS ALBATROSSES ❋

1935 – Gene Sarazen, fourth round, No. 15, 234 yards, 4-wood

1967 – Bruce Devlin, first round, No. 8, 248 yards, 4-wood

1994 – Jeff Maggert, fourth round, No. 13, 222 yards, 3-iron

❋ THE RYDER CUP TROPHY ❋

The gold trophy donated by Samuel A. Ryder in 1927 for presentation to the winning team stands 17 inches high, is nine inches from handle to handle and weighs four pounds. The golfing figure on the top of the trophy depicts Abe Mitchell, a former gardener, personal friend and golf instructor to Samuel A. Ryder. Appendicitis prevented Mitchell from participating in the inaugural official Ryder Cup in 1927. However, he returned to compete for Great Britain in 1929, 1931 and 1933, winning the trophy twice.

❋ OLYMPIC GOLF ❋

Golf, which will return at Rio de Janeiro 2016, was previously in the Olympic Games on two occasions, 1900 (Paris) and 1904 (St Louis).

❋ MOST WINS IN THE BRITISH OPEN ❋

6 – Harry Vardon, 1896, 1898, 1899, 1903, 1911, 1914
5 – James Braid, 1901, 1905, 1906, 1908, 1910; J.H. Taylor, 1894, 1895, 1900, 1909, 1913; Peter Thomson, 1954, 1955, 1956, 1958, 1965; Tom Watson, 1975, 1977, 1980, 1982, 1983

❋ THE REIGN OF THE HAIG ❋

In 1921 the reign of "The Haig" began at the US PGA Championship played Inwood CC in Far Rockaway, New York. Walter Hagen faced the 1916 and 1919 PGA Champion, Jim Barnes, in the final and won the match on the 34th hole to claim a famous 3 & 2 victory and the first of his five PGA Championship Wanamaker Trophies.

❋ A BIG DIFFERENCE ❋

When Henry Cotton won the first of his three British Open titles in 1934 he set the record for the biggest difference between rounds for the winning player, 14 shots. Cotton carded a second-round score of 65 and then hit a 79 in the final round. In 1904 Jack White carded a first-round score of 80 and bettered his score each round afterwards, culminating in a 69 in his final round. In the 1986 Open Championship at Turnberry, Greg Norman carded a first-round score of 74, a second-round score of 63 and a third-round score of 74 on his way to winning the famous Claret Jug.

❋ THE WEE ICE MAN ❋

In addition to his nickname of "The Hawk", Ben Hogan was also known as "The Wee Ice Man". This was believed to have been coined following his 1953 British Open Championship triumph at Carnoustie, Scotland, and was a reference to his steely and practically nerve-free demeanour on the golf course. Hogan very rarely spoke during competition, and many opponents failed to master his icy glare.

❋ THREE DECADES ❋

The following players won the British Open Championship in three different decades:

Harry Vardon, 1896, 1903, 1911
J. H. Taylor, 1894, 1900, 1913
Gary Player, 1959, 1968, 1974

❋ VARE TROPHY WINNERS ❋

In 1953 the Vare Trophy was presented to the Ladies Professional Golf Association. It is named after the legendary amateur lady golfer, Glenna Collett Vare, who won a record six US Women's Amateur Championships between 1922 and 1935. It is awarded annually to the LPGA golfer with the lowest scoring average, and to be eligible a golfer must have participated in a minimum of 70 official LPGA tournament rounds. The trophy was presented by Betty Jameson, who won the Texas Publinx Championship, aged just 13. In 1929, aged 15, she won the National Amateur Championship and retained the trophy the following year.

❋ GREAT GOLF COURSES OF THE WORLD (14) ❋

Shinnecock Hills, New York
Opened: 1891
Designer: William Dunn Jnr
Yardage: 7,445 Par: 72
Majors: US Open 1896, 1986, 1995, 2004

Shinnecock Hills Golf Club is a links-style golf course situated in Southampton, Long Island, NY, and founded in 1891. The course was originally designed and laid out by William Dunn Jnr with the help of members of the Shinnecock Indian Nation tribe. In 1894 it was one of the five clubs that founded the United States Golf Association. In 1896 it played host to the second US Open Championship, which was won by James Foulis, and has hosted the tournament four times in all. It is the only golf course to have hosted the US Open in three different centuries.

❋ US MASTERS WIRE-TO-WIRE WINNERS ❋

Craig Wood (1941)
Arnold Palmer (1960)
Jack Nicklaus (1972)
Raymond Floyd (1976)

❋ THE MASTERS TROPHY ❋

The permanent Masters Trophy was first introduced in 1961 and depicts the Clubhouse at the Augusta National Golf Club. It was made in England and consists of over 900 individual pieces of silver. The trophy rests on a pedestal, and bands of silver provide space to engrave the name of the winner and runner-up.

❋ DUFFERS' PARADISE ❋

The Duff House Golf Club came into existence following a gift of land to the towns of Banff and Macduff by the then Duke of Fife following his concern at "the want of ground for golf and other recreational sports". The original course in its present location was laid out in 1909 and was formally opened by a match between two of the great "Triumvirate" – J. H. Taylor (the then Open Champion) and James Braid. The par was 83 and Taylor scored 75 to Braid's 78. In 1923 the course was redesigned by the brilliant golf architects Dr A. and Major C.A. Mackenzie, Cypress Point in California and Royal Melbourne. On 5 August 1924 the Mackenzie course was formally opened with a match between Sandy Herd of Moor Park and Ted Ray of Oxley, both returning scores of 71. In the same year, Her Royal Highness the Princess Louise intimated that she desired that the club be known as Duff House Royal Golf Club, and on 1 January 1925 the two Banff clubs formally amalgamated as the Duff House Royal Golf Club.

❋ LEAVE IT TO ME ❋

Traditionally the winner of the previous year's Masters Tournament puts the green jacket on the new champion at the end of the tournament. In 1966, when Jack Nicklaus became the first player to win the tournament in consecutive years, he donned the famous jacket himself. However, when Nick Faldo (1990) and Tiger Woods (2002) became repeat champions, the chairman of the Augusta National Golf Club placed the green jacket on the winners.

❋ DEFENDING MASTERS ❋

Only three players, Jack Nicklaus (1965–66), Nick Faldo (1989–90) and Tiger Woods (2001–02), have successfully defended their Masters green jacket.

❋ BACK FROM THE DEAD ❋

In 1896 Harry Vardon trailed the leader of the British Open by 11 shots but went on to claim the famous Claret Jug; in 1920 George Duncan trailed the leader by 13 shots but went on to claim victory, and in 1999 Scotland's Paul Lawrie was 10 shots adrift of Jean Van de Velde after 54 holes but somehow managed to claw the deficit back and win the British Open.

WIT AND WISDOM OF GOLF (35)

"I only played three matches and hit only three fairways. My biggest contribution was to get the team colours for Sunday changed from green to my lucky blue."

Seve Ballesteros, speaking about his minor contribution to the European team, after they had won the 1995 Ryder Cup

US MASTERS HOLES-IN-ONE

There following 20 players have hit holes-in-one at the Masters:

Year	*Player*	*Hole*	*Distance*	*Club*
2010 –	Nathan Green	No. 16	176 yards	6-iron
2008 –	Ian Poulter	No. 16	167 yards	8-iron
2005 –	Trevor Immelman	No. 16	177 yards	7-iron
2004 –	Kirk Triplett	No. 16	177 yards	6-iron
2004 –	Padraig Harrington	No. 16	177 yards	6-iron
2004 –	Chris DiMarco	No. 6	198 yards	5-iron
1995 –	Raymond Floyd	No. 16	182 yards	5-iron
1992 –	Jeff Sluman	No. 4	213 yards	4-iron
1992 –	Corey Pavin	No. 16	140 yards	8-iron
1988 –	Curtis Strange	No. 12	155 yards	7-iron
1972 –	Charles Coody	No. 6	190 yards	5-iron
1968 –	Clive Clark	No. 16	190 yards	2-iron
1959 –	William Hyndman	No. 12	155 yards	6-iron
1954 –	Leland Gibson	No. 6	190 yards	4-iron
1954 –	Billy Joe Patton	No. 6	190 yards	5-iron
1949 –	John Dawson	No. 16	190 yards	4-iron
1947 –	Claude Harmon	No. 12	155 yards	7-iron
1940 –	Ray Billows	No. 16	145 yards	8-iron
1935 –	Willie Goggin	No. 16	145 yards	mashie
1934 –	Ross Somerville	No. 16	145 yards	mashie

THE GOLDEN BEAR OPEN

From 1963 to 1980, a period covering 18 Open Championships, Jack Nicklaus only finished outside the top 10 once, when he tied for 12th place in 1965. Jack's remarkable sequence included three wins (1966, 1970 & 1978), seven second-place finishes, including ties (1964, 1967, 1968T, 1972, 1976T, 1977 & 1979T) and two third-place finishes (1963 & 1974). The Golden Bear bade an emotional farewell to the Open in 2005 when he failed to make the cut at St Andrews.

❋ BRITISH OPEN LOWEST WINNING SCORE ❋

267 – Greg Norman, Royal St George's, 1993
268 – Tom Watson, Turnberry, 1977; Nick Price, Turnberry, 1994
269 – Tiger Woods, St Andrews, 2000
270 – Nick Faldo, St Andrews, 1990
271 – Tom Watson, Muirfield, 1980; Tom Lehman, Royal Lytham & St Annes, 1996
272 – Ian Baker-Finch, Royal Birkdale, 1991; Nick Faldo, Muirfield, 1992; Justin Leonard, Royal Troon, 1997; Louis Oosthuizen, St Andrews, 2010

❋ THE MASTERS CHAMPION ❋

In addition to the famous green jacket the winner of The Masters is honoured by having his name engraved on the permanent Masters Trophy which remains at the Augusta National Golf Club. He also receives a sterling silver replica of the Masters Trophy (since 1993), a Gold Medal (since 1993) and, of course, the prize money.

❋ THE VICTORIOUS 2010 RYDER CUP TEAM ❋

Captain: Colin Montgomerie
Vice Captains: Thomas Bjorn, Darren Clarke, Sergio Garcia and Paul McGinlay

The 2010 European Ryder Cup Team that beat the USA (14½–13½) at the Celtic Manor Club, Wales, on 1–4 October was selected on the basis of a points system. European contenders accumulated points on lists based on their final placings in official world golf ranking points tournaments between 1 September 2009 and 3 September 2010. The top four players from the Ryder Cup World Points List and the top five players from the European Points List automatically qualified and captain Colin Montgomerie added three wild-card picks to make the 12-man team.

Lee Westwood..........(Eng)
Martin Kaymer..........(Ger)
Rory McIlroy..........(NI)
Graeme McDowell..........(NI).
Ian Poulter..........(Eng)
Ross Fisher..........(Eng)
Francesco Molinari..........(Ita)
Miguel Angel Jimenez..........(Spa)
Peter Hanson..........(Swe)
*Luke Donald..........(Eng)
*Padraig Harrington..........(Ire)
*Edoardo Molinari..........(Ita)

* = ***Wild-card selection***

❋ HARRY VARDON (1870–1937) ❋

Harry Vardon was born on 9 May 1870 in Grouville, Jersey, Channel Islands, where he grew up. Vardon had little interest in golf until his older brother, Tom, introduced him to the game and encouraged him to turn professional when he was 20 years old. Within six years Vardon became one of the game's leading players, and in 1896 he won the first of his record six Open Championships. In 1900 his popularity in the sport was so high that he went on a tour of the United States of America and played in over 80 matches, including the US Open Championship, which he duly won. In 1903 Vardon was struck by tuberculosis, and although he was never quite the same prolific player ever again, he still was good enough to claim the British Open Championship in 1911 and 1914. His final Open triumph came when he was aged 44 years and 41 days, the second oldest player ever to lift the famous old Claret Jug.

On the course Vardon dressed in a buttoned jacket with dress shirt and knickers and, despite the cumbersome jacket, he was famous for his effortless, smooth, free-swinging motion. The World Golf Hall of Fame described his swing thus: "Vardon had a swing that repeated monotonously. His swing was more upright and his ball flight higher than his contemporaries, giving Vardon's approach shots the advantage of greater carry and softer landing. He took only the thinnest of divots." During his career, Vardon won 62 golf tournaments and popularized the "Vardon grip", which even today more than 90 per cent of professional golfers adopt. The "Vardon Flyer" branded gutta-percha golf ball is generally considered to be the first equipment deal for a golfer, and intriguingly he won Major Championships with both the gutta-percha and Haskell golf balls.

Towards the end of his playing career Vardon concentrated on golf course design and he designed several courses in Britain. He also wrote instructional books on golf, one of which, *The Gist of Golf,* is still considered a classic and influences up-and-coming golfers today. Following his death on 20 March 1937 in Totteridge, Hertfordshire, the PGA of America created the Vardon Trophy in his memory. First won by Harry Cooper in 1937, the trophy is awarded annually to the player on the US tour who possesses the year's lowest stroke average. In 1974 Harry Vardon was selected as one of the first 11 inductees into the PGA's World Golf Hall of Fame, and his most prestigious medals, including those from his six Open Championship victories, are on display at the museum in Florida. Harry Vardon was the first international golf celebrity and remains one of the most influential players the sport has ever seen.

❋ WIT AND WISDOM OF GOLF (36) ❋

"He comes on to a tee looking like a prize fighter climbing into the ring ready for a world championship bout."
Charles Price, US golf writer, describing Arnold Palmer

❋ A TRUE CHAMPION GOLFER ❋

James "Long Jim" Barnes won the inaugural PGA Championship in 1916 at Siwanoy Country Club, and after the First World War forced the suspension of the tournament from 1917 to 1918 he returned in 1919 and won his second successive PGA at Engineers, Roslyn, New York. During the war he took victory in the Western Opens of 1914 and 1917 as well as the 1919 event. In 1921, he added the US Open to his trophy collection, beating Fred McLeod by nine strokes at the Columbia Country Club in Chevy Chase, Maryland. On the 18th hole Barnes was serenaded by a Marine band and became the only champion ever to receive the trophy from a President of the United States, Warren G. Harding. A few days after his US Open triumph Barnes and McLeod were invited to the White House for lunch. Then in 1925 he defeated Archie Compston and Ted Ray for the British Open Golf Championship. The latter victory at Prestwick Golf Club meant that he had won all three of the professional Majors of the era (The Masters did not begin until 1934).

❋ CLOSE SHAVE AT AUGUSTA ❋

On his way to winning the 1998 US Masters, Mark O'Meara only led one hole outright, the 72nd and final hole.

❋ FOLLOW THE SUN ❋

In 1951 the movie *Follow the Sun: The Ben Hogan Story* was released, in which Glenn Ford starred as the legendary golfer.

❋ MASTERFUL DOUBLE EAGLES ❋

During the first round of the 1967 US Masters, Bruce Devlin scored a double eagle on the 8th hole. This was the first double eagle scored in the tournament since Gene Sarazen's on the 15th hole in 1935. Cliff Roberts, Chairman of the Augusta National Golf Club at the time, announced that a special trophy had been ordered for Devlin, a large crystal bowl, while Sarazen also received one.

❋ 50 MASTERS ❋

In 2004 Arnold Palmer, winner of four green jackets, competed in the US Masters for the last time, marking his 50th consecutive appearance at Augusta (a feat matched by Gary Player in 2007).

❋ THE LONG US OPEN ROAD ❋

The US Open Championship is open to any professional and to any amateur player possessing an up-to-date USGA Handicap Index not exceeding 1.4 under the Men's USGA Handicap System. A total of 156 players played in the first round of the 106th US Open at Winged Foot when play got under way on 15 June 2006. However, qualifying for the tournament began on 10 May 2006 at 110 clubs across the USA. All entrants not exempt from local and/or sectional qualifying competed in an 18-hole local qualifying round at stroke play. When the latter sifting was completed, around 750 entrants, including those exempt from local qualifying, were granted eligibility for sectional qualifying rounds. The Sectional Qualifying Rounds, consisting of 36 holes of stroke play, were played on 29 May, 5 June and 6 June at 14 clubs across the US, England and Japan to finally arrive at 2006's field of 156 entrants.

❋ US MASTERS YOUNGEST WINNER ❋

Tiger Woods, 1997 (21 years, 3 months, 14 days)

❋ LPGA PLAYER OF THE YEAR ❋

The LPGA Player of the Year Award was inaugurated in 1966 and has been awarded on an annual basis since. The award is based on a points system, under which points are earned during each LPGA season for victories, top 10 finishes and double points for a Major win. The inaugural LPGA Player of the Year winner was Kathy Whitworth, who also won the Vare Trophy in the same year (1966).

❋ THE OLD MEN OF THE OPEN ❋

Gary Player played in 46 British Open Golf Championships between 1956 and 2001, with three wins in 1958, 1969 and 1974. Jack Nicklaus played in 38 Open Championships from 1962 to 2005. Had Nicklaus played in all of the Open Championships after turning professional in 1961 he would have appeared 45 times.

❋ RYDER CUP RESULTS 1927–2010 ❋

Year	*Venue*	*Europe*	*USA*
2010	Celtic Manor Resort, Wales	14 ½	13 ½
2008	Valhalla GC, Kentucky	11 ½	16 ½
2006	The K Club, Ireland	18 ½	9 ½
2004	Oakland Hills, Michigan	18 ½	9 ½
2002	The De Vere Belfry, Sutton Coldfield	15 ½	12 ½
1999	The Country Club, Massachusetts	13 ½	14 ½
1997	Valderrama, Spain	14 ½	13 ½
1995	Oak Hill CC, New York	14 ½	13 ½
1993	The Belfry, Sutton Coldfield	13	15
1991	Ocean Course, South Carolina	13 ½	14 ½
1989	The Belfry, Sutton Coldfield	14	14
1987	Muirfield Village GC, Ohio	15	13
1985	The Belfry, Sutton Coldfield	16 ½	11 ½
1983	PGA National GC, Florida	13 ½	14 ½
1981	Walton Heath, Surrey	9 ½	18 ½
1979	Greenbrier, West Virginia	11	17
		GB/I	*USA*
1977	Royal Lytham & St Anne's, Lancashire	7 ½	12 ½
1975	Laurel Valley GC, Pennsylvania	11	21
1973	Muirfield, Scotland	13	19
1971	Old Warson CC, Missouri	13 ½	18 ½
1969	Royal Birkdale, Southport	16	16
1967	Champions GC, Texas	8 ½	23 ½
1965	Royal Birkdale, Southport	12 ½	19 ½
1963	East Lake CC, Georgia	9	23
1961	Royal Lytham & St Anne's, Lancashire	9 ½	14 ½
1959	Eldorado CC, California	3 ½	8 ½
1957	Lindrick, Sheffield	7 ½	4 ½
1955	Thunderbird CC, California	4	8
1953	Wentworth, Virginia Water	5 ½	6 ½
1951	Pinehurst CC, North Carolina	2 ½	9 ½
1949	Ganton, Scarborough	5	7
1947	Portland GC, Oregan	1	11
1939–45	*Second World War – no matches played*		
1937	Southport & Ainsdale, Southport	4	8
1935	Ridgewood CC, New Jersey	3	9
1933	Southport & Ainsdale, Southport	6 ½	5 ½
1931	Scioto CC, Ohio	3	9
1929	Moortown, Leeds	7	5
1927	Worcester CC, Massachusetts	2 ½	9 ½

❋ FORTRESS AMERICA ❋

In 2010, Graeme McDowell became the first European player to win the US Open since Tony Jacklin in 1970.

❋ THE GREEN JACKET ❋

In addition to a monetary prize the winner of The Masters is presented with a distinctive green jacket which has been awarded since 1949 when it was first presented to Sam Snead. The famous green jacket, much coveted among professional golfers, is actually the official coat worn by members of the Augusta National Golf Club while on the club grounds. Every Masters champion is automatically made an honorary member of the club. Masters winners keep their green jacket for the first year after their first victory and then return it to the club to wear during tournament week each following year. The green jacket is only permitted to be removed from the Augusta National Golf Club by the reigning champion who must then return it to the club prior to the next year's tournament. (When Gary Player won The Masters in 1961 he failed to return his green jacket despite the club's insistence that he should.)

❋ TEXAN MASTERS ❋

The state of Texas has produced more Masters Champions, 12, than any other state in the United States.

❋ BJORN FINED ❋

Thomas Bjorn heavily criticized the European team captain, Ian Woosnam, after he was left out of Europe's Ryder Cup team to defend the trophy at the K Club, Straffan, County Kildare in September 2006. Woosnam opted for Darren Clarke and Lee Westwood as his two captain's choices ahead of Bjorn. The Dane, who felt that he should have been told personally by Woosnam that he was left out of the team, instead of hearing the news on TV, described the Welshman as "the worst captain I have ever seen". Despite a sincere apology from Bjorn, he was fined £10,000 by the European Tour.

Did You Know That?
At the 1997 Ryder Cup in Valderrama, Spain, Woosnam partnered Bjorn, who was making his Ryder Cup debut, in the Four-Balls on Day 2 when they beat Justin Leonard and Brad Faxon 2&1.

❋ GREAT GOLF COURSES OF THE WORLD (15) ❋

Augusta National, Georgia
Opened: 1933
Designers: Alister Mackenzie and Bobby Jones
Yardage: 7,435 Par: 72
Majors: US Masters 1934–42 and 1946–present

The inaugural Masters tournament was held on 22 March 1934 and was won by Horton Smith. In 1942 Byron Nelson defeated Ben Hogan 69–70 in an 18-hole play-off, after which The Masters was suspended for the duration of the Second World War. Many memorable moments have occurred in The Masters including: Gene Sarazen holing a four-wood second shot at the 525-yard par five 15th to earn a very rare and priceless double-eagle two in 1935; Arnold Palmer's 1958 victory, beginning the tradition of Amen Corner; Jack Nicklaus becoming the first Masters Champion to successfully defend his green jacket in 1966; Nicklaus winning his record-breaking sixth Masters title in 1986, aged 46; and Tiger Woods's 2001 Masters victory, which meant he had won four consecutive Majors.

❋ WIT AND WISDOM OF GOLF (37) ❋

"No matter what happens – never give up a hole ... In tossing in your cards after a bad beginning you also undermine your whole game, because to quit between tee and green is more habit-forming than drinking a highball before breakfast."
Sam Snead

❋ AMATEUR SILVER AWARDS ❋

In 1952 The Masters tournament organizing committee presented their inaugural "Low Amateur Award", a Silver Cup. Two years later the low amateur runner-up began receiving a Silver Medal. However, in order to qualify for each award, the amateur must make the 36-hole cut.

❋ RYDER CUP GAMBLE ❋

A record £8 million was gambled on day one of the 2006 Ryder Cup according to bookmakers Ladbrokes. The sum bet works out at approximately £12,500 for every minute of play, beating all previous betting records for a golf event.

❋ WIT AND WISDOM OF GOLF (38) ❋

"There's an old saying. It's a poor craftsman who blames his tools. It's usually the player who misses those three-footers, not the putter."
Kathy Whitworth

❋ THE 60 BARRIER ❋

No player has ever shot all four rounds in the sixties in the Masters, but many have shot three rounds in the sixties, including winners Tiger Woods in 1997 (70–66–65–69). Phil Mickelson in 2010 (67–71–67–67) and Charl Schwartzel in 2011 (69–71–68–66).

❋ BEN AND JACK ❋

The legendary Ben Hogan's steely determination propelled him to four victories (1948, 1950, 1951 & 1953), the first coming 17 years after his debut on the US Tour. In direct contrast, Jack Nicklaus won the first of his four US Open titles in 1962 during what was his rookie season as a professional. Nicklaus also claimed victory in 1967, 1972 and 1980, making him one of only four golfers to win the US Open four times. The others are Willie Anderson (1901, 1903, 1904 & 1905), Jones and Hogan.

❋ THAT'S MY CLUB ❋

After he ended his professional playing career, Ben Hogan founded a golf club manufacturing company (now owned by the Callaway Golf Company), and clubs carrying his name are still used today.

❋ THE LEADING AMATEUR ❋

As far back as 1922 it was suggested that the leading amateur golfer at each Open Championship should be awarded a prize in recognition of his achievement. However, it was not until 1949 that a silver medal, of the same size and design as the winner's medal, was presented to the leading amateur. The medal bears the inscription "Golf Champion Trophy", with the addition of the words "First Amateur". Frank Stranahan of the US won the inaugural amateurs' silver medal and went on to win it again in 1950, 1951 and 1953.

Since 1972 all the amateurs who have played on the final day of the Open Championship, apart from the leading amateur, have received a bronze medal.

❋ THREE TROPHIES ❋

In 1993 Bernhard Langer won The Masters and, as well as receiving the famous green jacket, he became the first ever recipient of a sterling silver replica of the permanent Masters Trophy and a Gold Medal.

❋ CONGRESSIONAL GOLD MEDAL ❋

On 16 October 2006, just 20 days after Byron Nelson died, Congressman Michael C. Burgess's bill to award Byron Nelson the Congressional Gold Medal was signed into law by President George W. Bush. The following statement is attributed to Congressman Burgess: "This day is truly all about Byron Nelson. When this process began, I told Byron that he deserved this high distinction for all he had done, and he so graciously denied accolades. Byron's faith in God and strong character made him a beacon of hope to all who were lucky enough to know him. He was generous, gentlemanly and sincere in all areas of his life. While many may remember him as a legendary golfer, most remember him as a philanthropic leader. Today, I am very proud that the American people, and indeed our President, have honoured Byron Nelson and will award him the Congressional Gold Medal sometime next spring."

❋ LIGHTNING STRIKES ❋

During the 1975 Western Open at Medinah, Jerry Heard, Bobby Nichols and Lee Trevino were all struck by lightning. And they say it doesn't strike in the same place twice!

❋ TIGER DENIED SIX-IN-A-ROW ❋

After winning five consecutive tournaments the world number one, Tiger Woods, entered the 2006 World Matchplay Championship at Wentworth hoping to make it six-in-a-row and to take his winning streak into the following week's Ryder Cup at the K Club. However, the wind was taken out of Tiger's sails as he lost 4 & 3 to Shaun Micheel, ranked number 77 in the world, in the first round of the tournament.

❋ RED ARNIE ❋

Arnold Palmer helped negotiate the deal that saw the first golf course built in the People's Republic of China.

❋ BRITISH FIRST AND LAST ❋

The following table lists those players with the widest interval between their first and last victory in the Open Championship:

19 years, J. H Taylor, 1894–1913
18 years, Harry Vardon, 1896–1914
15 years, Gary Player, 1959–74
15 years, Willie Park, 1860–75
14 years, Henry Cotton, 1934–48

❋ WHEN IRISH EYES ARE SMILING ❋

In 2008, Padraig Harrington held off the challenge of Ben Curtis and Sergio Garcia to become the first European-born winner of the PGA Championship since 1930, when Scotland's Tommy Armour won at Fresh Meadows Country Club (during the tournament's matchplay era). Harrington also became the first Irish winner of the PGA Championship and, following his four-shot victory at the Open Championship at Royal Birkdale earlier in the year, became the first European player in history to win the Open and the PGA Championship in the same year.

❋ THE MASTER ARCHITECT ❋

Jack Nicklaus has helped to design in excess of 300 golf courses covering 30 US states and 25 countries around the world. His first solo design was for Glen Abbey GC in Oakville, Canada, where the course was opened for play in 1976. Today he runs his company, Nicklaus Design, in partnership with his four sons and his son-in-law. Outstanding designs by Nicklaus include Castle Pines, the PGA Centenary Course at Gleneagles Hotel and Muirfield Village. Course No. 300 was Sebonack GC, Southampton, NY.

❋ BRITISH OPEN'S NEARLY MEN ❋

Although Tiger Woods holds the record for the lowest aggregate score over four rounds in the British Open with 269 (at St Andrews in 2000), amazingly three players have also scored 269 to set the record for the lowest aggregate score by a runner-up in the British Open:

1977 – Jack Nicklaus (68, 70, 65, 66)	Turnberry
1993 – Nick Faldo (69, 63, 70, 67)	Royal St George's
1994 – Jesper Parnevik (68, 66, 68, 67)	Turnberry

❋ 22 CONSECUTIVE CUTS ❋

Fred Couples won The Masters in 1992 and did not miss a cut in his first 22 appearances at the tournament, until going home early in 2008 and 2009. He has enjoyed ten top 10 finishes at the Augusta National, including a sixth-place finish behind Phil Mickelson in 2010. Although it was the only PGA Major he entered, Couples did finish second in two of the Majors on the Champions Tour.

❋ RECORD US RYDER CUP APPEARANCES ❋

Up to 2010, only eight American golfers have played in seven or more Ryder Cups:

Rank	*Name*	*Appearances*	*Rookie Year*	*Last Played*
1	Billy Casper	8	1961	1975
	Raymond Floyd	8	1969	1993
	Lanny Wadkins	8	1977	1993
	Phil Mickelson	8	1995	2010
5	Sam Snead	7	1937	1959
	Gene Littler	7	1961	1975
	Tom Kite	7	1979	1993
	Jim Furyk	7	1997	2010

❋ MAGNIFICENT HAGEN ❋

Perhaps Walter Hagen's greatest achievement was winning five PGA Championships, including four in a row, when it was a match-play tournament. He took his first PGA title in 1921, didn't play in 1922, lost to Gene Sarazen in the 1923 final and then won each year from 1924 to 1927. During those six years of competition, he lost just one match out of 23.

❋ BLOWING HOT & COLD ❋

There is a heating and cooling system under holes 12 and 13 at the Masters course at Augusta National Golf Club, Georgia.

❋ CHAMPIONSHIP CONSISTENCY ❋

Densmore "Denny" Shute won the 1933 Open Championship at St Andrews after carding four rounds in which he scored 73 each time (excluding the play-off).

❋ WIT AND WISDOM OF GOLF (39) ❋

"Don't be in such a hurry. That little white ball isn't going to run away from you."
Patty Berg

❋ THE BOB JONES AWARD ❋

The Bob Jones Award, named in honour of Bob Jones Snr, was inaugurated in 1955 and is the highest honour awarded by the United States Golf Association. It is presented by the USGA to a golfer in recognition of his or her distinguished sportsmanship in the game.

❋ THE US PGA CHAMPIONSHIP ❋

The US PGA Championship was first played in 1916 at Siwanoy, Bronxville, New Jersey and was won by James Barnes. However, since 1916 many of golf's greatest ever players have never won this Major Championship. Furthermore, as a result of PGA rules and travel difficulties many of the best non-Americans did not participate from the 1930s through the 1950s (for example Peter Thomson and Bobby Locke).

❋ OGILVY WINS US OPEN ❋

By winning the 106th US Open Championship at Winged Foot Golf Club's West Course in June 2006, Australia's Geoff Ogilvy became only the third player in US Open history to win without ever being under par in a round. The others were Corey Pavin in 1996 at Shinnecock Hills Golf Club and Lou Graham in 1975 at Medinah Country Club. He also became the first Australian golfer to win the US Open since David Graham claimed victory at Merion Golf Club in Ardmore, Pennsylvania, in 1981. Of the five US Opens played at Winged Foot, Ogilvy's five-over-par winning score bettered only Hale Irwin's seven-over finish in 1974 and Bobby Jones's six-over score in 1929.

❋ FALDO CLAWS HIS WAY BACK ❋

Nick Faldo won the 1996 Masters tournament by five strokes from Greg Norman despite starting the final round six strokes behind Norman, who led the competition going into the final round.

⁂ TOM WATSON (1949–) ⁂

Thomas Sturges Watson was born on 4 September 1949 in Kansas City, Missouri. Watson first took up golf when he attended the Pembroke-Country Day School, and after graduating with a degree in Psychology from Stanford University in 1971 he began his career as a professional golfer. During the early years of his golf career Watson unfortunately earned the tag of being a "choker", and this was the case at the 1974 US Open at Winged Foot GC, when he went into the final round with a one-stroke lead, only to card a disastrous 79 to lose to Hale Irwin. But he turned his fortunes around to win the 1974 Western Open, the first of 39 on the PGA Tour.

When Watson arrived at Carnoustie for the 1975 British Open, the eyes of golf were on other players, including Jack Nicklaus. Indeed, Watson crossed the Atlantic after poor showings that year in both The Masters and the US Open. But a different, steely Watson, possessing new-found self-belief after his second PGA win (in the Byron Nelson Classic), went about his business at Carnoustie and after holing a long birdie on the final hole he set a score that only one man, Jack Newton, could match. However, the next day Watson claimed the Open Championship, the first of his eight Majors, after defeating Newton in a play-off. Watson would go on to win the Open Championship a further four times during his career. A barren 1976 was followed by a fruitful 1977, when he won five PGA Tour events including two Majors: The Masters and his second Open Championship. On the final day of the 1977 Open at Turnberry, Watson and Nicklaus were tied after 16 holes. Nicklaus missed a putt for a birdie on 17, as Watson made his birdie. On the 18th Nicklaus made a sensational 30-foot birdie putt but watched on as Watson holed from three feet to win the old Claret Jug again.

In 1978 and 1979 he bagged five PGA titles, and went two better in 1980 – his most prolific season – including a third Open Championship in six years. More Major success followed in 1981, when winning his second green jacket and two Major victories in 1982, the US Open and a fourth silver medal when he won the Open at Royal Troon. His eighth and final Major came in 1983 in the shape of his fifth Open title when he led the field home at Royal Birkdale. In 2009, aged 59, he needed a par on the 72nd hole at Turnberry to win his sixth Open Championship. Sadly, he made a bogey and then lost a four-hole playoff to Stewart Cink.

Watson was PGA Player of the Year six times (1977–80, 1982 and 1984) – only Tiger Woods has won more (10); he won the Vardon Trophy three times (1977–9); played on four Ryder Cup teams.

❋ WIT AND WISDOM OF GOLF (40) ❋

"I regard golf as an expensive way of playing marbles."
G.K. Chesterton

❋ SOLHEIM CUP GOES TO IRELAND ❋

On 14 December 2006, Alexandra Armas, Executive Director of the Ladies European Tour (LET), announced at a press conference at the National Museum, Dublin, that the 2011 Solheim Cup would take place at Killeen Castle, County Meath, Ireland. The LET and Failte Ireland also announced a five-year agreement to stage a new tournament on the Ladies European Tour, the Irish Ladies Open. In 2008, Norway's Suzann Pettersen won the inaugural Irish Ladies Open at Portmarnock Golf Club.

❋ THE AUSTRALIAN OPEN ❋

The Australian Open, which was inaugurated in 1904, is one of the major annual tournaments on the PGA Tour of Australasia. The winner of the Australian Open receives the Stonehaven Cup. Gary Player has won the competition on most occasions (seven).

❋ THE OLDER THE BETTER ❋

Allen Doyle did not turn professional until he was 46 (1994). In 1995 he won three times on the second tier Nike Tour, and in July 1998 became eligible to play on the Senior PGA Tour. In 1999, aged 51, he won four times on the Champions Tour including the Senior PGA Championship. In 2001 Allen won his second Senior Major, the Senior Players Championship, and was top of the Seniors Tour money list. Then in 2005 he secured his third Major when he won the most lucrative Senior tournament of them all, the US Senior Open, after wiping out a nine-stroke deficit when he carded a final-round 63. Doyle successfully defended his US Senior Open title in 2006 to become the oldest winner of the US Senior Open Championship aged 57 years, 11 months and 17 days. On the Champions Tour he has won in excess of $11 million.

❋ QUICK PLAY-OFFS ❋

In the history of The Masters no sudden-death play-off has lasted more than two extra holes.

❋ THE SAND WEDGE IS BORN ❋

Gene Sarazen invented the modern sand wedge in 1932. At the time golfers struggled when their ball hit a bunker, because the lofted clubs of the day bit into the sand. So Sarazen took a club with a broad sole and added lead solder to raise the height of the rear. He used the club for the first time at the 1932 British Open Golf Championship, which he duly won, and called it a sand iron.

❋ LUCKY NO. 7 ❋

In 1994 Jose-Maria Olazabal became only the seventh international player to win The Masters and then in 1999, Olazabal became one of only fifteen multiple winners of the event (as of 2010 there have been seventeen multiple winners).

❋ GREAT GOLF COURSES OF THE WORLD (16) ❋

Cypress Point, California
Opened: 1928
Designer: Alister Mackenzie
Yardage: 6,612 Par: 72
Majors: None

Cypress Point is known throughout the world for its trio of holes that play along the Pacific Ocean, the 15th, 16th and 17th, that are regularly rated among the best golf holes in the world. The course was designed by Alister Mackenzie, who was the architect behind Augusta National. In 1991 Cypress Point was dropped by the PGA Tour because it would not admit women and was replaced as a PGA tournament venue by Poppy Hills Golf Course. In 2006 Cypress Point was named the No. 1 golf course in *Golfweek Magazine*'s America's Top 100 Classic Courses (it was No. 4 in 2005).

❋ RECRUITS FACE-OFF ❋

In 1942 Jim Turnesa, a US Army Corporal, and Sam Snead, a US Navy recruit, who was scheduled to report to duty a day later, met in the final of the PGA Championship. Snead went to lunch after the opening 18 holes three down before fighting back in true Snead style to level the match on the 27th hole. Snead closed the match on the 35th, holing a monster 60-foot chip shot for a birdie and a 2 & 1 victory. It was his first Major championship.

❋ WIT AND WISDOM OF GOLF (41) ❋

"When it's breezy, hit it easy."
Davis Love Jnr

❋ WINNING BRITISH OPEN DEBUTS ❋

In the 146-year history of the Open Championship only ten players have won the famous Claret Jug at their first attempt. The first to achieve this feat was Willie Park at Prestwick in 1860, the inaugural British Open Championship, and the last to do so was Ben Curtis, when he won at Sandwich in 2003. In between the following players have all made a winning Open debut:

Tom Kidd	St Andrews	1873
Mungo Park	Musselburgh	1874
Harold Hilton	Muirfield	1892
Jock Hutchison	St Andrews	1921
Densmore Shute	St Andrews	1933
Ben Hogan	Carnoustie	1963
Tony Lema	St Andrews	1964
Tom Watson	Carnoustie	1975

❋ FRIENDSHIP PUT TO ONE SIDE ❋

Jimmy Demaret came up against his close friend Ben Hogan in the semi-final of the 1946 US PGA Championship in Portland, Oregon. However, for this particular encounter friendship was put to one side as Demaret went two up after the 3rd hole. However, Hogan hit back when he birdied holes 4, 5 and 6, and after nine holes he was three up. The unrelenting Hogan, seeking his first US PGA win, extended his lead to six up by the end of the morning's 18 holes. In the afternoon Hogan was in sensational form and carded a scintillating 31 on the first 9 to bring the match to an end with a convincing 10 & 9 victory, the second biggest margin in PGA Championship match-play history. Afterwards, when asked by reporters what he thought was the turning-point in the match, Demaret jokingly replied, "When Hogan showed up at the first tee."

❋ NELSON EDGES OUT HOGAN ❋

Byron Nelson shot five under par over the final 13 holes to defeat Ben Hogan 69–70 in a play-off for the 1942 Masters title.

❋ GRAND SLAM MASTERS ❋

The PGA Grand Slam of Golf, open to the winners of the four Majors each year, was contested from 1979–82, 1986 and annually since 1988. It was played in Hawaii until 2007 and in Bermuda ever since. Five men have won this Grand Slam more than once: Tiger Woods (1998, 1999, 2000, 2001, 2002, 2005 and 2006), Greg Norman (1986, 1993 and 1994), Andy North (1979 and 1990), Jim Furyk (2003 and 2008) and Ernie Els (1997 and 2010).

❋ RECORD-BREAKING TIGER ❋

On his way to winning the 1997 Masters, Tiger Woods set a total of 20 Masters records and tied six others. In the 2000 US Open Championship, Woods broke or tied a total of nine tournament records, and became the PGA Tour's all-time career money leader. Then at the 2000 Open Championship, which he won by eight strokes, Woods set the record for lowest score to par (-19) in any Major, and he holds at least a share of that record in all four Majors.

❋ MASTERS SELL-OUT ❋

The first Masters tournament sold out prior to its start was the 1966 championship. Jack Nicklaus won his third green jacket at the event.

❋ BRITISH OPEN TOP FIVE ❋

The following players hold the record for the most top-five finishes in the British Open Championship:

16 – J. H. Taylor, Jack Nicklaus ❖ 15 – Harry Vardon, James Braid

❋ THE ST ANDREWS OF EUROPE ❋

Pau Golf Club was founded in France in 1856 and was the first golf club built outside the British Isles. The course is also referred to as the "St Andrews of Europe" because of its flatness.

❋ A MONSTER OF A HOLE ❋

Since records were kept in 1942 the monstrous tenth hole (Camellia), a 495-yard par four has traditionally been the hardest hole to play in the US Masters. The hole has not played under par in any one of the seventy-five Masters tournaments staged.

❋ CONSECUTIVE HOLES-IN-ONE ❋

Claude Harmon (1968) and Toshi Izawa (2002) both hit consecutive holes-in-one during the par-three contest prior to the start of that year's Masters tournament. Claude Harmon had won The Masters 20 years earlier, in 1948.

❋ THE CLARET JUG ❋

In September 1872, three clubs, Prestwick, the Honourable Company of Edinburgh Golfers (Musselburgh) and the Royal & Ancient Golf Club at St Andrews, agreed to host the Open in alternate years, with St Andrews hosting it in 1873 and Musselburgh in 1874. The winner would receive a medal and each of the three clubs would contribute £10 towards the cost of a new trophy, which was to be a silver claret jug, the Golf Champion Trophy. However, as the new trophy was not ready in time for the 1872 Open, the winner, Tom Morris Jnr, was awarded with a gold medal instead. The new trophy was made by Mackay Cunningham & Company of Edinburgh and was hallmarked 1873. The first Open Champion to receive the new trophy was the 1873 winner, Tom Kidd, but Tom Morris Jnr's name was the first to be engraved on it as the 1872 champion. From 1873 to 1927 no fewer than 28 different players held the original Claret Jug aloft, including Harry Vardon on a record six occasions. In 1920 all responsibility for the Open Championship was handed over to the Royal & Ancient Golf Club at St Andrews. After Bobby Jones claimed victory in the Open at St Andrews in 1927, the Championship Committee decided to retain the Claret Jug from 1928 onwards and to present the winner with a replica. Walter Hagen in 1928 was the first recipient of the replica Claret Jug. Since 1990 further replicas have been made for display in the new British Golf Museum at St Andrews and for use in travelling exhibitions. The original Golf Champion Trophy is on permanent display in the R&A Clubhouse at St Andrews and sits alongside the original first prize, the Challenge Belt, which was donated to the club by the grandchildren of Tom Morris Snr in 1908.

❋ HONOUR ARNIE ❋

Arnold Palmer owns "Arnold Palmer's Bay Hill Club and Lodge", which is the venue for the PGA Tour's "Arnold Palmer Invitational" (renamed from the Bay Hill Invitational with effect from 2007). Palmer, a World Golf Hall of Famer, was awarded the PGA Lifetime Achievement Award in 1998.

❋ MOST US RYDER CUP POINTS ❋

Rank	*Name*	*Points*
1.	Billy Casper	23 ½
2.	Arnold Palmer	23
3.	Lanny Wadkins	21 ½
4.	Lee Trevino	20
5.	Jack Nicklaus	18 ½
6.	Gene Littler	18
7.	Tom Kite	17
8.	Hale Irwin	14
9.	Raymond Floyd	13 ½
10.	Phil Mickelson	13
11.	Davis Love III	11 ½
12.	Julius Boros	11
	Tiger Woods	11

Up to and including the 2010 Ryder Cup

❋ TIGER NICKS FALDO'S RECORD ❋

On his way to winning the Open at St Andrews in 2000, Tiger Woods broke Nick Faldo's record for the lowest aggregate score in relation to par when he fired a 269 for a score of 19 under par at St Andrews. Faldo hit a 270 (18 under par) when he won the Open in 1990 on the same course.

❋ TENTH TIME LUCKY ❋

It took Ben Hogan 10 attempts before he won his first Masters title in 1951. Two years later he won his second green jacket.

❋ OPEN DE FRANCE ❋

The Open de France was inaugurated in 1906 and won by the home favourite, Arnaud Massy. It has the distinction of being the oldest national open in continental Europe and has been a European Tour event since the tour's inception in 1972. The tournament used to be played at various venues across France but now has a permanent home at the Le Golf National near Paris. In 1980 the tournament was sponsored for the first time in its 74-year history. However, in 2002 the Fédération Française de Golf, the organizing body for the tournament, dropped sponsorship completely to increase the stature of the event.

❋ WIT AND WISDOM OF GOLF (42) ❋

"I'm disappointed, but I'm not going to run around like Dennis Rodman and head-butt somebody."
Greg Norman, on losing a six-stroke lead in the 1996 Masters

❋ A CLOSE TRIUMVIRATE ❋

Three of the greatest ever golfers the sport has ever seen were all born within six or seven months of one another in 1912:

Byron Nelson	4 February
Sam Snead	27 May
Ben Hogan	13 August

❋ AUGUSTA'S LONGEST ❋

The second hole is the longest on the Augusta National golf course, playing at 575 yards, par five.

❋ SAME OLD FACES ❋

The following players have made the most appearances on the final day of the Open Championship since official records were maintained in 1892:

Appearances	*Player*	*Appearances*	*Player*
32	Jack Nicklaus	26	Peter Thomson
31	Alex Herd	26	Gary Player
30	J. H. Taylor	26	Nick Faldo
27	Harry Vardon	23	Dai Davies
30	James Braid	22	Henry Cotton

❋ ROYAL CALCUTTA GOLF CLUB ❋

Royal Calcutta Golf Club was founded in Kolkata, India in 1829 and is the second oldest golf club in the world after the Royal and Ancient at St Andrews. RCGC is a par-72 18-hole golf course with a yardage of 7,195. King George V and Queen Mary conferred the "Royal" patronage on the club in 1911 to commemorate their visit to Calcutta. Apart from a golf course, the RCGC provides tennis courts and a swimming pool and facilities for lawn bowls. October to March is the best time to play the course.

❋ NINE-HOLE OPEN ❋

The inaugural US Open Championship, organized by the United States Golf Association (USGA), was played on 4 October 1895 on the nine-hole course at Newport (Rhode Island) Golf and Country Club. The maiden US Open was considered by many sports journalists at the time to be nothing more than a "sideshow" to the inaugural US Amateur Golf Championship, which was played on the same course and during the same week. Only 11 players (10 professionals and 1 amateur) started in the 36-hole event, comprising four rounds of the nine-hole Newport course in one day. The surprise winner was Horace Rawlins, 21, an English professional who was the assistant at the Newport (Rhode Island) Golf and Country Club course. Rawlins carded a score of 173 using a gutta-percha ball and picked up the winner's prize of $150 (total prize money was $3,350). Rawlins also received a gold medal and the custody of the US Open Championship Cup for his club for one year.

❋ INAUGURAL GREEN JACKET WINNER ❋

The first green jacket, presented to the winner of The Masters championship, was awarded to Sam Snead in 1949.

❋ SILENCE IN THE CROWD ❋

On 22 January 2007, the R&A announced that spectators would be banned from taking mobile phones on to the Carnoustie course at the 2007 Open Championship. Their decision came after players complained about the number of phones in use during the 2006 Open played at Hoylake. "We have so far resisted the call to ban mobile phones, as it may be an inconvenience to the public. However, after receiving complaints, we feel there is no reasonable option other than a complete ban," said a spokesman. The policy followed that adopted by the three other Majors and the 2006 Ryder Cup, he said. All fans entering the course would be searched at security checks.

❋ HIS BEST YEAR ❋

In 1989 Mark Calcavecchia won the British Open Championship in a year that marked his only multi-win season on the PGA Tour with two other titles (the Phoenix and the Nissan Los Angeles Opens) complementing his Major victory.

❋ GREAT GOLF COURSES OF THE WORLD (17) ❋

ST ANDREWS, SCOTLAND
Opened: Unknown
Designer: Anon.
Yardage: 7,125 Par: 72
Majors: Open Championship 1873, 1876, 1879, 1882, 1885, 1888, 1891, 1895, 1900, 1905, 1910, 1921, 1927, 1933, 1939, 1946, 1955, 1957, 1960, 1964, 1970, 1978, 1984, 1990, 1995, 2000, 2005, 2010

The Old Course at St Andrews, Fife, is one of the oldest golf courses in the world and is held in trust by the St Andrews Links Trust under an Act of Parliament. The clubhouse of the Royal and Ancient Golf Club sits adjacent to the first tee. The first written record of golf being played at the Old Course dates from 1506, when King James IV purchased a set of golf clubs at St Andrews. One unique feature of the Old Course at St Andrews is unquestionably its massive double greens, with seven greens shared by two holes each (only the 1st, 9th, 17th and 18th holes enjoy their own greens). Another is that it can be played in either direction, clockwise or anti-clockwise, while its 17th hole is the most famous in golf. In 2005 the Old Course was ranked as the greatest golf course outside the US by *Golf Digest* magazine. St Andrews has hosted a record 28 Open Championships.

❋ WIT AND WISDOM OF GOLF (43) ❋

"The worst advice in golf is, 'Keep your head down'."
Patty Sheehan

❋ JAMES BARNES SWINGS IN PRINT ❋

In 1919 James Barnes published a book entitled *Picture Analysis of Golf Strokes*. This best-selling golf instruction manual was the first such book to use still photographs on flip pages to create the illusion of movement.

❋ ARNIE'S ONLY US OPEN VICTORY ❋

At the 1960 US Open Championship Arnold Palmer made a record comeback win when he fired a final-round score of 65 to come from seven strokes off the lead to win his first and only US Open title.

❋ TIGER WOODS (1975–) ❋

Eldrick "Tiger" Woods was born on 30 December 1975 in Cypress, California. When he was born his father nicknamed him "Tiger" after Vuong Dang Phong, a Vietnamese friend of Earl's who served with him in Vietnam. Tiger was born to play golf, a child prodigy who first played the game at the age of two. In 1978 he appeared on *The Mike Douglas Show* on television displaying his talent, and when he was only three he shot a 48 over nine holes. In 1984 he won the 9–10 boys' event at the Junior World Golf Championships aged only eight; he won the Junior World Championships six times.

Aged 15 in 1991, he became the youngest ever US Junior Amateur Champion. The following year he successfully defended his title and competed in his first PGA Tour event, the Nissan Los Angeles Open. In 1993 Tiger won his third consecutive US Junior Amateur Championship, and remains the youngest ever and only multiple winner. He became the youngest to win the US Amateur Championship in 1994, and defended the title in 1995 and 1996.

In 1995 Tiger participated in his first Major, The Masters, in which he tied for 41st place, and then in 1996 he equalled the British Open record for an amateur with an aggregate score of 281. After turning professional in August 1996, he signed endorsement deals worth $40 million from Nike and $20 million from Titleist. Tiger won two events in his first three months as a professional, thereby qualifying for the Tour Championship. In 1997 Tiger won the first of his 12 Majors when he won The Masters by a record margin of 12 strokes, becoming the youngest ever green jacket winner and the first Masters winner of African or Asian descent. Tiger won a further three PGA Tour events in 1997, and on 15 June 1997 he took the number-one position in the official world rankings after only 42 weeks on the Tour. In 2000 Tiger won three straight Majors, nine PGA Tour events (six of them consecutively) and set or tied 27 PGA Tour records. His six consecutive wins were the most since Hogan in 1948 and only five behind Byron Nelson's record of 11 in a row. In 2002 he won The Masters and the US Open, and in 2005, after two years without adding to his tally of Majors, he won The Masters and the Open. Majors 11 and 12 came in 2006, and his place in the history of golf is already assured. In 2007, Tiger won the PGA Championship for a fourth time and the following year landed his fourteenth Major with a third US Open title. He has been named PGA Tour Player of the Year a record 10 times.

Tiger's personal world fell apart after an incident at home in November 2009, which led to a divorce, while a string of injuries have hampered his golfing progress and he remains stuck on 14 Majors.

❃ US MASTERS WINNERS ❃

2011 Charl Schwartzel
2010 Phil Mickelson
2009* Angel Cabrera
2008 Trevor Immelman
2007 Zach Johnson
2006 Phil Mickelson
2005* Tiger Woods
2004 Phil Mickelson
2003* Mike Weir
2002 Tiger Woods
2001 Tiger Woods
2000 Vijay Singh
1999 Jose-Maria Olazabal
1998 Mark O'Meara
1997 Tiger Woods
1996 Nick Faldo
1995 Ben Crenshaw
1994 Jose-Maria Olazabal
1993 Bernhard Langer
1992 Fred Couples
1991 Ian Woosnam
1990* Nick Faldo
1989* Nick Faldo
1988 Sandy Lyle
1987* Larry Mize
1986 Jack Nicklaus
1985 Bernhard Langer
1984 Ben Crenshaw
1983 Seve Ballesteros
1982* Craig Stadler
1981 Tom Watson
1980 Seve Ballesteros
1979* Fuzzy Zoeller
1978 Gary Player
1977 Tom Watson
1976 Ray Floyd
1975 Jack Nicklaus
1974 Gary Player
1973 Tommy Aaron
1972 Jack Nicklaus
1971 Charles Coody
1970* Billy Casper
1969 George Archer
1968 Bob Goalby
1967 Gay Brewer
1966* Jack Nicklaus
1965 Jack Nicklaus
1964 Arnold Palmer
1963 Jack Nicklaus
1962* Arnold Palmer
1961 Gary Player
1960 Arnold Palmer
1959 Art Wall
1958 Arnold Palmer
1957 Doug Ford
1956 Jack Burke Jr
1955 Cary Middlecoff
1954* Sam Snead
1953 Ben Hogan
1952 Sam Snead
1951 Ben Hogan
1950 Jimmy Demaret
1949 Sam Snead
1948 Claude Harmon
1947 Jimmy Demaret
1946 Herman Keiser
1945 *Not held – Second World War*
1944 *Not held – Second World War*
1943 *Not held – Second World War*
1942* Byron Nelson
1941 Craig Wood
1940 Jimmy Demaret
1939 Ralph Guldahl
1938 Henry Picard
1937 Byron Nelson
1936 Horton Smith
1935* Gene Sarazen
1934 Horton Smith

* *won in a playoff.*

❋ BRITISH OPEN MASTERS ❋

The following players hold the record for the most consecutive victories in the British Open Championship:

4 – Young Tom Morris, 1868–72 (tournament not played in 1871)

3 – Jamie Anderson, 1877–79; Bob Ferguson, 1880–82; Peter Thomson, 1954–56

2 – Old Tom Morris, 1861–62; J. H. Taylor, 1894–95; Harry Vardon, 1998–99; James Braid, 1905–06; Bobby Jones, 1926–27; Walter Hagen, 1928–29; Bobby Locke, 1949–50; Arnold Palmer, 1961–62; Lee Trevino, 1971–72; Tom Watson, 1982–83; Tiger Woods, 2005–06; Padraig Harrington, 2007–08

❋ WOODS ACHIEVES A MAJOR HAT-TRICK ❋

In the summer of 2000, Tiger Woods won both the US Open and British Open titles, which gave him the chance of becoming the first golfer in history to win all four modern Majors in succession. Next up for Woods was the US PGA Championship at Valhalla. After 72 holes of play Woods and Bob May were tied for the lead. Later that afternoon Woods and May emerged from the clubhouse for a three-hole play-off, the first in the tournament's history. On the first hole, the par-four 16th, Woods recorded a birdie for a one-stroke lead, and then on the 17th hole the duellists both made unbelievable par saves. At the third play-off hole, the par-five 18th, Woods smacked his drive to the left, hitting a sycamore tree, and then he landed his approach in the rough. Woods's third shot drifted into a green-side bunker. May, sensing his chance to get back in the match, hit his drive across the fairway and landed it in the left rough, and his approach shot also found the rough, this time on the right. May's third shot finished 40 feet shy of the cup. Woods hit his bunker approach shot to within two feet, while May narrowly missed his birdie attempt, to lose the tournament by one shot. After claiming his third consecutive Major, Woods said: "It's got to go down as one of the best duels in the game, in a major championship."

❋ FINALLY MADE IT ❋

Among Open champions, Nick Price from Zimbabwe holds the record of having played in the highest number of Opens, 16, before actually winning the old Claret Jug (in 1994 at Turnberry). When Mark O'Meara won the Open Championship at Royal Birkdale in 1998, it was at his 14th attempt.

❋ NOT ON THE PASSENGER LIST ❋

In 1912 Harry Vardon, already a winner of six Majors, was taken ill and had to cancel one of his many transatlantic trips to play in the USA. Vardon, the US Open winner in 1900, had been due to sail on the *Titanic*'s maiden voyage to the US. Two years later Vardon won a record sixth Open Championship, a record that still stands today.

❋ KEEPING IT IN THE FAMILY ❋

In 1869 Young Tom Morris, aged just 17, won the first of his four British Open Championships, and his father, Old Tom Morris, finished second. It is the only time in the history of golf that a father and son have occupied the top two places in one of the four Majors. The Liverpool Golf Club was also founded at Hoylake in 1869, later renamed "Royal Liverpool".

❋ US OPEN CHAMPIONS' NO-SHOWS ❋

Seven US Open Champions failed to defend their title at the following year's tournament: Harry Vardon (1901, after winning in 1900), Alex Smith (1907), Jerome Travers (1916), Ted Ray (1921), Bobby Jones (1931), Ben Hogan (1949) and Payne Stewart (2000). Stewart died in a plane crash a few months after winning the 1999 US Open Championship.

❋ CRYSTAL PRIZES ❋

In 1954 The Masters' tournament organizing committee began awarding trophies for various notable feats by golfers during the tournament. A crystal vase was presented for the day's lowest score; a crystal bowl was presented to any golfer who scored a hole-in-one; and a pair of crystal goblets went to a golfer who managed an eagle.

❋ THE CHAMPION OF THE US OPEN ❋

Jack Nicklaus won the US Open four times (1962, 1967, 1972 & 1980) and is tied with other golf legends Willie Anderson, Bobby Jones and Ben Hogan for the most victories in the Major. However, Nicklaus is the only player to win the title in three different decades. In his 44 consecutive appearances he also took four runner-up places and made the cut 35 times.

❋ BENT GRASS WINNER ❋

In 1981 Tom Watson won the first ever Masters played on bent grass greens. It was his second green jacket (1977).

❋ EUROPEAN RYDER CUP APPEARANCES ❋

The following table lists those golfers who have played against the US in the Ryder Cup on at least seven occasions, taking into consideration they played for at least one of the following teams:

Great Britain: 1921 to 1971
Great Britain & Ireland: 1973 to 1977
Europe: 1979 to 2010

Rank	*Name*	*Appearances*	*Rookie Year*	*Last Played*
1.	Nick Faldo	11	1977	1997
2.	Bernhard Langer	10	1981	2002
	Christy O'Connor Snr	10	1955	1973
4.	Dai Rees	9	1937	1961
5.	Colin Montgomerie	8	1991	2006
	Ian Woosnam	8	1983	1997
	Seve Ballesteros	8	1979	1995
	Sam Torrance	8	1981	1995
	Bernard Gallacher	8	1969	1983
	Neil Coles	8	1961	1977
	Peter Alliss	8	1953	1969
	Bernard Hunt	8	1953	1969
13.	Jose-Maria Olazabal	7	1987	2006
	Mark James	7	1977	1995
	Tony Jacklin	7	1967	1979
	Harry Weetman	7	1951	1963
	Lee Westwood	7	1997	2010

Did You Know That?
Nick Faldo holds the record for most appearances in the Ryder Cup by either a European or an American golfer.

❋ WIT AND WISDOM OF GOLF (44) ❋

"Through years of experience I have found that air offers less resistance than dirt."
Jack Nicklaus, on why he tees his ball high

❋ 23-YEAR GAP ❋

There was an interval of 23 years between Jack Nicklaus's first Masters victory in 1963 and his sixth in 1986.

❋ BRITAIN'S US AMATEUR CHAMPION ❋

In 2006, 23-year-old Richie Ramsay became Britain's first US Amateur Champion in 95 years when he beat American, John Kelly, 4 & 2 at Hazeltine National Golf Club. The Scot's victory earned him exemptions into 2007's Masters, British Open and US Open provided he remains an amateur. Ramsay, a Stirling University student from Aberdeen, will partner defending champion Phil Mickelson in the first two rounds of The Masters at Augusta in April 2007. Ramsay became the first British winner of the prestigious US Amateur Championship event since Harold Hilton in 1911 and the first British golfer to reach the final since Jack McLean in 1936. Ramsay's name appears on the Havemeyer Cup along with Arnold Palmer, Jack Nicklaus, Phil Mickelson and Tiger Woods.

❋ THE CHALLENGE TOUR ❋

The Challenge Tour is the second-tier men's professional golf tour in Europe and is organized by the PGA European Tour. However, some of the Tour's events are actually played outside Europe. The inaugural tour was played in 1986 and at the time was known as the Satellite Tour. Three years later the European Order of Merit was established, with the top five players on the Satellite Tour winning membership of the European Tour for the following year. In 1990, the tour was renamed the Challenge Tour and from 1986 to 1993 the Challenge Tour rankings were based on each player's best few results. However, since 1994 the Order of Merit has been calculated on tournament winnings, with every result counting. The biggest incentive for players on the Challenge Tour being that the top 10 automatically qualify for membership of the European Tour the following year, while it also has an annual Qualifying School. From 1986 to 1988 the Challenge Tour rankings were calculated in British pounds sterling, but since 1999 they have been calculated in euros.

Did You Know That?
There are three third-level developmental tours below the Challenge Tour: the Alps Tour, the EPD Tour and the PGA EuroPro Tour.

❋ PLAY-OFF HIGHS & LOWS ❋

Nick Faldo won two of his three Masters titles in play-offs (1989 against Scott Hoch and 1990 against Raymond Floyd), whereas Ben Hogan lost two Masters titles in play-offs (1942, 1954).

❋ THE BIRTH OF THE RYDER CUP ❋

Although the English seed merchant from St Albans, Hertfordshire, Samuel A. Ryder, is widely regarded as the founder of the Ryder Cup, there is a debate among the golfing hierarchy as to who actually first suggested the idea of a golf match between Britain and the US. It is said that in December 1920 James Harnett, a journalist with *Golf Illustrated* magazine, suggested a similar idea to the USPGA, but his idea was ignored. The following year Sylvanus Germain, the president of a golf club in Toledo, raised the idea of a cross-Atlantic competition once again. Germain's idea came to fruition when an unofficial match took place in 1921, won 9–3 by Britain, and another match in 1926, won 13½–1½ by Britain. Samuel Ryder attended the 1926 match, which was held on the East Course at Wentworth, in Surrey. Ryder was so impressed with the idea of a competition between Britain and the US that he offered to sponsor the competition, and thus the Ryder Cup was born. The first official Ryder Cup was hosted by Worcester County Club, Massachusetts, in 1927 and was won by the USA 9½–2½. Ryder donated a gold cup and agreed to pay £5 to each of the winning team. The competition has been held on a two-year rotating cycle (hosted by the US and Britain/Europe), with the exception of 1939 to 1945, when it was suspended owing to the Second World War.

❋ WIT AND WISDOM OF GOLF (45) ❋

"You create your own luck by the way you play. There is no such luck as bad luck. Fate has nothing to do with success or failure, because that is a negative philosophy that indicts one's confidence, and I'll have no part of it."
Greg Norman

❋ STRAIGHT-SHOOTING ERNIE ❋

Ernie Els of South Africa holds the British Open record for firing the most consecutive under-par rounds in the competition, with seven of them from 1993 to 1994.

❋ MULTIPLE US AMATEUR CHAMPIONS ❋

Since the inaugural US Amateur Championship was held in 1895, only 18 players have won the tournament on more than one occasion up to and including 2010:

5 wins: Bobby Jones
4 wins: Jerome Travers
3 wins: Walter Travis, Tiger Woods
2 wins: H. J. Whigham, H. Chandler Egan, Robert A. Gardner, Charles Evans Jnr, Francis Ouimet, Lawson Little, Marvin H. Ward, William Turnesa, Harvie Ward, Charles Coe, Jack Nicklaus, Deane Beman, Gary Cowan, Jay Sigel

❋ SIX CHAIRMEN AT AUGUSTA ❋

To date there have only ever been six Chairmen of the Augusta National Golf Club: Cliff Roberts, Bill Lane, Hord Hardin, Jack Stephens, Hootie Johnson and Billy Payne. Roberts, Chairman of the Club from 1931 to 1976, along with Bobby Jones, was a co-founder of the Masters championship in 1934.

❋ GREAT GOLF COURSES OF THE WORLD (18) ❋

PINEHURST COUNTRY CLUB (NO. 2 COURSE), NORTH CAROLINA
Opened: 1895
Designer: Donald Ross
Yardage: 7,020 Par: 72
Majors: US PGA Championship 1936. US Open 1992, 2005.
Ryder Cup: 1951. US Amateur 2008.

Pinehurst was the idea of James W. Tufts, a Boston-based soda fountain magnate. His idea was to build a resort in the south where the residents of New England could spend the winter. In 1895 Tufts founded Pinehurst Country Club in North Carolina. The course was designed by Donald Ross, and in 1907 a second Ross-designed course was opened, Pinehurst No. 2. The No. 2 course has hosted significant championships down the years, including the US Open twice and the US PGA Championship. Today Pinehurst Country Club boasts eight courses in total. The legendary Sam Snead described Pinehurst No. 2 as his all-time favourite course, because it constantly challenges the player.

❋ THE A–Z OF MAJOR WINNERS ❋

The names of players who have won one or more of golf's four Major tournaments form almost a complete A–Z. The only letters of the alphabet not represented are Q, U and X.

Azinger, Paul
Ballesteros, Seve
Charles, Bob
Duval, David
Els, Ernie
Faldo, Nick
Goosen, Retief
Hagen, Walter
Irwin, Hale
Jacklin, Tony
Kite, Tom
Langer, Bernhard
Mickelson, Phil
Norman, Greg
Olazabel, Jose-Maria
Palmer, Arnold
Rogers, Bill
Snead, Sam
Trevino, Lee
Vardon, Harry
Woods, Tiger
Yong-eun, Yang
Zoeller, Fuzzy

❋ AMATEUR BEGINNINGS ❋

The US Amateur champion is invited to play in The Masters, while 11 Masters champions first played in the tournament as amateurs.

❋ LORD BYRON ❋

Byron Nelson was nicknamed "Lord Byron" by the Atlanta sports journalist O. B. Keeler for the dignity he showed during his golfing career. He turned professional in 1932 as a result of not being able to secure long-term employment during America's Great Depression. During his career Byron won five Majors and achieved a total of 54 PGA Tour event wins, his last coming in the 1955 French Open.

❋ TIGER'S FURY OVER TOPLESS SHOTS ❋

Prior to the start of the 2006 Ryder Cup played at the K Club in Ireland, an Irish magazine and an Irish newspaper linked photos of Tiger Woods's wife, Elin, to a number of pornographic websites. An enraged Woods appeared on television and ripped into the publication for falsely linking his wife to the websites, while the publishers, were quick to issue an apology. The world No. 1 took it seriously enough to contact his legal team with a view to bringing a law suit against the company.

❋ WIT AND WISDOM OF GOLF (46) ❋

"My favourite shots are the practice swing and the conceded putt. The rest can never be mastered."
Lord Robertson

❋ THE OLD BOY ❋

In 1986 Jack Nicklaus won The Masters aged 46 years, 2 months and 23 days, to become the oldest player ever to win it. It was his sixth and last Masters victory, a record for the tournament.

❋ STILL SLAMMIN' ❋

In 1979 Sam Snead became the first PGA Tour golfer to shoot his age (67) when he carded a 67 in the second round of the 1979 Quad Cities Open. Amazingly, Slammin' Sam carded a 66 in his final round. Snead won seven Majors during his career.

❋ THE DUNHILL CHAMPIONSHIP ❋

The Dunhill Championship is a European Tour event which is played in South Africa. First established in 1959 and formerly known as the South African PGA Championship, it has been part of the European Tour's schedule since 1995. Along with the South African Open, also sanctioned as a European Tour event, it forms part of the Southern African "Sunshine Tour".

❋ LEFT AND RIGHT ❋

Although Vijay Singh is a right-handed golfer, he once stated during a television interview that he was "about a six handicap" left-handed.

❋ 70 FINALLY BREACHED ❋

In 1904 a score of 70 for a single round was broken for the first time in the 44-year history of the Open when J. H. Taylor carded a 68, James Braid carded a 69, and the winner, Jack White, carded a 69 at Royal St George's.

Did You Know That?
Jack White worked as a caddie from the age of 10.

❋ BABE ZAHARIAS (1911–56) ❋

Mildred Ella "Babe" Didrikson Zaharias was born on 26 June 1911 in Port Arthur, Texas. She was nicknamed "Babe" after she hit five home runs in one game of baseball with the Employers Casualty Insurance Co., Dallas, Texas, but her employment was merely a ruse to enable her to play basketball for one of the "industrial teams" in Amateur Athletic Union (AAU) competitions. She led her team to an AAU basketball championship in 1931 and also represented her company in the 1932 national athletics championships, winning six of the eight events she entered. Amazingly, she set five world records in a single afternoon at the championships. Babe was a sporting phenomenon and gained world fame in track and field at the 1932 Olympics in Los Angeles. She won gold medals in the 80 metres hurdles and the javelin, setting a new Olympic record in each; and in the high jump she tied for first place, sharing an Olympic record with Jean Shiley, but was awarded a silver medal because she used the "Western Roll" (jumping over head-first). She achieved All-American status in basketball, was an excellent tennis player, an accomplished baseball and softball player and was an expert diver, roller-skater and bowler.

Babe began to play golf seriously in 1935, and after being denied amateur status she competed in the 1938 Los Angeles Open, a men's PGA tournament. She was teamed with George Zaharias, a famous professional Greek wrestler and sports promoter whom she married 11 months later. It would be almost 60 years before another woman entered a men's PGA Tour event. During her golf career, Babe had no equal in her sex. She won every Major professional championship at least once, and in 1947 she became the first American to capture the British Women's Amateur Championship and the first player to win both the US Women's Amateur and the British Women's Amateur Championships. She totally dominated the sport in the 1940s and the early 1950s, winning 17 amateur tournaments in a row, including the British Amateur, the US Amateur and the All-American (a feat unequalled even by Tiger Woods). Babe's greatest year was in 1950, when she became the fastest LPGA golfer to ever reach 10 wins, completed the Grand Slam of the three women's majors of the day, the US Open, the Titleholders Championship and the Western Open, as well as leading the money list. After being diagnosed with colon cancer in 1953 and undergoing surgery, she made a comeback in 1954 and won the US Women's Open Championship, her tenth and final Major. She died in 1956, having won 82 tournaments during her 20-year golf career.

❋ WIT AND WISDOM OF GOLF (47) ❋

"A hole-in-one is amazing when you think of the different universes this white mass of molecules has to pass through on its way to the hole."
Mac O'Grady

❋ PGA WORLD GOLF HALL OF FAME ❋

The PGA World Golf Hall of Fame was opened in September 1974 in Pinehurst, North Carolina, but moved to its new premises in Saint Augustine, Florida, on 19 May 1998. There is a museum which houses galleries on Hall of Fame inductees and various exhibitions covering the history of golf. The organization is managed by a consortium of 26 golf organizations from across the globe. Membership of the Hall of Fame is open to both men and women, and new members are inducted each October. By 2011, there were 135 members, 102 men and 33 women.

❋ LOW SCORES IN THE BRITISH OPEN ❋

The following players hold the record for the lowest scores in the British Open Championship:

First Round (63)
Rory McIlroy.......2010.......St Andrews

Second Round (63)
Mark Hayes.......1977.......Turnberry
Greg Norman.......1986.......Turnberry
Nick Faldo.......1993.......Royal St George's

Third Round (63)
Isao Aoki.......1980.......Muirfield
Paul Broadhurst.......1990.......St Andrews

Fourth Round (63)
Jodie Mudd.......1991.......Royal Birkdale
Payne Stewart.......1993.......Royal St George's

Did You Know That?
Rory McIlroy did not shoot a round in the seventies at the 2010 Open. Unfortunately he fired 80 in round two to go with his 63–69–68.

❋ INAUGURAL US PGA, OR THE SECOND? ❋

In the programme of the 1945 US PGA Championship played at Morraine, Dayton, Ohio, Jim Barnes, the inaugural PGA Champion in 1916 (and winner again in 1919) recalled that he was the only PGA champion who had to win the event twice to claim the title: "Say, you know that PGA Championship record list is actually in error. I won that 1916 Championship at Siwanoy all right, but that wasn't the first professional golf championship in the United States. The spring of that year, the New York Newspapermen's Golf Club put on a medal play tournament at Van Courtland Park, which they labelled the 'Professional Golfers Championship'. They put up a cup. I should know. I have it yet. I won it. My winning score was 276 and I think I made it with four rounds of 69 each. I know the late Clare Briggs drew a cartoon in which one fellow was kidding the other and advising him to go see Jim Barnes who might pass along a tip for making '69s. Clare gave me the original cartoon. I have it yet."

❋ SHARK MOVES IN FOR THE KILL ❋

Greg Norman of Australia holds the British Open Golf Championship record for the best closing round in the tournament. At Royal St Georges in 1993, Greg carded a final-round score of 64 on his way to a final 72-hole score of 267 (-13) and the famous old Claret Jug. The previous best was a closing 65 and was held by three players: Tom Watson, Turnberry 1977; Severiano Ballesteros, Royal Lytham 1988; Justin Leonard, Royal Troon 1997.

❋ JONES'S LOVE AFFAIR ❋

Bobby Jones's victory in the Open at St Andrews in 1927 was a very popular win. The British public immediately fell in love with him when he asked the Royal & Ancient Golf Club's permission to allow the famous Claret Jug to remain with his friends at St Andrews rather than take it back to the USA with him. In 1958 he was named a "Freeman of the City" of St Andrews, becoming only the second American to be so honoured, the other being Benjamin Franklin in 1759.

❋ FIRST SOUTH AMERICAN US MASTER ❋

In 2009, Argentina's Angel Cabrera held his nerve in a playoff to become the first South American to win the Masters at Augusta.

❋ WIT AND WISDOM OF GOLF (48) ❋

"If there is any larceny in man, golf will bring it out."
Paul Gallico

❋ THE MAGNIFICENT FIVE ❋

Five golfers have been honoured at the Augusta National Golf Club. Three of golf's legends (Ben Hogan, Byron Nelson and Gene Sarazen) have bridges named after them, while two more golf legends (Jack Nicklaus and Arnold Palmer) have plaques bearing their names.

❋ SAM FRIGHTENS LEE ❋

In 1974 Sam Snead, aged 62, fired a one-under-par 279 to finish in third place at the PGA Championship at Tanglewood in Clemmons, North Carolina, and just three shots behind the winner, Lee Trevino.

❋ THE OLDEST US GOLF HOLE ❋

The Oakhurst Golf Club was founded in White Sulphur Springs, Virginia, in 1884. Oakhurst's first hole is considered to be the oldest surviving golf hole in the United States and it is now the No. 1 hole at the Homestead Resort in Virginia.

❋ EARLY GOLF LESSONS ❋

The first book on golf instruction, published in 1857, was *The Golfer's Manual* by "A Keen Hand". In 1857 Prestwick GC instituted the first ever championship meeting, a foursomes competition played at St Andrews which was attended by eleven golf clubs. George Glennie and J. C. Stewart won the competition for Blackheath GC.

❋ LOWEST AT THE PAR-THREE COURSE ❋

The lowest winning score at the nine-hole par-three course at the Augusta National Golf Club, Georgia, home to The Masters, is 20. The record is held jointly by Art Wall (1965) and Gay Brewer (1973).

❋ BUTLER CABIN BECOMES TV STUDIO ❋

The Butler Cabin was first used as a television studio during the 1965 Masters tournament.

❋ FOREIGN-BORN US OPEN WINNERS ❋

The 2010 and 2011 champions Graeme McDowell and Rory McIlroy, respectively, joined an elite group of non-American winners of US Open. Amazingly, McDowell, from Portrush, and McIlroy, Hollywood, Belfast, grew up just 64 miles apart, the second and third golfers from Northern Ireland (Fred Daly, winner of the 1947 British Open) to win Major championships.

Year		*Player*	*Country*
2011	—	Rory McIlroy	Northern Ireland
2010	—	Graeme McDowell	Northern Ireland
2007	—	Angel Cabrera	Argentina
2006	—	Geoff Ogilvy	Australia
2005	—	Michael Campbell	New Zealand
2004	—	Retief Goosen	South Africa
2001	—	Retief Goosen	South Africa
1997	—	Ernie Els	South Africa
1994	—	Ernie Els	South Africa
1981	—	David Graham	Australia
1970	—	Tony Jacklin	England
1965	—	Gary Player	South Africa
1927	—	Tommy Armour	Scotland
1925	—	William Marfarlane	Scotland
1924	—	Cyril Walker	England
1921	—	James Barnes	England
1920	—	Edward Ray	England
1910	—	Alex Smith	Scotland
1909	—	George Sargent	England
1908	—	Fred McLeod	Scotland
1907	—	Alex Ross	Scotland
1906	—	Alex Smith	Scotland
1905	—	Willie Anderson	Scotland
1904	—	Willie Anderson	Scotland
1903	—	Willie Anderson	Scotland
1902	—	Laurence Auchterlonie	Scotland
1901	—	Willie Anderson	Scotland
1900	—	Harry Vardon	England
1899	—	Willie Smith	Scotland
1898	—	Fred Herd	Scotland
1897	—	Joe Lloyd	England
1896	—	James Foulis	Scotland
1895	—	Horace Rawlins	England

❋ PRESIDENTIAL MEMBER ❋

In 1948 the future 34th President of the United States, Dwight David Eisenhower, joined the Augusta National Golf Club. A number of objects bearing his name are situated at the club, including the Eisenhower Cabin, the Eisenhower Tree at the 17th hole, and Ike's Pond at the par-three course.

❋ HISTORY OF THE PGA ❋

On 12 April 1901, a letter from a golf professional from North Wales was published in *Golf Illustrated* in which he called for his fellow pros to form a group to protect their interests. On 9 September 1901, the leading golfers of the day, led by the legendary J. H. Taylor, banded together to form the London and Counties Golf Professionals' Association (subsequently renamed the Professional Golfers' Association at the organization's inaugural AGM on 2 December 1901). The founder members comprised 59 professionals with 11 assistants and funds of just over £47. Today the PGA is based at Centenary House, the De Vere Belfry, England and has a membership of over five thousand professionals. Among the PGA's activities is the organization of golf tournaments, including the Ryder Cup.

❋ GREAT GOLF COURSES OF THE WORLD (19) ❋

BALLYBUNION (OLD COURSE), IRELAND
Opened: 1893
Designer: Anon.
Yardage: 6,503, Par 71
Majors: None

Ballybunion Golf Club is located in what many describe as the most beautiful county in Ireland, County Kerry (nicknamed "The Kingdom"). In its early years the golf club experienced financial difficulties and in 1896, an investment from Colonel Bartholomew saved the club with nine new holes laid out. In 1927, the course was expanded to 18 holes while 10 years later it was redesigned to be a 6,542-yard, par-71 course. Tom Watson fell in love with the course in 1981 and personally re-designed it in 1995 which is the same course that remains today. In 2005, Ballybunion was ranked by *Golf Digest* magazine as the seventh best course in the world outside the USA.

❋ RYDER CUP CAPTAINS ❋

GB: 1927–71
GB & Ire: 1973–77
Europe: 1979–present

Year	Captain	Year	Captain
2010	Colin Montgomerie	1971	Eric Brown
2008	Nick Faldo	1969	Eric Brown
2006	Ian Woosnam	1967	Dai Rees
2004	Bernhard Langer	1965	Herry Wheetman
2002	Sam Torrance	1963	Johnny Fallon
1999	Mark James	1961	Dai Rees
1997	Seve Ballesteros	1959	Dai Rees
1995	Bernard Gallacher	1957	Dai Rees
1993	Bernard Gallacher	1955	Dai Rees
1991	Bernard Gallacher	1953	Henry Cotton
1989	Tony Jacklin	1951	Arthur Lacey
1987	Tony Jacklin	1949	Charles Whitcombe
1985	Tony Jacklin	1947	Henry Cotton
1983	Tony Jacklin	1939–45	
1981	John Jacobs	1937	Charles Whitcombe
1979	John Jacobs	1935	Charles Whitcombe
1977	Brian Huggett	1933	J. H. Taylor
1975	Bernard Hunt	1931	Charles Whitcombe
1973	Bernard Hunt	1929	George Duncan
		1927	Ted Ray

United States

Year	Captain	Year	Captain
2010	Corey Pavin	1971	Jay Hebert
2008	Paul Azinger	1969	Sam Snead
2006	Tom Lehman	1967	Ben Hogan
2004	Hal Sutton	1965	Byron Nelson
2002	Curtis Strange	1963	Arnold Palmer
1999	Ben Crenshaw	1961	Jerry Barber
1997	Tom Kite	1959	Sam Snead
1995	Lanny Wadkins	1957	Jack Burke
1993	Tom Watson	1955	Chick Harbert
1991	Dave Stockton	1953	Lloyd Mangrum
1989	Ray Floyd	1951	Sam Snead
1987	Jack Nicklaus	1949	Ben Hogan
1985	Lee Trevino	1947	Ben Hogan
1983	Jack Nicklaus	1937	Walter Hagen
1981	Dave Marr	1935	Walter Hagen
1979	Billy Casper	1933	Walter Hagen
1977	Dow Finsterwald	1931	Walter Hagen
1975	Arnold Palmer	1929	Walter Hagen
1973	Jack Burke	1927	Walter Hagen

❋ WIT AND WISDOM OF GOLF (49) ❋

"Every golfer worthy of the name likes to think that he is just as good at the man-to-man competition as he is shooting against par."
***Ben Hogan,** 1947*

❋ MONTY'S AMERICAN CENTURY ❋

Colin Montgomerie, searching for his first win in 100 starts in the United States, finished in a three-way tie with Jim Furyk and Phil Mickelson for second place in the 2006 US Open Championship.

❋ SOUTH KOREA'S NEW STAR ❋

In 2009, South Korea's Yang Yong-eun became the first Asian-born player to win a Major Championship (although the third of Asian descent, following Tiger Woods and Vijay Singh). Yang's victory in the PGA Championship was all the more remarkable as he won by three strokes over Woods (it the first time the American had failed to win a Major after he had had at least a share of the 54-hole lead).

❋ GERMANY BECOME WORLD CHAMPIONS ❋

On 10 December 2006, Germany's Bernhard Langer and Marcel Siem beat the Scottish pairing of Colin Montgomerie and Marc Warren in a play-off to claim the World Golf Championship (Barbados World Cup). Both countries finished on 16 under par after 72 holes to set up a thrilling play-off at a rain-soaked Sandy Lane course in Saint James, Barbados. It was Langer's and Germany's second World Cup win, Germany's first coming in 1990 when Langer partnered Torsten Gideon to victory in Florida. "It just shows that the golf ball doesn't know how old you are!" said a beaming Langer. Wales's Bradley Dredge and Stephen Dodd, winners in 2005, finished in a tie for eighth while the pre-tournament favourites, England, endured a disappointing week as Luke Donald and David Howell could only manage a share of 15th place overall.

Did You Know That?
Langer, aged 49, was making his first appearance in the competition since 1996 but went into the event after partnering his 16-year-old son Stefan to victory in a fathers and sons tournament in Orlando the previous week. Raymond Floyd won the fathers and sons tournament with Ray Jnr and Robert, his sons.

❋ WORLD'S GREATEST AMATEUR GOLFER ❋

Without doubt the most prolific amateur golfer the sport has ever seen is Frank Stranahan. During his amateur career (1936 to 1954) he won over 70 amateur championships. Frank won two Major Championships (as they were classed at the time), the 1948 and 1950 British Amateur Championships, and remarkably for an amateur he finished runner-up in five other Major Championships, including the British Amateur Championship, the Open Championship, the US Amateur Championship and The Masters. After finishing runner-up to Arnold Palmer in the 1954 US Amateur Championship he finally turned professional and in 1958 claimed his greatest victory as a pro, the Los Angeles Open.

❋ PLAY IT WITH FLOWERS ❋

The course at Augusta National Golf Club is renowned for its beauty; because The Masters is held in early spring, the flowers of the trees and shrubs bordering the course are in full bloom during the tournament. Every hole on the course is named after the tree or shrub with which it has become associated:

1	Tea Olive	10	Camellia
2	Pink Dogwood	11	White Dogwood
3	Flowering Peach	12	Golden Bell
4	Flowering Crab Apple	13	Azalea
5	Magnolia	14	Chinese Fir
6	Juniper	15	Firethorn
7	Pampas	16	Redbud
8	Yellow Jasmine	17	Nandina
9	Carolina Cherry	18	Holly

❋ THE TIGER SLAM ❋

Tiger Woods won the last three Majors of 2000, the US Open, the Open and the US PGA, and then in April 2001 he captured his second Masters title, thereby marking the only time (within the era of the modern "Grand Slam") that any player held all four Majors at the same time. This feat has become known as the "Tiger Slam". Tiger's adjusted scoring average of 67.79 in 2000 was the lowest in PGA Tour history, while his actual scoring average of 68.17 was also the lowest in PGA Tour history, bettering Byron Nelson's 68.33 average in 1945.

❋ LIGHTNING START TO BRITISH OPEN ❋

In 1983 Denis Durnian carded a 28 for the first nine holes of the 1983 Open at Royal Birkdale. The next best score for nine holes, 29, is held by nine other players, including Ian Baker-Finch who did it twice: over the first nine at St Andrews in 1990 and over the first nine at Royal Birkdale in 1991. The other eight players in addition to Baker-Finch (Peter Thomson 1958, Tom Haliburton 1958, Tony Jacklin 1970, Bill Longmuir 1979, David J. Russell 1988, Paul Broadhurst 1990, Paul McGinley 1996 and Ernie Els 2002) all carded their 29 over the Open's first nine holes.

❋ HAGEN'S WILLOW TREE ❋

During the 1921 US PGA Championship at Inwood Country Club, Far Rockaway, New York, Walter Hagen played the 17th hole by driving his tee shot down the parallel 18th fairway so that he had a good lie for his second shot at the flag. At dinner on the evening of the first day's play a few PGA officials argued that a tree should be planted on the 17th, dividing the two fairways and thereby preventing similar shots to Hagen's. After hearing this, Jack Mackie, the golf professional at Inwood CC, and Morton Wild, a landscaper, uprooted a 15-foot weeping willow that they found in the woods adjacent to the 17th fairway. The pair planted the tree as suggested, dividing the two fairways. When Hagen arrived on the 17th tee the following day, he saw the tree and remarked: "I never saw such fast-growing trees in my life." Just before he made his tee shot a strong wind blew, causing the wires that were supporting the tree to snap, and Hagen watched as the willow fell to the ground. With both fairways open again, Hagen smacked his drive on to the 18th fairway and went on to win the US PGA Championship. In his autobiography Hagen discusses the incident: "The green on the seventeenth was trapped on the short and left side, and almost at right angles to the line of play from the seventeenth fairway. If I played over on to the parallel eighteenth, I could open up the hole and come in from the right-hand side with my second shot."

❋ WHAT'S IN A NAME – "CADDIE" ❋

The term "caddie" derives from the French word "le cadet", which translated means "the boy" or the youngest of the family. The word "cadet" appears in English from 1610 and the word "caddie" appears from 1634.

❋ WOODS MATCHES HOGAN ❋

When Tiger Woods defeated Bob May in a three-hole play-off to win the 2000 US PGA Championship at Valhalla, he became the only player apart from Ben Hogan in 1953 to win three professional Majors in one season.

❋ A NEW MARK AT THE SA OPEN ❋

On 15 December 2006, Sweden's Patrik Sjoland shot a course record round of 64 to take the half-way lead at the South African Airways Open in Port Elizabeth, South Africa. Sjoland played the first nine holes in only 30 shots, five under, parred the next five holes and then finished his round with four straight birdies. "I only played two events in Europe this past year but, you know, the break from the game did me a lot of good. After 10 straight years on tour it was nice to stay at home and spend time with the family. I went to Q-School refreshed," said the 35-year-old Sjoland, who had lost his European Tour card in 2005 and only regained it at the recent qualifying school.

❋ MAGNOLIA DELIGHT ❋

There are 61 magnolia trees lining Magnolia Lane, the 5th hole of the US Masters championship at the Augusta National Golf Club, Georgia. Although the trees that line Magnolia Lane date back to the late 1850s, the lane has only been paved since 1947.

❋ THE ARNOLD PALMER HOSPITAL ❋

The Arnold Palmer Hospital for Children in Orlando, Florida, is a world-class medical facility named after the legendary golfer, Arnold Palmer. The hospital was originally called "The Arnold Palmer Hospital for Children and Women" until, in 2006, a new campus was built adjacent to it and named "The Winnie Palmer Hospital for Women and Babies" in honour of his wife Winnie.

❋ ONE JACKET ONLY ❋

Despite winning a record six Masters championships, Jack Nicklaus has only one green jacket. This is because a multiple winner of the tournament will receive only one jacket unless his size dramatically changes.

❋ WIT AND WISDOM OF GOLF (50) ❋

"Golf and sex are about the only things you can enjoy without being good at."
Jimmy Demaret

❋ GOING DOWN TO GO TOP ❋

Five players have won the Open Championship after carding four rounds of which each was completed in fewer shots than the previous round:

1904	Jack White	Sandwich (80, 75, 72, 69)
1906	James Braid	Muirfield (77, 76, 74, 73)
1937	Henry Cotton	Carnoustie (74, 73, 72, 71)
1953	Ben Hogan	Carnoustie (73, 71, 70, 68)
1959	Gary Player	Muirfield (75, 71, 70, 68)

❋ US MASTERS OLDEST WINNER ❋

Jack Nicklaus, 1986 (46 years, 2 months, 23 days)

❋ TIGER HITS THE SILVER SCREEN ❋

Tiger Woods's life was profiled in the 1998 movie, *The Tiger Woods Story*, which showed highlights of his early years over the background story of his 1997 Masters victory. Tiger was played by Khalil Kian, while has father, Earl Woods, was portrayed by Keith David.

Did You Know That?
In 1996 Tiger Woods enrolled at Stanford University and won his first collegiate event, the William Tucker Invitational.

❋ A DINNER FIT FOR MASTERS ❋

In 1952 the reigning Masters champion, Ben Hogan, started the tradition of the Masters Club dinner (Champions dinner).

❋ NO MORE MAJORS ❋

After missing the cut at the 2005 US Senior Open by 21 strokes, Arnold Palmer announced that he would not enter any more Senior Majors. He won five Senior Majors in his career.

❋ OLDEST AND YOUNGEST MASTER ❋

Jack Nicklaus is the oldest winner of The Masters (46 years old when 1986 champion) and Tiger Woods the youngest winner (aged 21 when 1997 champion). Nicklaus has six green jackets to Woods's four.

❋ GREAT GOLF COURSES OF THE WORLD (20) ❋

Wentworth (The West Course), England
Opened: 1924
Designer: Harry Colt
Yardage: 7,308, Par 72
Majors: None
Ryder Cup: 1953

Wentworth Golf Club was founded in 1924 in Virginia Water, Surrey with only the East Course at the time but today boasts three 18-hole golf courses including the famous West Course designed by Harry Colt. The club was the vision of one man, Walter George Tarrant, the son of a Portsmouth policeman, who bought 200 acres of the Wentworth estate including the late-eighteenth-century gothic-style country house, originally built for the brother-in-law of the future Duke of Wellington. Wentworth GC is the headquarters of the European Tour and each year it plays host to the BMW Championship and the HSBC World Matchplay Championship. Although Wentworth has never hosted a Major it has hosted the Ryder Cup (1953), the Curtis Cup (1952), the World Cup (1956) and the Women's British Open (1980).

❋ LOW SCORES BUT NO TROPHY ❋

In the 150-year history of the British Open Golf Championship two players have carded four rounds of scores under 70 but not been victorious in the tournament:

Year	*Venue*	*Player*	*Scores*	*Winner*
1993	Royal St George's	Ernie Els	68–69–69–68	Greg Norman 267 (–13)
1994	Turnberry	Jesper Parnevik	68–66–68–67	Nick Price 268 (–12)
2004	Royal Troon	Ernie Els	69–69–68–68	Todd Hamilton 274 (–10)*

* *Won after a play-off*

❋ WIT AND WISDOM OF GOLF (51) ❋

"Golf … is the infallible test. The man who can go into a patch of rough alone, with the knowledge that only God is watching him, and play the ball where it lies, is the man who will serve you faithfully and well."
P. G. Wodehouse

❋ FIRST INDIAN MASTER ❋

When Jeev Milkha Singh carded a level score of 72 after the 1st round of the 2007 US Masters, he became the first Indian to play in the tournament in its 73-year history. The average score on the opening day was 76.2, over four shots over par.

❋ CELEBRITY GOLFERS ❋

The great game of golf has recruited many illustrious names to its ranks. Here are a few of the stars of screen and stage, comedians and sporting personalities who have regularly swung a golf club in earnest.

Bing Crosby ◈ Michael Douglas ◈ Catherine Zeta Jones
Kenny Lynch ◈ Jasper Carrott ◈ Sean Connery ◈ Kenny Dalglish
Clint Eastwood ◈ Pat Jennings ◈ Eddie Irvine ◈ Cindy Crawford
Dame Kiri Te Kanawa ◈ Jimmy Tarbuck ◈ Bruce Forsyth
Ronnie Corbett ◈ Michael Bolton ◈ Kevin Costner ◈ Kenny G
Emmitt Smith ◈ Bill Murray ◈ Michael Jordan ◈ Bob Hope
Alice Cooper ◈ Burt Lancaster ◈ Jackie Stewart

❋ A BIT OFF THE BEATEN TRACK ❋

Some people would go a long way for a game of golf … and you can't go much further than the tiny South Atlantic island of St Helena, famous for being the place of exile for Napoleon following his defeat at the Battle of Waterloo in 1815. "Saint" is now an exotic destination for scuba divers and sport-fishing enthusiasts, and in Longwood boasts a golf course that can claim to be the remotest in the world. Though not especially long at 4,783 yards, it can be challenging, according to the St Helena tourist office, and benefits from modest green fees. Mind you, you'd have to fork out quite a bit to get yourself there in the first place: it is over 1,250 miles from the nearest major landmass and it doesn't currently have an airport!

❋ GOLF'S "FIFTH MAJOR" ❋

The TPC Sawgrass's famed stadium course plays host each spring to The Players Championship. It is often called golf's "Fifth Major".

The Players Championship

2011 K.J. Choi (South Korean)........TPC Sawgrass
2010 Tim Clark (South Africa)........TPC Sawgrass
2009 Henrik Stenson (Sweden)........TPC Sawgrass
2008 Sergio Garcia (Spain)........TPC Sawgrass
2007 Phil Mickelson (USA)........TPC Sawgrass
2006 Stephen Ames (Canada)........TPC Sawgrass
2005 Fred Funk (USA)........TPC Sawgrass
2004 Adam Scott (Australia)........TPC Sawgrass
2003 Davis Love III (USA)........TPC Sawgrass
2002 Craig Perks (New Zealand)........TPC Sawgrass
2001 Tiger Woods (USA)........TPC Sawgrass
2000 Hal Sutton (USA)........TPC Sawgrass
1999 David Duval (USA)........TPC Sawgrass
1998 Justin Leonard (USA)........TPC Sawgrass
1997 Steve Elkington (USA)........TPC Sawgrass
1996 Fred Couples (USA)........TPC Sawgrass
1995 Lee Janzen (USA)........TPC Sawgrass
1994 Greg Norman (Australia)........TPC Sawgrass
1993 Nick Price (Zimbabwe)........TPC Sawgrass
1992 Davis Love III (USA)........TPC Sawgrass
1991 Steve Elkington (USA)........TPC Sawgrass
1990 Jodie Mudd (USA)........TPC Sawgrass
1989 Tom Kite (USA)........TPC Sawgrass
1988 Mark McCumber (USA)........TPC Sawgrass

Tournament Players Championship

1987 Sandy Lyle (Scotland)........TPC Sawgrass
1986 John Mahaffey (USA)........TPC Sawgrass
1985 Calvin Peete (USA)........TPC Sawgrass
1984 Fred Couples (USA)........TPC Sawgrass
1983 Hal Sutton (USA)........TPC Sawgrass
1982 Jerry Pate (USA)........TPC Sawgrass, Ponte Vedra Beach, FL
1981 Raymond Floyd (USA)........Sawgrass CC
1980 Lee Trevino (USA)........Sawgrass CC
1979 Lanny Wadkins (USA)........Sawgrass CC
1978 Jack Nicklaus (USA)........Sawgrass CC
1977 Mark Hayes (USA)........Sawgrass CC, Ponte Vedra Beach, FL
1976 Jack Nicklaus (USA)........Inverrary CC, Fort Lauderdale, FL
1975 Al Geiberger (USA)........Colonial CC, Fort Worth, TX
1974 Jack Nicklaus (USA)........Atlanta CC, Marietta, GA

❋ THE OLDEST MEMBER ❋

P. G. Wodehouse, the acclaimed English humourist (1881–1975), perhaps best known for his comic creations Bertie Wooster and Jeeves, was a great golf enthusiast who claimed it was the only important pursuit of his life. "Plum" wrote more than 30 short stories with a golfing theme – most of which were narrated by "The Oldest Member", a retired golfer who frequented the nineteenth hole of his local golf club and delighted in regaling the unwary with lengthy anecdotes about unfortunate mishaps and curious occurrences on the links. Prominent among the redoubtable raconteur's reminiscences were the following tales:

The Clicking of Cuthbert ❖ A Mixed Threesome ❖ Ordeal by Golf
The Long Hole ❖ The Rough Stuff ❖ The Heart of a Goof
The Magic Plus Fours ❖ Rodney Fails to Qualify
Jane Gets off the Fairway ❖ There's Always Golf

❋ EASING THE CADDIE'S BURDEN ❋

A golf cart is a small vehicle designed to transport two golfers and their clubs around the golf course. They were first mass-produced in the United States in the early 1950s. Initially fitted with small gas engines, they are now normally battery operated. Three of the leading manufacturers of golf carts today are Club Car, EZ-Go and Yamaha. Golf carts can be customized at the whim of the owner or even purchased as miniaturized versions of popular full-size vehicles, such as mini-Jeeps, Rolls-Royces, Cadillacs and Mercedes. There is even a "Hummer" golf cart available at the modest purchase price of US$25,000. Enterprising dealers now market golf carts – or Electric Utility Vehicles as they are known in the trade – beyond the golfing community to gardeners with a lot of lawn-cutting equipment to transport and property owners with substantial grounds to patrol.

Did You Know That?
Peachtree City, Georgia, a planned urban development chartered in 1959, has a system of golf cart paths that criss-cross the city. Many of its citizens use a golf cart to get about town, and students are encouraged to use their golf carts to drive to school. The golf cart paths are also popular with walkers, joggers and pedestrians. The McIntosh High School in Peachtree has its very own golf cart parking lot situated on the campus.

❋ WIT AND WISDOM OF GOLF (52) ❋

"Hockey is a sport for white men. Basketball is a sport for black men. Golf is a sport for white men dressed as black pimps."
Tiger Woods

❋ MONSTER OF GOLF ❋

Heavy metal rocker Alice Cooper – renowned for his outlandish appearance, boa constrictor as part of his act and allegedly biting the head off a chicken on stage (something he's always denied) – discovered golf after a successful sojourn in an alcohol rehab unit. Reportedly, he plays golf on at least 300 days of the year and has a handicap of five. He has participated in several celebrity golf pro-am competitions and has appeared in commercials for Callaway golf equipment. Since 1997 he has hosted the Alice Cooper Celebrity Amateur Golf Tournament, with the proceeds of the annual competition going to his charity, the Solid Rock Foundation, and in August 2006 he took part in the Northern Rock All Stars Cup – a celebrity version of the Ryder Cup. His autobiography *Alice Cooper – Golf Monster: A Rock 'n' Roller's 12 Steps to Becoming a Golf Addict* describes the debt he owes to the game. "I traded one addiction for another. Once I took [golf] seriously, I loved it. It absolutely saved my life."

❋ SPYGLASS HILL (PEBBLE BEACH RESORTS) ❋

The holes at Spyglass Hill are named after characters, locations and incidents in Robert Louis Stevenson's famous pirate adventure story *Treasure Island*, which was first published in 1883, and the golf course logo is a peg-legged pirate looking through a telescope. The story goes that the Scottish writer, when on a visit to Monterey, was witnessed wandering the coastline seeking inspiration for his novel.

1 .... Treasure Island
2 .... Billy Bones
3 .... The Black Spot
4 .... Blind Pew
5 .... Bird Rock
6 .... Israel Hands
7 .... Indian Village
8 .... Signal Hill
9 .... Captain Smollett
10 .... Captain Flint
11 .... Admiral Benbow
12 .... Skeleton Island
13 .... Tom Morgan
14 .... Long John Silver
15 .... Jim Hawkins
16 .... Black Dog
17 .... Ben Gunn
18 .... Spyglass

❋ THE WORLD GOLF HALL OF FAME ❋

The World Golf Hall of Fame is located in St Augustine, Florida. Inaugurated in 1998, it honours both men and women golfers. Mickey Wright, Betsy Rawls, Patty Berg, Betty Jameson, Louise Suggs and Babe Zaharias were all first in the Women's Golf Hall of Fame (with their year of induction).

Ernie Els (2011) *South Africa*
Doug Ford (2011)
Jock Hutchison (2011) *Scotland*
Masashi "Jumbo" Ozaki (2011) *Jap*
George H.W. Bush (2011)
(former US president)
Frank Chirkinian (2011)
(television executive)
Christy O'Connor Snr (2009) *Ire*
José María Olazábal (2009) *Spain*
Lanny Wadkins (2009)
Dwight D. Eisenhower (2009)
(former US president)
Bob Charles (2008) *New Zealand*
Denny Shute (2008)
Carol Semple Thompson (2008)
Craig Wood (2008)
Pete Dye (2008)
(Golf course architect)
Hubert Warren Wind (2008)
(Golf writer)
Joe Carr (2007) *Ireland*
Hubert Green (2007)
Charles B. Macdonald (2007)
Kel Nagle (2007) *Australia*
Se Ri Pak (2007) *South Korea*
Curtis Strange (2007)
Larry Nelson (2006)
Henry Picard (2006)
Vijay Singh (2006) *Fiji*
Marilynn Smith (2006)
Mark McCormack (2006)
(Sports agent)
Ayako Okamoto (2005) *Japan*
Willie Park Sr (2005) *Scotland*
Karrie Webb (2005) *Australia*
Bernard Darwin (2005) *England*
(Golf writer)
Alister Mackenzie (2005) *England*
(Golf architect)
Isao Aoki (2004) *Japan*
Tom Kite (2004)
Charlie Sifford (2004)
Marlene Stewart Streit (2004) *Can*
Leo Diegel (2003)
Hisako "Chako" Higuchi (2003) *Jap*
Nick Price (2003) *Zimbabwe*
Annika Sorenstam (2003) *Sweden*
Tommy Bolt (2002)
Ben Crenshaw (2002)
Marlene Bauer Hagge (2002)
Tony Jacklin (2002) *England*
Bernhard Langer (2002) *Germany*
Harvey Penick (2002)
(Golf instructor)
Donna Caponi (2001)
Greg Norman (2001) *Australia*
Allan Robertson (2001) *Scotland*
Payne Stewart (2001)
Judy Bell (2001)
(Administrator)
Karsten Solheim (2001)
(Golf equipment manufacturer)
Sir Michael Bonallack (2000) *Eng*
Jack Burke, Jr. (2000)
Neil Coles (2000) *England*
Beth Daniel (2000)
Juli Inkster (2000)
John Jacobs (2000) *England*
Judy Rankin (2000)
Deane Beman (2000)
(Administrator)

Amy Alcott (1999)
Seve Ballesteros (1999) *Spain*
Lloyd Mangrum (1999)
Nick Faldo (1998) *England*
Johnny Miller (1998)
Betsy King (1995)
Dinah Shore (1994)
(Celebrity friend of golf)
Patty Sheehan (1993)
Harry Cooper (1992)
Hale Irwin (1992)
Chi-Chi Rodriguez (1992) *PR*
Richard Tufts (1992)
(Administrator)
Pat Bradley (1991)
Gene Littler (1990)
Paul Runyan (1990)
Horton Smith (1990)
William Campbell (1990)
(Administrator)
Jim Barnes (1989)
Roberto De Vicenzo (1989) *Arg*
Ray Floyd (1989)
Peter Thomson (1988) *Australia*
Tom Watson (1988)
Bob Harlow (1988)
(Promoter)
Nancy Lopez (1987)
Robert Trent Jones, Sr (1987)
(Golf architect)
Cary Middlecoff (1986)
Jimmy Demaret (1983)
Bob Hope (1983)
(Celebrity)
Julius Boros (1982)
JoAnne Carner (1982)
Ralph Guldahl (1981)
Lee Trevino (1981)
Henry Cotton (1980) *England*
Lawson Little (1980)
Walter Travis (1979)
Billy Casper (1978)
Bing Crosby (1978)
(Celebrity)
Harold Hilton (1978) *England*

Dorothy Campbell Hurd Howe
(1978) *Scotland/USA*
Clifford Roberts (1978)
(Administrator)
John Ball, Jr (1977) *England*
Sandra Haynie (1977)
Bobby Locke (1977) *South Africa*
Carol Mann (1977)
Herb Graffis (1977)
(Golf writer)
Donald Ross (1977) *Scotland/USA*
(Golf architect) –
Tommy Armour (1976) *Sco/USA*
James Braid (1976) *Scotland*
Tom Morris, Sr (1976) *Scotland*
Jerry Travers (1976)
Willie Anderson (1975) *Scotland*
Chick Evans (1975)
Tom Morris, Jr (1975) *Scotland*
J. H. Taylor (1975) *England*
Glenna Collett Vare (1975)
Joyce Wethered (1975) *England*
Kathy Whitworth (1975)
Fred Corcoran (1975)
(Promoter & Administrator)
Joseph Dey (1975)
(Administrator)
Walter Hagen (1974)
Ben Hogan (1974)
Bobby Jones (1974)
Byron Nelson (1974)
Jack Nickl*Aus* (1974)
Francis Ouimet (1974)
Arnold Palmer (1974)
Gary Player (1974) *South Africa*
Gene Sarazen (1974)
Sam Snead (1974)
Harry Vardon (1974)
Mickey Wright (1964)
Betsy Rawls (1960)
Patty Berg (1951)
Betty Jameson (1951)
Louise Suggs (1951)
Babe Zaharias (1951)

❋ WIT AND WISDOM OF GOLF (53) ❋

"Golf appeals to the idiot in us and the child. Just how childlike golf players become is proven by their frequent inability to count up to five."
John Updike

❋ THE WALKER CUP ❋

The Walker Cup is an event for men contested biennially between amateur teams from the United States and Great Britain and Ireland. Organized by the R&A and the USGA, it was established in the aftermath of the First World War and named in honour of George Herbert Walker, President of the USGA in 1920, and great-grandfather of the former US President George W. Bush.

Year	*Venue*	*Winner*
1922	National Golf Links of America	US
1923	St Andrews	US
1924	Garden City GC	US
1926	St Andrews	US
1928	Chicago GC	US
1930	Royal St George's GC	US
1932	The Country Club	US
1934	St Andrews	US
1936	Pine Valley GC	US
1938	St Andrews	GB & Ireland
1940–46	*Tournament not held due to the Second World War*	
1947	St Andrews	US
1949	Winged Foot	US
1951	Royal Birkdale GC	US
1953	The Kittausett Club	US
1955	St Andrews	US
1957	The Minikahda Club	US
1959	Muirfield	US
1961	Seattle GC	US
1963	Westin Turnberry Resort	US
1965	Baltimore CC	US
1967	Royal St George's GC	US
1969	Milwaukee CC	US
1971	St Andrews	GB & Ireland
1973	The Country Club	US
1975	St Andrews	US

1977	Shinnecock Hills GC	US
1979	Muirfield	US
1981	Cypress Point	US
1983	Royal Liverpool GC	US
1985	Pine Valley GC	US
1987	Sunningdale GC	US
1989	Peachtree GC	GB & Ireland
1991	Portmarnock GC	US
1993	Interlachen CC	US
1995	Royal Porthcawl GC	GB & Ireland
1997	Quaker Ridge GC	US
1999	Nairn GC	GB & Ireland
2001	Ocean Forest GC	GB & Ireland
2003	Ganton GC	GB & Ireland
2005	Chicago GC	US
2007	Royal County Down GC	US
2009	Merion GC	US

❋ A HAPPY BLACK KNIGHT ❋

In the opening round of the 2007 US Masters, 71-year-old Gary Player carded an 11-over-par score of 83. It was the 50th time the Black Knight had played in the Masters tournament, the tournament's first international champion. Arnold Palmer and Gary Player are the only golfers to compete in 50 Masters.

❋ BOHEMIAN RHAPSODY ❋

The Czech Republic enjoys the longest history of golf of any of the former Eastern bloc countries. In 1904, the spa town of Karlsbad opened the country's first 9-hole golf course, and today there are 36 championship courses in operation, many designed by some of golf's top names including Gary Player and Miguel Angel Jiménez. The Marianske Lazne Golf Course, the Czech Republic's oldest operating golf club, was officially opened by His Majesty King Edward VII when he cut the inaugural ribbon on 21 August 1905. He then signed his name in the memorial book of the course with a gold pen to become the first foundation member of the Marianske Lazne Golf Club. Indeed, King Edward VII made a total of ten trips to Marianske Lazne, his last in 1909. In 2003, Queen Elizabeth II granted the golf club in Marianske Lazne the right to use the title Royal Golf Club. The first championship in the country was won by Diaz Albertini in 1904: he was from the Paris Golf Club.

❋ MRS DOUBTFIRE ❋

Colin Montgomerie had to endure unkind jibes from some of the less charitable elements of the American golfing public. He was dubbed Mrs Doubtfire for the passing resemblance he was supposed to bear the Robin Williams character in the film of the same name. His sometimes irascible approach did nothing to endear him to the gallery, but in the latter part of his career Monty is becoming something of a favourite in the States.

❋ GOLFING ON THE MOON ❋

In 1971 Apollo 14 astronaut Alan Shepard smuggled aboard a club and balls inside his space suit. Engaged in his mission to gather moon rock, he had to take the longest moonwalk thus-far attempted, but his nine-hour stint did not deter him from hitting two balls just before getting back into the lunar module and preparing for lift-off. By is own account, he drove them "miles and miles and miles". Eat your heart out, Tiger!

❋ AFRICAN-AMERICAN TRAILBLAZER ❋

In 1975 Lee Elder broke the colour barrier at Augusta as the first African American to play at The Masters; previously talented golfers from his community, such as Charlie Sifford and Pete Brown, had been debarred. Four years later, he also became the first African American to play on a Ryder Cup team. Born in Dallas, Texas, in 1934, much of his childhood was a struggle against poverty. He would sneak on to golf courses at night to teach himself the game, and as a teenager he posed as a caddy to earn money. Fittingly, this trailblazer for the African-American community was present during Tiger Woods's historic victory at The Masters in 1997. In his career to date, he has recorded a combined 12 victories on the PGA and Senior Tours.

❋ GOLF IN THE DESERT ❋

The Dubai Desert Classic is an annual golf tournament played in Dubai, part of the United Arab Emirates. Contested in February or March, it forms part of the European Tour and was first held in 1989. It is now played on the "Majlis" course at Emirates Golf Club, although it was hosted by the Dubai Creek Golf Club in 1999 and 2000. There are two other European Tour events in the Gulf States: namely the Abu Dhabi Golf Championship and the Qatar Masters.

❋ GATOR AID ❋

There are some golf courses in the world where retrieving lost balls from the water can be a hazardous business, as Vernon Messier found to his cost at New Port Richey, Florida, in March 2007. He had been steadfastly engaged in extricating golf balls from the waterholes at the course for purposes of resale when a 7ft-long alligator emerged from beneath the surface, clamped one of his feet in its jaws and tried to drag him under. Alerted by the victim's cries for help, Tom Arundel, a pensioner from Basildon, Essex, and his American friend Pat McGuire, who had been playing a nearby hole, rushed to his aid and were able to help him escape from the would-be man-eater. The fortunate Mr Vernon drove himself to hospital, and was confident of making a full recovery. The luckless alligator was later caught and killed. There's a moral in the story somewhere!

❋ KNICKERBOCKER GLORY ❋

A popular and always conspicuous figure on the golf course due to his predilection for wearing loud golfing attire (Tam o'Shanter caps and his trademark plus fours), Payne Stewart won three Majors (US PGA 1989 and US Open 1991 and 1999) and appeared in five Ryder Cups between 1987 and 1999. He had just won his third Major, when aged 42 his career was tragically cut short by a fatal airplane accident. The Lear jet in which he was flying from Orlando bound for Dallas, Texas, strayed off course and eventually came down near Mina, South Dakota, killing him and five other people, including Bruce Borland an acclaimed golf architect. Payne Stewart was posthumously inducted into the World Golf Hall of Fame in 2001.

❋ WIT AND WISDOM OF GOLF (54) ❋

"I would like to deny all allegations by Bob Hope that during my last game I hit an eagle, a birdie, an elk and a moose."
Gerald Ford

❋ OUT OF KILTER ❋

The 2001 Ryder Cup was postponed for a year because of the 9/11 terrorist attacks in the US, and thereafter it was decided to stage the Ryder Cup in even-numbered years instead of odd-numbered years.

❋ THE WORLD'S GREATEST GOLF COURSES (21)

TPC Sawgrass
Opened: 1980
Designers: Pete & Alice Dye
Yardage: 6,954, Par 72 (The Stadium Course)
Majors: None

The Tournament Players Club (TPC) at Sawgrass is one of the best known, and toughest, golf courses in the USA and is located in Ponte Vedra Brach, Florida. Sawgrass has two courses, the Stadium Course and the Valley Course and is also the home of the PGA Tour's headquarters. The Stadium Course has played host to the Players Championship, the PGA Tour's flagship tournament since 1982. The best known hole on the Stadium Course is the par-3, 132-yard 17th, known simply as the "Island Green", one of golf's most instantly recognisable and most difficult holes. Designed by the well-known and respected golf course architects Pete and Alice Dye, Sawgrass was built over 415 acres of swampland, while fans attending the Players Championship sit in "stands" made from raised mounds of grass. The TPC is a chain of American public and private golf clubs operated by the PGA Tour.

❋ INDOOR GOLF ❋

Launched in 1935 by Parker Brothers, the property-trading board game Monopoly quickly established itself as a firm family favourite in the United States, Britain and then the rest of the world. Now there is a bespoke version of the popular parlour game aimed at the golfing community, with prestigious US golf courses to acquire instead of famous streets; caddyshacks and clubhouses to build instead of houses and hotels; and Community Chest and Chance cards replaced by "Drive for Show" and "Putt for Dough" cards – it's enough to have everybody squabbling and sulking as if they were playing in their local golf club's annual fourballs competition!

❋ TEE IN CHINA ❋

Mission Hills Golf Club is located near the city of Shenzhen in China, not far from neighbouring Hong Kong. With its 12 championship courses, designed by some of the biggest names in world golf, including Jack Nicklaus, Greg Norman and Ernie Els, it is deemed to be the world's largest golf and leisure complex.

❋ US OPEN TAKES OFF ❋

In 1913, the US Open really caught the public's attention when Francis Ouimet, a 20-year-old American amateur, stunned the golf world by defeating two famous English professionals, Harry Vardon and Ted Ray, in a play-off. Despite wins by golf legends such as Walter Hagen (1914 & 1919), Ted Ray (1920) and Gene Sarazen (1922), it was not until 1923 that the US Open truly came to prominence in terms of "Major" championship stature when an amateur named Bobby Jones won the US Open four times (1923, 1926, 1929, 1930). Indeed, spectator tickets were first sold in 1922 and a boom in tournament entries caused the USGA to introduce sectional qualifying for the 1924 event. In 1926, the format was changed again to 18 holes played on each of two days, followed by 36 holes on the third day. In 1933 John Goodman became the fifth and last amateur to win the US Open, following Francis Ouimet (1913), Jerome D. Travers (1915), Charles Evans Jnr (1916) and Bobby Jones (who first won in 1923).

❋ NAMES OF THE HOLES AT PRESTWICK ❋

The holes at Prestwick Golf Club in Ayrshire, Scotland are evocatively named as follows:

1	Railway	10	Arran
2	Tunnel	11	Carrick
3	Cardinal	12	Wall
4	Bridge	13	Sea Headrig
5	Himalayas	14	Goosedubs
6	Elysian Fields	15	Narrows
7	Monkton Miln	16	Cardinals Back
8	End	17	Alps
9	Eglington	18	Clock

❋ HOGAN IN HEAVEN ❋

In episode 50 of the HBO television series *Curb Your Enthusiasm*, Larry David meets Ben Hogan during his brief visit to Heaven.

❋ ALWAYS THERE ❋

Only one player has made more final-day appearances in the Open Championship than the 31 Alex Herd notched up: Jack Nicklaus with 32 final-day shows.

❋ WIT AND WISDOM OF GOLF (55) ❋

"If you drink, don't drive. Don't even putt."
Dean Martin

❋ GET YOUR KNICKERS ON ❋

Harry Vardon's first Major victory came in 1896 when he won the Open Championship. Throughout the competition Vardon played in what would become his signature attire during his illustrious career: knickerbockers (he was the first golfer to play in knickerbockers), dress shirt, tie and buttoned jacket.

❋ NINETEEN PUTTS ❋

During a round at Augusta Country Club in 1926 the legendary amateur player, Dorothy Campbell Hurd, holed out from the fairway on the 18th hole to complete her round with only 19 putts.

❋ GARY PLAYER'S 10 COMMANDMENTS ❋

1. Change is the price of survival.
2. Everything in business is negotiable except quality.
3. A promise made is a debt incurred.
4. For all we take in life we must pay.
5. Persistence and common sense are more important than intelligence.
6. The fox fears not the man who boasts by night, but the man who rises early in the morning.
7. Accept the advice of the man who loves you, though you like it not at present.
8. Trust instinct to the end, though you cannot render any reason.
9. The heights of great men reached and kept were not attained by sudden flight, but that while their companions slept were toiling upward in the night.
10. There is no substitute for personal contact.

Did You Know That?
Gary Player was awarded the "Order of Ikhamanga" by President Mbeki of South Africa for his outstanding excellence in golf and his contribution to non-racial sport in South Africa. He has also been featured on a South African stamp and has designed more than 350 golf courses around the world.

❋ GOD HELPS ZACH TO MASTERS GLORY ❋

The USA's Zach Johnson carded a three-under-par 69 on a dramatic final day's play at the 2007 US Masters in Augusta to score a one-over total of 289, enough to secure the 31-year-old from Iowa City the green jacket. His one over par score is the joint highest winning score in US Masters history, while his win was only his second victory on the PGA Tour. Tiger Woods, chasing his fifth green jacket, finished two shots back in joint-second place along with the South African pair of Retief Goosen and Rory Sabbatini. Justin Rose, the co-leader after the first round, finished in a tie for fifth place with Jerry Kelly (USA). Johnson, a committed Christian, picked up the $664,000 winner's cheque along with the most famous blazer in sport. Johnson was 200–1 to win the tournament before the first round began.

❋ DISTINGUISHED PRO-AM CREW ❋

In the respective 115-year histories of both events, only 11 players have won both the US Amateur and US Open Championships up to and including the 2010 tournaments:

Jerome Travers: Amateur 1907, 1908, 1912, 1913; Open 1915
Francis Ouimet: Amateur 1914, 1931; Open 1913
Charles Evans Jr*: 1916; Amateur 1920; Open 1916
Bobby Jones*: 1924; Amateur 1925, 1927, 1928, 1930; Open 1923, 1926, 1929, 1930
Lawson Little: Amateur 1934, 1935; Open 1940
Johnny Goodman: Amateur 1937 Amateur; Open 1933
Gene Littler: Amateur 1953 Amateur; Open 1961
Arnold Palmer: Amateur 1954 Amateur; Open 1960
Jack Nicklaus: Amateur 1959, 1961; Open 1962, 1967, 1972, 1980
Jerry Pate: Amateur 1974; Open 1976
Tiger Woods: Amateur 1994, 1995, 1996; Open 2000, 2002, 2008

(won both in the same year)*

❋ HORSES FOR COURSES ❋

Gary Player bred the racehorse Broadway Flyer, which competed in the 1994 Epsom Derby, and has had over 1,000 wins with horses produced at his thoroughbred stud farm. He has been in the bloodstock business since 1965, and has a passion for horse-racing.

❋ HOPE IN THE OPEN ❋

By the time of the 1960 US Open, Arnold Palmer had already stamped his name in the history books of golf by twice winning The Masters. However, it was the 1960 US Open that sealed his legend status. After three rounds Palmer trailed the leader by six strokes but had a feeling that a final-round 65 might make him champion. He completed the first nine in 30 and then parred his way home as his two closest rivals, the ageing Ben Hogan and a young Jack Nicklaus, faltered. He went on to win four more Majors.

❋ TILTING AT WINDMILLS ❋

Much beloved of day-trippers to the seaside, miniature golf, goofy golf, crazy golf, carpet golf (call it what you will), is played over 9 or 18 holes, and the pertinacious putter has to negotiate pipes, shoots, tunnels, wishing wells and flailing windmills to card the best score. Its "kiss-me-quick" image is surely the very antithesis of the starchy gentility of the golf clubhouse. Strangely then, the roots of miniature golf can be traced to the manicured lawns of the home of golf itself. This adaptation of the game – admittedly not yet embellished by artificial obstacles – was adopted by the Ladies' Putting Club at St Andrews in 1867. These Victorian ladies liked to play golf, but were wary of attracting the social opprobrium that swinging clubs above the shoulder would bring.

Did You Know That?
The annual British Crazy Golf Championships is held in Hastings in Sussex. The event takes place in March and is open to all "nutters with putters" over the age of 14 who are prepared to stump up the modest entrance fee.

❋ GOLF IN THE GAMES ARCADE ❋

There have been lots of golf video games and computer games. The Jack Nicklaus series was very popular, now the Tiger Woods series from EA Sports dominates the market – no surprise there then!

Big Event Golf ❖ Birdie King ❖ Fuji Golf ❖ Golden Tee
Hot Shots Golf (series) ❖ Jack Nicklaus Golf (series)
Links 2003 ❖ Mario Golf ❖ Ninja Golf ❖ Outlaw Golf 2
Pang Ya ❖ Meier's SimGolf ❖ Super Swing Golf ❖ Swingerz Golf
Tiger Woods PGA Tour (series) ❖ True Golf: Wicked 18

❋ THE OLDEST SWINGER IN TOWN ❋

Bob Hope (1903–2003), professional boxer, crooner, movie star, double-act partner of Bing Crosby (another fanatical golfer), US trooper's trouper and entertainer extraordinaire, maintained for 70 years that his true profession was golf. Equally at home on the fairway as treading the boards, he played in a few PGA tour events and was a pioneer of celebrity pro-am golf tournaments and golfing buddy of a succession of US presidents from Ike to George W. He even utilized a golf club as an on-stage prop in the manner of a Vaudevillian's cane. He was famous for his wisecracks; several of his witty asides with a golfing theme can be found elsewhere in this book. In 1960 the Palm Springs Classic was renamed the Bob Hope Chrysler Classic in his honour. Part of the pro-golf tour, the event now takes place in January at Coachella Valley, California, and has a unique format with its five daily 18-hole rounds played over four courses and attracts a retinue of celebrity golfers and top pros. His autobiography was entitled *Confessions of a Hooker: My Life Long Love Affair with Golf*. Bob Hope won the prestigious Bob Jones Award in 1978 (with Bing Crosby) and was elected to be a member of the Golf Hall of Fame in 1983.

❋ SNAKE IN THE GRASS ❋

During a practice round with Sam Torrance in preparation for the Volvo PGA at Wentworth in 1992, Northern Ireland's David Feherty (now a much-respected commentator in America) mishit a drive into the deep rough at the 15th. Scrambling around in undergrowth in an attempt to find his ball, he disturbed a Black Adder and got bitten on the hand. Undeterred by his painful encounter with a highly poisonous snake (and eager not to forfeit the modest side bet that he had going with his playing partner), he struggled on and completed his round. After returning to the clubhouse, on doctor's advice he had to be rushed to hospital with a massively swollen hand. Later when asked how the patient was getting on, Torrence jocularly remarked: "Well, he'll be OK, but I'm not sure how the snake will be after biting David!"

❋ WIT AND WISDOM OF GOLF (56) ❋

"Golf is popular because it is the best game in the world at which to be bad."
A. A. Milne

❋ PHIL MICKELSON (1970–❋

Philip Alfred Mickelson was born on 16 June 1970 in San Diego, USA to Phil Sr. and Mary. Phil Sr was a retired US Navy fighter pilot who turned to commercial flying whilst Mary was a nurse. In 1988, he graduated from the University of San Diego High School and attended Arizona State University on a golf scholarship, graduating in 1992. Phil was the most dominant amateur collegiate golfer of his time, winning three NCAA individual championships and three Haskins Awards (1990–92). In 1990, he became the first left-handed golfer to win the US Amateur Championship. During his four years at Arizona State, Mickelson earned first-team All-American honours to become only the second collegiate golfer to do so. In total Phil won 34 San Diego County junior titles while working with teaching professional Dean Reinmuth and in 1991 he won his first PGA Tour event, the Northern Telecom Open, thereby becoming only the fourth amateur player in PGA history to win on the PGA Tour. A year later he turned professional aged 22.

Between 1996 and 2002, Phil was a regular victor on the PGA Tour and a polificic money-winner. However, he had to wait until 2004 to win his first Major, holding off the challenge of Ernie Els to win the Masters. Phil was only the third left-handed golfer to win a Major (Bob Charles –1963 Open Championship – and Mike Weir – 2003 Masters – are the others). Mickelson won his second Major in 2005, the PGA Championship at Baltusrol finishing one shot clear of Thomas Bjorn and Steve Elkington. In 2006, Phil claimed his second green jacket and was ranked the No.2 golfer in the world, his highest ranking of his career. However, he missed the cut at the 2007 US Open at Oakmount, the first time he had failed to make the cut in a Major since the 1999 Open at Carnoustie, 31 Majors. When he won the 2009 Northern Trust Open it was his 35th PGA Tour victory, surpassing Vijay Singh as the current PGA Tour wins leader. At the 2009 US Open he finished second for the fifth time in the tournament, a record and then in late 2009, he won the Tour Championship for a second time.

Phil won the Masters for a third time in 2010, his –16 beating Lee Westwood by three strokes. It was his fourth Major and left him second to Tiger Woods (14) in Majors wins among active players.

Did You Know That?

Phil, nicknamed "Lefty", although actually right-handed, swings the club with his left hand as he developed his swing by watching his right-handed father practice his own swing in front of a mirror at home.

❋ US VICTORY AT VALHALLA ❋

In 2008, the US reclaimed the Ryder Cup for the first time since 1999 with a 16½ - 11½ victory over Europe at Valhalla Golf Club. Jim Furyk secured the winning point, beating Spaniard Miguel Angel Jiménez on the 17th green in Louisville, Kentucky to take the US Team's total points score to an insurmountable 14½ points. In the end, Paul Azinger's men won by a score of 16½–11½ over Nick Faldo's team, Team USA's largest margin of victory since 1981. The format for the 2008 Ryder Cup differed from the previous two; for the first time since 1999, the opening matches featured foursomes. Foursomes was used in the first sessions of every Ryder Cup since 1981 until Seve Ballesteros, the European captain, opened with better ball (four-ball) in 1997 at Valderrama. Then in 1999, Ben Crenshaw, the USA captain, switched back to alternate shot in 1999 at Brookline.

❋ TIGER DEPOSED ❋

At the start of November 2010, Lee Westwood ended Tiger Woods' record consecutive stay of 281 weeks as the No.1 ranked golfer in the world. Westwood's climb to the top of the rankings left Woods just one week short of 12 years in total as the World's No.1 in his career (an incredible 623 weeks). In December 2010, no fewer than five British golfers occupied slots in the Top 10 of the world's leading golfers: Lee Westwood (1), Paul Casey (7), Ian Poulter (8), Luke Donald (9) and Rory McIlroy (10) whilst Germany's Martin Kaymer was No.3 to make it a European dominated table.

❋ NO TWEETING ❋

When Europe's 2010 Ryder Cup Captain, Colin Montgomerie, read about Kevin Pietersen's, problems following a tweet the England cricketer put on the internet, he told his players not to tweet during the three days of play at the 2010 Ryder Cup played at Celtic Manor. The USA Team Captain, Corey Pavin, made a similar request.

❋ BIRDIE SMILES ❋

Anthony Ha-Jin Kim, a Korean-American, set a record for most birdies in a round at the Masters with 11 in 2009 during his second round. The previous year, Kim won his first PGA Tour tournament at the Wachovia Championship whilst his winning 16-under par 272 total score is the lowest score in the tournament's history.

❋ WIT AND WISDOM OF GOLF (57) ❋

"We went to the High Street to get some pizzas and on our way back we got our arm twisted and went in for a pint."
Jim Furyk at the 2007 Open Championship at Carnoustie

❋ CADDIE RAKES IN THE MONEY ❋

In 2008, *Forbes Magazine* published the top-earning caddies on the world golf circuit. Not surprisingly the highest paid caddy for the 2006-07 season was New Zealand's Steve Williams, caddie to Tiger Woods, who earned a whopping $1.27 million.

❋ SUPER SWEDE ❋

In February 2007, Sweden's Henrik Stenson won the WGC-Accenture Match Play Championship after defeating the defending champion, Geoff Ogilvy (Australia), in the final and moved up to fifth place in golf's official world rankings, the highest position ever attained by a Swedish male golfer. Amazingly, it was also the first time that an American failed to reach the final.

❋ A TADD TOO GOOD ❋

On 12 January 2007, sixteen year-old Tadd Fuikawa, a Japanese-American, became the youngest player in 50 years to make the cut at a PGA Tour event after shooting rounds of 71 and 66 at the Sony Open in Hawaii. Fuikawa finished the tournament tied for 20th place.

❋ A TIMELY VICTORY ❋

In April 2007, Lorena Ochoa overtook Annika Sorenstam as the No.1 ranked female golfer in the world and topped off her season by winning the 2007 Ricoh Women's British Open to claim her first major. Sorenstam had held the No.1 spot for 60 weeks, since the women's world rankings were introduced in February 2006. Not surprisingly Ochoa also won the LPGA Player of the Year Award and LPGA Vare Trophy in 2007.

❋ CHOW FOR VICTORY ❋

The inaugural Indian Masters was played in 2008 and home player Shiv Shankar Prasad Chowrasia won it. His nickname is "Chow".

❋ COLT FIRING ON ALL CYLINDERS ❋

Colt Knost won the US Amateur Public Links title in July 2007 and one month later claimed the US Amateur Championship to become only the second man to win both the US Amateur Public Links and US Amateur titles in the same year, and only the sixth person to win two USGA individual championships in the same year.

❋ YOUNG GIRLS ❋

In June 2008, Taiwanese teenager and LPGA Tour rookie, Yani Tseng, became the youngest ever LPGA Championship winner and the first Taiwanese golfer to win a major. Tseng's success was followed that same month by Inbee Park who won the US Women's Open Championship to become the youngest ever winner in the tournament's 63-year history.

❋ WHEN THE CAT CREPT IN ❋

Eduardo Romero won the 2008 US Senior Open at The Broadmoor GC, Colorado, beating Fred Funk by four strokes. He was only the second golfer from Argentina to win the US Senior Open (Roberto De Vicenzo was the first in the inaugural year, 1980). Romero's victory followed that of his compatriot, Angel Cabrera, who three months earlier won the US Open. Romero is nicknamed "El Gato" (the cat).

❋ NEW KIDS ON THE BLOCK ❋

New Zealand's Danny Lee won the 2008 US Amateur Championship aged 18 years and one month. He became the tournament's youngest ever winner beating Tiger Woods's record. Woods was six months older than Lee when he won the first of his three consecutive US Amateur Championships in 1994. However, the following year Lee's record was beaten by An Byeong-hun from South Korea.

❋ ACE IN THE HOLE ❋

In October 2010, at the Justin Timberlake Shriners Hospital Open at TPC Summerlin, Las Vegas, Jonathan Byrd ended the play-off spectacular style. At the 204-yard 17th hole (the fourth of sudden death), playing with defending champion Martin Laird and Cameron Percy, Byrd looked on in stunned amazement as his 6-iron sent the ball bouncing and rolling straight into the hole. It was the first time in PGA history a play-off had been decided by a hole-in-one.

❋ GREAT GOLF COURSES OF THE WORLD (23) ❋

CELTIC MANOR RESORT
Opened: 1982
Designers: Robert Trent Jones Jnr. (The Wentwood Hills golf course)
Yardage: 7,493
Majors: None

The Celtic Manor (Twenty Ten) golf course, situated at the Celtic Manor Resort, Newport, Wales, was specifically built to host the 2010 Ryder Cup. The resort at Celtic Manor was conceived and developed by Sir Terence Matthews in the late 1970s. In September 1999, the Wentwood Hills course opened for play and was designed by Robert Trent Jones Jnr. In July 2007, the first course to be built specifically for the Ryder Cup opened its tees for play, the result of a partnership between the European PGA, golf course architects and tour professionals. The course features nine new holes that have been routed through the Usk Valley plus nine holes from the former Wentwood Hills course that were significantly reshaped. The Celtic Manor (Twenty Ten) course has six signature holes with a par of 71 and has water hazards on half of its holes. Celtic Manor is also the current home of the Welsh Open.

❋ HOW TO STOP THE TIGER ❋

Kelly Tilghman was the PGA Tour's first female golf commentator and also appears on the Golf Channel. However, on 4 January 2008, Tilghman was involved in a very controversial incident during a PGA Tour telecast on the second day of the Mercedes-Benz Championship. On the show Tilghman and her co-host, Nick Faldo, were talking about how young players could maybe bring an end to Tiger Woods's dominance of golf. Faldo joked that they should gang up on Tiger whilst Tilghman suggested that they should lynch him in a back alley. Rev. Al Sharpton, a civil rights activist, demanded that Tilghman be sacked immediately. Five days after her remark Tilghman was suspended for two weeks by the Golf Channel. After Tilghman's remark *Golfweek* magazine published a story about the incident and on the cover of their magazine they showed a photograph of a hanging noose. The choice of cover drew criticism from all parts and it resulted in the sacking of the magazine's editor, Dave Seanor. Tilghman returned to commentary booth after her suspension and her voice has since been used as a commentator on the Tiger Woods PGA Tour golf video games.

❋ WATSON ALSO RIPS UP HISTORY BOOKS ❋

The 2009 Open Championship, the 138th in history, was played at Turnberry and 32 years after lifting the famous Claret Jug on the course in the famous "Duel in the Sun" with Jack Nicklaus in 1977, Tom Watson almost won his sixth Open title. He was in scintillating form ending the first three rounds tied for second, tied for first and leading outright – setting records as the oldest man to lead after two and three rounds of a Major tournament. Unfortunately, needing a par at the 72nd hole to win the Champoinship, he bogeyed it, and finished at –2, tied with fellow countryman Stewart Cink. In the four-hole playoff, the younger man prevailed.

❋ PRETTY IN PINK ❋

On 20 May 2009, Phil Mickelson announced that his wife, Amy, had been diagnosed with breast cancer which immediately led to Phil suspending his PGA Tour schedule indefinitely. During the final round of the 2009 MBW PGA Championship his close friend, John Daly, wore a pair of bright pink trousers in support of Amy. The following week at the Crowne Plaza Invitational at Colonial a "Pink Out" day was organised by the PGA Tour with all of the players wearing pink that day as their gesture of support to the Mickelson family.

❋ TIGER'S AWAY DAY BLUES ❋

On 27 November 2009, Tiger Woods was involved in a car crash which culminated in media frenzy and eventually the end of his marriage to Elin Nordegren. In the early hours of the morning he was driving his SUV, a Cadillac Escalade, and struck a hedge, a fire hydrant and finally a tree close to his Orlando, Florida home. Woods was treated for cuts to his face and charged with wreckless driving. The accident came less than two days after a story had been published in the *National Enquirer* claiming that he had an extramarital affair. Woods later admitted to having an affair and on 23 August 2010 he and Elin got divorced.

❋ WHAT AN ENTRANCE ❋

In May 2004, Michael Allen won the Senior PGA Championship in what was his first ever Champions Tour event. Allen, winner of just one European PGA Tour event in his career, the 1989 Bell's Scottish Open, became the first player since Jack Nicklaus in 1990 to win a Major on his Champions Tour debut.

❋ WIT AND WISDOM OF GOLF (58) ❋

"Can I have 12 wild cards and just take this team over? Just give them a cat's lick, some deodorant and clean shirts and just start over!"
Nick Faldo, incoming 2008 European Ryder Cup Team Captain, talking about the 2006 European team which had just beaten the USA 18½–9½

❋ A YEAR OF MAJOR FIRSTS ❋

In April 2009, Brittany Lincicome (USA) won on the LPGA Tour for the third time by claiming her first Major, the Kraft Nabisco Championship. Lincicome fired an eagle on the last hole. Swedish rookie, Anna Nordqvist, won the 2009 LPGA Championship in June 2009 to claim her first Major. The following month Eun-Hee Ji from South Korea scored a one shot victory over Candie Kung to claim her first Major, the US Women's Open, and her second LPGA victory. Then in August 2009, Catriona Matthew became the first Scottish woman to win a Major when she won the Ricoh Women's British Open.

❋ FOLLOWING IN TONY'S FOOTSTEPS ❋

Graeme McDowell from Portrush, Northern Ireland won the US Open at Pebble Beach Golf Links by one stroke from Gregory Havret (France) France's and became the first European to win the Major since Tony Jacklin's victory at the Hazeltine National Golf Club in 1970.

❋ DUMPING THE ALBATROSS ❋

South Africa's Tim Clark went into The Players Championship in 2010 having won more money than anyone else on the PGA Tour without ever winning a PGA Tour event. However, Clark finally removed the albatross from around his neck by winning the event by one shot over Australia's Robert Allenby.

❋ INDIA'S FIRST PGA TOUR EVENT WINNER ❋

In August 2010, Arjun Atwal made PGA Tour history by becoming the first Indian-born player to win on the PGA Tour when he claimed victory in the Wyndham Championship. He was also the first Monday qualifier to win on the PGA Tour since 1986.

❋ BASHFUL PRINCE CARDS RECORD ROUND ❋

On 2nd May 2010, Ryo Ishikawa became the first golfer to card a 58 on a major professional golf tour. Ishikawa, from Japan, shot his amazing 12 under par score in the final round of The Crowns event on the Japan Golf Tour. His round consisted of 12 birdies and 6 pars. He is known by the nickname "*Hanikami Ōji*" ("*Bashful Prince*").

❋ CREAMING THE FIELD ❋

Paula Creamer from the USA was the only player to finish under par to claim a four stroke victory in the 2010 US Women's Open, her ninth win on the LPGA Tour and her first career Major win.

❋ GERMANY RULES EUROPE ❋

Martin Kaymer became Europe's youngest No.1 golfer for 21 years by claiming top spot in the money list after his final round at the 2010 Dubai World Championship. The 25-year old German won the event after his nearest rival in the money stakes, Graeme McDowell, missed out on a Top 3 finish. The event was won by Sweden's Robert Karlsson following a dramatic play-off against Ian Poulter.

❋ EUROPE TRIUMPHS IN THE 2010 RYDER CUP ❋

In 2010, for the second successive time, the format to the Ryder Cup changed and this time began with 4 four-ball (better ball) matches on the first morning of competition. The event was played on a specially built course for the event on the Twenty Ten Course at the Celtic Manor Resort, Wales. A torrential downpour of rain on the first day meant that the competition went into a fourth day for the first time in its history. Colin Montgomerie, no stranger to past Ryder Cup battles and a winner as a player no less than five times, captained the European side and led the team to a memorable 14½ to 13½ victory. Graeme McDowell clinched the all-important final point on offer for Monty's Heroes when he defeated Hunter Mahan 3&1.

❋ A LONG WAY TO GO TO WIN IN EUROPE ❋

Belgium's Nicolas Colsaerts won his first European Tour event at the Volvo China Open, staged at Luxe Hill Country Club in Chengdu province. It is 5,000 miles from his home town of Schaerbeek.

❋ HOLLYWOOD LEGEND ❋

On the opening day of the 2011 US Open Championship at Congressional CC, Bethesda, Maryland, Rory McIlroy, from Hollywood Golf Club, in Northern Ireland, carded a six-under-par 65, three shot clear of 2011 Masters winner, Charl Schwartzel from South Africa, and South Korea's Y.E. Yang. McIlroy broke several US Open scoring records in his second round: a birdie at the 17th took him to 13-under-par, the first player in US Open history to reach that total. McIlroy ended the third day on –14, eight shots clear of his closest rival, Yang. On the final day McIlroy played majestic golf and carded a 69 to give him a final score of 268 (16-under-par) to win his first Major by eight shots from 2011 Masters runner-up Jason Day of Australia. After his final putt, Rory McIlroy was greeted by his father, Gerry, put his arms around him and said "Happy Father's Day."

❋ GMAC QUELLS TIGER'S ROAR ❋

On 5 December, the 2010 US Open Champion, Northern Ireland's Graeme McDowell ended an outstanding campaign spectacularly as he came from four shots behind to defeat Tiger Woods on the first play-off hole to win the Chevron World Challenge, at Sherwood Country Club, Thousand Oaks, California. This was McDowell's fourth title of the year, a personal best. But it was a record of a different sort for the beaten Woods, who, for the first time in his professional career failed to win a tournament during a season.

❋ WESTWOOD RULES THE WORLD ❋

World No.1 Lee Westwood went into his final tournament of the season, the 2010 Nedbank Golf Challenge in South Africa, knowing a top-two finish would guarantee him the world's year-end top ranking. He did it in style, firing a 17-under-par 271, and defeating his nearest rival, South Africa's Tim Clark, by eight shots.

❋ ALWAYS THE BRIDESMAID ❋

These players have the most top five finishes in Majors without having won one:

11	Harry Cooper
10	Macdonald Smith
9	Sergio Garcia, Jay Haas
8	Bobby Cruickshank, Doug Sanders

❋ A JITTERY TIGER ❋

Tiger Woods put his first shot of the 2006 Ryder Cup into the River Liffey at the K Club in the four-balls of the first day's play. However, luckily for Tiger his partner, Jim Furyk, was in fine form and the Americans beat Colin Montgomerie and Padraig Harrington 1-up.

❋ A CHAMPION IN THE MAKING ❋

When Phil Mickelson was three years old he tried to run away from home because his parents didn't think that he was old enough to join his father for a weekend golf game at the local public course.

❋ BONNIE LAIRD ❋

The only Scots playing on the 2011 PGA Tour, David Laird has enjoyed plenty of success. The winner of a 2009 event at TPC Southwind, Las Vegas, he was the first European to triumph in 2011 when he won the Arnold Palmer Invitational at Bay Hill Country Club, Florida.

❋ BACK ON THE MAINLAND ❋

Britain and Europe will play the United States for the Ryder Cup on the European mainland for only the second time in 2018. Le Golf National at Saint-Quentin-en-Yvelines, France, was chosen ahead of bids from Spain, Germany, Portugal and the Netherlands.

❋ THIRTEEN OF THE BEST ❋

In the 24-year history of the No.1 rankings (up to December 2010) only 13 players have held the status of being ranked the official World No.1; Tiger Woods (623 weeks), Greg Norman (331 weeks), Nick Faldo (97 weeks), Seve Ballesteros (61 weeks), Ian Woosnam (50 weeks), Nick Price (44 weeks), Vijay Singh (32 weeks), Fred Couples (16 weeks), David Duval (15 weeks), Ernie Els (9 weeks), Lee Westwood (5 weeks), Bernhard Langer (3 weeks) and Tom Lehman (1 week).

❋ VEGAS CONQUERS CALIFORNIA ❋

Jhonattan Vegas became the first Venezuelan ever to win on the PGA Tour when he triumphed in a playoff against Bill Haas and Gary Woodland to take the 2011 Bob Hope Classic, Palm Desert, California.

❋ WIT AND WISDOM OF GOLF (59) ❋

"Hey, this ain't a funeral, you know."
Tom Watson (as solemn faced journalists entered the interview room after Tom missed an 8 foot putt to win the 2009 Open at Turnberry aged 59, before losing to Stewart Cink in a play-off)

❋ THE LAND OF THE RISING KID ❋

Japan's Ryo Ishikawa, aged 17, became the youngest ever player to reach the Official World Golf Rankings Top 50 on 8 September 2009, taking the record from Northern Ireland's Rory McIlroy.

❋ THE EYE OF THE TIGER ❋

The 2010 Masters, won by Phil Mickelson, attracted the third highest television audience in the history of the tournament, behind only Tiger Woods's historic wins in 1997 and 2001.

❋ BIG TOM'S MAJOR SUCCESS ❋

Tom Lehman won the 2010 Senior PGA Championship, the first Senior Major of his career. The losing 2006 Ryder Cup captain claimed victory on the first hole of a sudden-death play-off over fellow American Fred Couples and South African, David Frost.

❋ TWO LIONS GO TO WAR ❋

In February 2010, Ian Poulter defeated fellow countryman Paul Casey 4&2 in the WGC-Accenture Match Play Championship.

❋ JIM'S MEGABUCKS PAY DAY ❋

Amazingly, both Tiger Woods and Vijay Singh, who between them had won the three previous FedEx Cup titles, failed to qualify for The Tour Championship in September 2010. Jim Furyk won the title by one shot over Luke Donald to claim the megabucks $10 million prize.

❋ LANGER THE OLD MASTER ❋

In July 2010, Bernhard Langer won his first senior Major, the Senior British Open. Two weeks later, Langer won a second senior Major, the US Senior Open.

❋ NATTY DRESSERS ❋

The Payne Stewart Award was first made in 2000 by the PGA Tour. An annual award, it goes to the player who shows most respect for golf's traditions; displays commitment to uphold its heritage of charitable support; and the professional and meticulous presentation of himself and the sport through his dress and conduct.

❋ SAM'S THE MAN ❋

In 2009, Scotland's Sam Torrance MBE, OBE, the man who famously sank the winning putt in the 1985 Ryder Cup at The Belfry which meant that it was the first time in 28 years the Americans did not hold the trophy, topped the European Seniors Tour Order of Merit with earnings of €170,696.

❋ THE TIGER RULES DOWN UNDER ❋

In November 2009, Tiger Woods was paid $3.3 million to play in the JBWere Masters at Kingston Heath, Melbourne, Australia. Woods' appearance meant that the tournament was sold out for the first time and he went on to win the event with a score of -14, his 38th European Tour win and his first win on the PGA Tour of Australasia.

❋ LEE'S DUBAI ADVENTURE ❋

In November 2009, Lee Westwood won the inaugural Dubai World Championship played at the Jumeirah Golf Estates and on his way to victory set a course record of 64 in the final round to win by six strokes.

❋ HIGH FIVES ❋

Team Great Britain & Ireland defeated Team Continental Europe 16½–11½ to win the 2009 Vivendi Trophy (The Seve Trophy), their fifth consecutive win in the competition.

❋ OH, DANNY BOY ❋

In February 2009, Danny Lee from New Zealand won the Johnnie Walker Classic to become only the second ever amateur golfer to win a European Tour event. He also became the youngest ever winner on the European Tour.

❋ COLIN MONTGOMERIE, OBE ❋

Colin Stuart Montgomerie was born in Glasgow on 23 June 1963, though he grew up in Yorkshire, where his father, James, worked. In his early years Colin was tutored at the Ilkley Golf Club by the past professional Bill Ferguson. Monty was educated at Leeds Grammar School and Strathallan School, Perthshire and was one of the first British golfers to attend an American university, when he went to Houston Baptist. He played for the university golf team and was their best player. Before turning professional, Colin won three prestigious Scottish amateur championships; the 1983 Youths, 1985 Stroke Play and 1987 Amateur. Monty turned professional after winning the Scottish Amateur Championship and was Europe's Rookie of the Year in 1988. In 1989, he won his first PGA Tour event with an 11-shot victory in the Portuguese Open.

Monty became Europe's No.1 player in 1993, retaining top spot for an unprecedented seven consecutive years and in 1994 broke into the world's Top 10. One of the most successful years of his career was 1999 when he claimed a record equalling five victories on the European Tour and never finished outside the Top 20 in any tournament. In 2002, he won his first title in Asia, the TCL Classic in China, just one week after sharing first place with Bernhard Langer in the 2002 Volvo Masters, his 27th European title. Colin was the leading European golfer for an eighth time in 2005 thanks to a runners-up spot in the Open Championship and victory in the Alfred Dunhill Links Championship.

Probably the greatest ever golfer never to win a Major, Colin has had other near-misses, including three second place finishes in the US Open and a runners-up place at the 1995 PGA Championship in 1995. However, Monty was exceptional in the Ryder Cup. He played in all eight between 1991 and 2006 and spearheaded the team to glory in 1995, 1997, 2002, 2004 and 2006. But his greatest and proudest moment in the Ryder Cup came in 2010 when he captained the European to victory over the USA 14½–13½ at Celtic Manor. Colin won 41 tournaments worldwide and claimed more European Tour wins than any other British golfer. His last victory was the 2007 Omega World Cup, with Marc Warren, helping Scotland's win a first World Cup.

Did You Know That?

Colin Montgomerie never lost a singles match in the Ryder Cup winning six and halving the other two of his eight matches. His overall Ryder Cup reads: played 36, won 20, halved 7, lost 9.

❋ TIGER'S THREE WORLD TITLES ❋

When Tiger Woods won the WGC-Accenture Match Play Championship for the third time in 2008, he became the first golfer to simultaneously hold all three individual World Golf Championship titles.

❋ FIJI'S INTERNATIONAL SUPERSTAR ❋

In July 2008, Vijay Singh won the WGC-Bridgestone Invitational to claim his first World Golf Championship event. It was also his 32nd win on the PGA Tour, placing him in the record books for most victories by an international player.

❋ BABY FACE ❋

On 21 November 2008, Hong Kong's Jason Hak, aged just 14 years and 304 days, became the youngest player ever to make the cut in a European Tour event at the UBS Hong Kong Open.

❋ THE OLD DRAGON ❋

Ian Woosnam topped the Order of Merit on the 2008 European Seniors Tour with earnings of €320,120.

❋ MONTY DOES HIS SUMS ❋

As well as studying at Houston Baptist University, Colin Montgomerie did an accountancy degree at the University of Stirling, 1988–91.

❋ A YEAR OF AWARDS ❋

In 2009, Tiger Woods's stranglehold on world of golf relentless. He topped the 2009 PGA Tour Money Winners List, earning $10,508,163 and also claimed a $10 million bonus ($9 million up front and $1 million deferred) for winning the FedEx Cup points race. His list of achievements was pretty impressive:

PGA Player of the Year ❖ FedEx Cup Winner
Vardon Trophy ❖ Byron Nelson Award
Player of the Year (Jack Nicklaus Trophy)
Leading money winner (Arnold Palmer Award)

Indeed the only major golf award which Tiger failed to collect was The Payne Stewart Award which was won by Kenny Perry.

❋ WIT AND WISDOM OF GOLF (60) ❋

"I'm very disappointed and I will be for the next few days, but I've got to take the positives out of this week. I led this tournament for 63 holes and that will build a bit of character in me."
Rory McIlroy, after shooting 80 in his final round, blowing a four-shot lead in the 2011 Masters

❋ RELIVING NORMAN'S NIGHTMARE ROUND ❋

Rory McIlroy led the 2011 US Masters after the first three rounds and went into the last day with a four-shot lead over the field on 12 under par. However, the 21-year old golfer from Northern Ireland capitulated in the final round and after shooting a 37 on the front nine he carded a 43 over the back nine to finish on –4, ten shots behind the winner Charl Schwartzel. McIlroy is the youngest ever player to lead the US Masters at the end of the first day, but he also set an unwanted record as he shot the worst round in history by any professional golfer leading after the third round of the Augusta tournament. The previous worst final round by a leader had come in 1986, when Australia's Greg Norman went into his final round holding a six-shot lead over the field. However, Norman shot a 78 on the Sunday whilst his playing partner Nick Faldo shot a 67 to win his second successive green jacket. In the end, Norman finished the 1996 Masters five shots behind Faldo.

❋ SEVENTH HEAVEN FOR ERNIE ❋

In October 2007, Ernie Els extended his own record by winning his seventh HSBC World Match Play Championship. In the final he defeated Angel Cabrera by the comprehensive score of 6&4.

❋ NO ONE DOMINATES ❋

Between the 2009 US PGA Championship and 2011 US Open, 11 different players won the 11 Majors, eight winning for the first time. No American won a Major after Phil Mickelson in the 2010 Masters.

❋ TIGER'S DOUBLE WGC TREBLE ❋

In 2007, Tiger Woods won the WGC-CA Championship for the third consecutive year, and for the sixth time in his career and also claimed the WGC-Bridgestone Invitational for the third year in a row.

❋ McILROY REWRITES THE RECORD BOOKS ❋

Northern Ireland's Rory McIlroy set a number of records as he won the 2011 US Open Championship at Congressional Country Club, just outside Washington DC. Here are some of the records he broke or equalled:

Lowest 72-hole score:	268 (65–66–68–69, previous best was 272, by Jack Nicklaus, 1980, Lee Janzen, 1993, Tiger Woods, 2000, Jim Furyk, 2003)
Most shots under par (finish):	16 (previous best was Tiger Woods –12 in 2000)
Most shots under par (in play):	13, 14, 15, 16, 17 (Woods' –12 in 2000 was the previous best)
Lowest score after 36 holes:	131 (65–66, 11 under par)
Biggest lead after 36 holes:	6 shots (shared with Woods, 2000)
Lowest score after 54 holes:	199 (65–66–68, 14 under par)
Youngest post-war champion:	22 years, 1 month, beat Jack Nicklaus, 22 years, 4 months)
Youngest European winner:	22 years, 1 month
Four rounds in sixties:	Fifth player to achieve

❋ 50 YEARS ON ❋

Charl Schwartzel from South Africa won the 2011 Masters by two strokes from Adam Scott and Jason Day. Scott and Day were bidding to be the first Australian to wear the green jacket but in the end Schwartzel became the third South African after Gary Player (1961, 1974 and 1978) and Trevor Immelman (2008) to win the Masters.

❋ THE ITALIAN WONDERKID ❋

In June 2009, Matteo Manassero, a 16-year old from Italy, won the British Amateur Championship to become the youngest ever winner of the competition and the first Italian to do so.

❋ BEWARE THE WOUNDED TIGER ❋

Despite being in much pain, Tiger Woods beat Rocco Mediate in a playoff at Torrey Pines, California, to win the 2008 US Open. A few days later, Woods had surgery to reconstruct his left knee and discovered he had played with a stress double-fracture of his tibia.

⚹ INDEX ⚹